The Bond Market Association is the trade association representing securities firms and banks that underwrite, trade, and sell debt securities, both domestically and internationally. The bond markets represent one of the most liquid securities markets in the world, with nearly $15 trillion outstanding. The Association's membership collectively accounted for more than 97 percent of the nation's bond underwriting activity in 1999.

At the end of 1999, the outstanding supply of municipal securities represented more than $1.5 trillion. Together, the Association's members accounted for approximately 90 percent of the nation's municipal bond underwriting activity.

The Association is composed of approximately 200 member and associate-member firms and twenty affiliates. Almost three-fourths of the members are securities firms. The balance of the membership is commercial banks or their securities subsidiaries, which include large, multiproduct firms and companies with special market niches.

More than one-fourth of the Association's members specialize in a particular bond market, and nearly two-thirds of all members are headquartered outside New York City. Many member firms are substantially owned by foreign institutions. Almost 10 percent are predominately American-owned multinationals.

The Bond Market Association actively speaks for the bond industry, advocating its positions and representing its interests in Washington, DC, New York, Europe, and Asia. Additionally, the Association oversees two affiliate membership organizations, The Asset Managers Forum and The European Securitisation Forum.

As part of its educational programs, The Bond Market Association organizes several conferences, roundtables, and seminars on industry issues and trends for members and other professionals. The Association produces a series of Investor's Guide publications for individual investors each focusing on different aspects of the bond market. The Association also maintains several award-winning websites and conducts a wide variety of fixed-income market research. In addition, the Association publishes manuals outlining the standards for industry practices.

Through the Association, The Bond Market Foundation was established to broaden public understanding of the bond markets, helping individuals learn more about investing for a secure future, as well as reaching out to broader audiences to stimulate thoughtful dialogue on public policy issues affecting the bond markets.

The Bond Market Association—New York   Washington   London
Headquarters: 40 Broad Street, New York, NY 10004 / 212.440.9400
Washington: 1399 New York Avenue, NW, Washington, DC 20005 / 202.434.8400
Association: *www.bondmarkets.com*
Foundation: *www.bondmarkets.org*
Investor Information: *www.investinginbonds.com*

The Fundamentals of
municipal bonds

Fifth Edition

The Bond Market Association

Written by
JUDY WESALO TEMEL

John Wiley & Sons
New York • Chichester • Weinheim • Brisbane • Singapore • Toronto

This book is printed on acid-free paper. ∞

Fifth Edition

Copyright © 1981, 1982, 1987, 1989, 1990, and 2001 by The Bond Market Association. All rights reserved.

Published by John Wiley & Sons, Inc.
Published simultaneously in Canada.

First printing 1981
Second edition printing 1982
Third edition printing 1987, 1989
Fourth edition printing 1990
Fifth edition printing 2001

Although the information and data contained in this book is from sources believed to be reliable, The Bond Market Association assumes no responsibility for any errors, inaccuracies, omissions or inconsistencies.

This publication is designed to provide general information in regard to the subject matter covered. It is sold with the understanding that The Bond Market Association is not engaged in rendering financial, investment, legal, accounting, or other professional service. If financial, investment, legal advice or other expert assistance is required, the services of a competent professional should be sought.

Library of Congress Cataloging-in-Publication Data
The Bond Market Association.
      The fundamentals of municipal bonds / The Bond Market Association ; Judy Wesalo Temel.
— 5th ed.
          p. cm. — (Wiley Finance)
      Previous eds. entered under title. 1981–1990.
      Includes bibliographical references (p.).
      ISBN 0-471-39365-7 (cloth : alk. paper)
      1. Municipal bonds — United States.   I. The Bond Market Association.   II. Fundamentals of municipal bonds (Public Securities Association).   III. Title.   IV. Wiley finance series.
HG4952.F86 2001
332.63′233′0973—dc21

                                                                                          00-063347

Printed in the United States of America.

10 9 8 7 6 5 4 3 2 1

contents

preface

A lexis de Tocqueville, author of *Democracy in America,* the visionary observation of the United States published in 1835, wrote, "A nation may establish a free government, but without municipal institutions it cannot have the spirit of liberty." He admired the system of towns, counties, and states with their advantages of independence and authority that were, at that point, uniquely American. The municipal institutions of modern America continue to encourage this spirit of liberty. One way that happens is through the municipal bond market, which provides the arena for state and local governments to borrow money for capital projects and certain other needs. This ability of the more than 87,500 state and local governments to determine their own capital needs and then finance them is a hallmark of the American Federal system of government.

The size and scope of the municipal bond market are vast. In 1999 more than $263 billion in long- and short-term bonds were sold, encompassing every state in the nation, the District of Columbia, and U.S. territories and possessions. The proceeds of these bonds were used to construct facilities for education, transportation, health care, affordable housing, water supply and sewers, governmental offices, and electric power, and for many other purposes. More than $1.5 trillion in municipal bonds were outstanding in 1999, attesting to the longevity of this business. The holders of those outstanding bonds are a diverse group: households (either directly or through mutual funds), property and casualty insurance companies, commercial banks, and other investors with a well-placed degree of confidence that these securities will pay interest and repay principal as scheduled.

Technological advances and initiatives affect nearly every aspect of the municipal market, from operations, to sales and trading, to dissemination of documents. For example, the growth of electronic trading systems for fixed-income financial products continues at a rapid pace. In the fall of 1997 The Bond Market Association published a survey that had identified 11 systems allowing market participants to buy or sell bonds electronically. In the fall of 2000 there are more than 70 systems identified in The Bond Market Association's survey, and that number of systems grows on an almost weekly basis. This directory of fixed income-trading systems is available online at *www.bondmarkets.com,* enabling the reader of this book to keep current with this continuously changing environment.

Other areas affected by technology may be less dramatic but no less significant in the ever-changing and evolving municipal markets. *The Fundamentals of Municipal Bonds, Fifth Edition,* incorporates many current developments, while still giving the reader a solid survey of the basics of the market. It outlines the process by which state and local governments borrow money and how the financial markets operate to facilitate that borrowing.

It is safe to say that wherever you are in the United States, or, increasingly, throughout the world, you have either used or been touched by a project or facility that was built by municipal bonds.

The Fundamentals of Municipal Bonds has long been regarded as a basic text about the municipal securities market. This is the fifth edition, which has been rewritten to reflect the many changes that have occurred in the municipal market since the fourth edition was published in 1990. Originally published under the auspices of the Investment Bankers Association of America (IBAA), it was updated and reprinted in 1973 by the Securities Industry Association (SIA) through the efforts of its Public Finance Information and Education Committee. The Public Securities Association (PSA), which was established in 1976 to continue the work of the IBAA and the SIA in serving the members of the public securities industry, published an expanded edition of *Fundamentals* in 1981. In 1997, PSA changed its name to The Bond Market Association.

The Association is deeply grateful to the writer, Judy Wesalo Temel, for her work on this book and appreciates the dedication and valuable industry experience she brought to the task. The Association wishes to thank its many members and industry professionals who contributed to the writing of this book and who enthusiastically responded to her requests for comments and feedback on the manuscript. The spirit of cooperation among the members, along with their competitive drive which yields innovation, have enabled state and local governments to access capital efficiently, at the lowest possible cost, while satisfying the needs of investors.

Heather L. Ruth
President and Chief Executive Officer
The Bond Market Association

acknowledgments

The Bond Market Association and the writer, Judy Wesalo Temel, are deeply indebted to the many members and industry professionals who made such important contributions to the fifth edition of *The Fundamentals of Municipal Bonds*. We are particularly grateful to the following people, without whom this major revision could not have been written:

D. Bruce Gabriel, Michael G. Meissner, and Thomas Havener from Squire Sanders & Dempsey LLP, who rendered exhaustive work on legal, regulatory, disclosure, and tax issues throughout the book; and Dr. Maury N. Harris of PaineWebber Incorporated for his work on the chapter on interest rates.

Three respected professionals commented extensively on the final manuscript, and their invaluable insights were incorporated into the book: Gedale B. Horowitz, Senior Managing Director, Salomon Smith Barney; Alan L. Anders, Treasurer, New York City Transitional Finance Authority; and Ronald A. Stack, Managing Director, Lehman Brothers.

Deeply appreciated is the expert advice of the following professionals who clarified many of the nuances of the business: Edward B. Droesch, Managing Director, Salomon Smith Barney; Richard G. Kolman, Managing Director, Goldman, Sachs & Co.; Charles J. Paviolitis, Executive Vice President, PaineWebber Incorporated; Richard W. Meister, Chief Executive Officer, eBondTrade; Kevin Carey, Managing Director, Deutsche Bank Securities, Inc.; Peter Allegrini, Managing Director, Prudential Investment Corporation; Gary R. Pollack, Vice President, Deutsche Bank Securities, Inc.; James E. Spiotto, Partner, Chapman & Cutler, Steven D. Conlon, Partner, Katten Muchin & Zavis; Mark G. Muller, Senior Vice President, Loews Corporation; John Mousseau, formerly of Lord Abbett; Andrew Garvey, Managing Director, Morgan Stanley Dean Witter & Co.; Sam Gruer, Capital Markets Division, Chase Securities; Milton S. Wakschlag, Partner, Katten Muchin & Zavis; Thomas Quinn, Product Manager, U.S. Capital Markets Group, Thomson Financial Securities Data; and Theodore Payne, DPC Data.

The following individuals gave valuable and extensive comments on drafts of the book: Jeffrey M. Baker, Vice President, Chase Manhattan Bank; Edward C. Brisotti, Vice President, Goldman, Sachs & Co.; Hyman Grossman, Managing Director, Standard & Poor's; Moira J. McGrane, Vice President & Director, The Bank of New York; Joyce L. Miller, Vice President &

Director, Griffin, Kubik Stephens & Thompson, Inc.; and Linda T. Ray, Senior Research Analyst, Newman & Associates, Inc.

This book stands on the shoulders of those individuals within the municipal bond industry who worked to produce the first four editions. Although each of them cannot be acknowledged by name, the Association joins the author in acknowledging their extraordinary efforts. This book has been called a real workhorse in explaining the basics and fundamentals of the business to those who are entering it and a continuing reference work for those who are veterans in the field. That tradition was respected as the current edition was made relevant for the future.

writer's acknowledgments

want to thank my many colleagues in the industry and in the issuer community for encouraging me to write this book. It has indeed been an honor to write *Fundamentals,* and to be a professional in this important industry.

I want to thank again all of the people named in the acknowledgments for their extensive contributions to this book. Their understanding of the business is indeed impressive. There are so many other people, though not specifically cited, whom I have been fortunate to know and to work with and whose influence is woven throughout the book. I particularly want to thank the former and current professionals at The Bond Market Association for their help and their unwavering support of this project.

Finally, I want to thank my husband, Charles S. Temel, my children, Erica, Laura, and Dan, and my mother, Blanche B. Wesalo, for being the extraordinary people that they are. We have a running commentary in my family whenever we drive over a bridge, walk into a school, or pass by a hospital. I will say, "How did they build that?" They will invariably answer, "With bonds!" I hope that with the publication of this book more people will understand and appreciate how the infrastructure of our country is financed and built. It is to my children—the future of our country—that I dedicate this book.

Overview of the Municipal Bond Market

INTRODUCTION

Municipal bonds, or municipal securities, represent a promise by state or local governmental units (called the *issuers*) or other qualified issuers to repay to lenders (*investors*) an amount of money borrowed, called *principal,* along with *interest* according to a fixed schedule. Municipal bonds generally are repaid, or *mature,* anywhere from one to 40 years from the date they are issued. At the end of 1999, there were $1.5 trillion in municipal bonds outstanding, representing the cumulative issuance of bonds over many years. These bonds have been used to finance a vast array of projects, a small sample of which includes

- Elementary and secondary school buildings
- Streets and roads
- Government office buildings
- Higher-education buildings, research laboratories, and dormitories
- Transportation facilities, including bridges, highways, roads, airports, ports, and surface transit
- Electric power–generating and –transmission facilities
- Water tunnels and sewage treatment plants
- Resource recovery plants
- Hospitals, healthcare and assisted living facilities, and nursing homes
- Housing for low- and moderate-income families

The municipal bond market is composed of thousands of dedicated professionals throughout the United States who have the diverse skills needed to raise money in the capital markets for state and local governments. Distinct roles are played by state and local government officials, public finance investment bankers, underwriters, salespeople, traders, analysts, lawyers, financial advisors, rating agencies, insurers, commercial bankers, investors, brokers, technology developers and vendors, the media, and regulators; yet all are working together toward the common goal of providing funds to state and local government units to build needed public projects and infrastructure.

Municipal bonds are also commonly called *tax-exempts,* because the interest paid to the investor is subject neither to federal income taxes nor (sometimes) to state or local taxation. With regard to tax exemption, it must be noted that each household and organization's tax status is unique and different. Although this book delineates the general principles of municipal bonds, investors should consult with their own financial advisors when considering the purchase or sale of municipal securities. There has developed, however, a market for taxable *municipal bonds,* issued by state and local governments or other qualified issuers and on which the interest income is taxable. This is because there are certain uses for municipal bonds that are not eligible for tax exemption due to limiting provisions in the U.S. tax code. Throughout this book, references to municipal bonds are to tax exempt securities, except where it is expressly stated that they are taxable.

One of the statistics that is key to understanding the municipal bond market is the dollar volume of new bond issues that are sold each year. Fluctuations in volume can reflect national economic trends as well as events that are unique and specific to the municipal bond market. The causes and effects of volume changes in the municipal market will be examined in great detail throughout this book, and there will also be a general discussion of the overall level of interest rates. Table 1.1 tracks 25 years of new-issue volume.

The municipal bond market consists of the primary market, which deals in the new securities of issuers, and the secondary market, where securities are bought, sold, and traded after they have been issued. Figure 1.1 presents the flow of funds through the primary market.

The process begins when an issuer sees a need for money to pay for capital improvements or to fill gaps in its cash flow. The issuer then takes a series of steps that lead to the primary market. There, the municipal bond dealer, who may be independent or part of a securities firm or a bank, purchases the issuer's bonds through a process called *underwriting.* The bonds are resold to institutional and individual investors, who pay the dealer directly for the debt they have purchased. The dealer uses these funds to reimburse itself for its capital that was used to purchase the bonds from the issuer. If an issue is underwritten and there are no buyers, the underwriter assumes the risk of holding the bonds in inventory until they are eventually sold. Both principal and interest are paid to the investors by the issuer, usually through a bank acting as paying agent, on a fixed schedule.

The secondary market consists of the activity and trading in securities after they have been sold as new issues. This market also supports the primary market by providing liquidity to investors who are more likely to buy a security if they know they can sell that security at a fair market price prior to its

TABLE 1.1 Total Long-Term and Short-Term Municipal Issuance 1975–1999 ($ billions)

Year	Long-Term Issuance	Short-Term Issuance	Total Municipal Issuance
1975	25.3	0.6	26.0
1976	33.2	0.3	33.5
1977	42.3	0.3	42.6
1978	46.3	0.2	46.5
1979	41.2	0.1	41.3
1980	46.3	9.0	55.4
1981	45.6	14.2	59.8
1982	77.9	16.6	94.5
1983	85.5	19.3	104.8
1984	105.6	23.4	129.1
1985	206.9	22.4	229.3
1986	150.7	22.2	172.9
1987	105.1	20.8	125.8
1988	117.4	23.9	141.3
1989	125.0	30.0	155.0
1990	128.0	35.3	163.3
1991	172.8	44.7	17.5
1992	234.7	43.4	278.1
1993	292.5	47.8	340.3
1994	165.1	40.6	205.7
1995	160.0	38.5	198.5
1996	185.0	42.2	227.2
1997	220.6	46.3	266.9
1998	286.2	34.8	321.0
1999	226.8	37.1	263.8

Source: Thomson Financial Securities Data.

stated maturity. Most municipal bond dealers have trading departments that make secondary markets in outstanding bond issues.

THE ISSUERS

According to the 1997 U.S. Census, there were more than 87,500 units of state and local governments. The Census categorizes governmental units as states, counties, municipalities, towns and townships, school districts, and special districts. Municipal bonds are issued by state and local governmental units, either directly under their own names or through a special authority. An *authority* is a separate state or local governmental issuer expressly created

FIGURE 1.1   Flow of Funds in the Primary Market

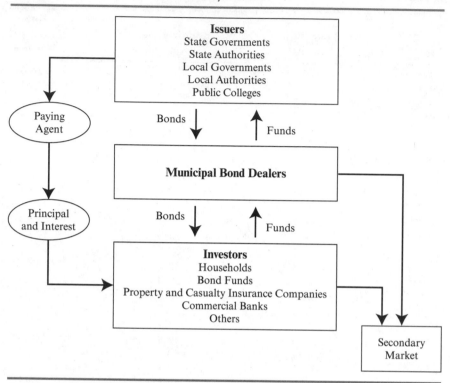

Source: The Bond Market Association.

to issue bonds or to run an enterprise, or both. Authorities such as those for transportation or power can issue bonds on their own behalves. Other authorities can issue bonds for the benefit of other, qualified, nongovernmental parties, such as not-for-profit hospitals, private colleges, and private companies engaged in pollution-control activities.

Municipal bonds are authorized and issued pursuant to express state and local laws, which impose restrictions on the size and financial structure of the debt. Moreover, each new issue requires the approval of the legislative body of the issuer, often through an ordinance or resolution. Bonds are generally sold to provide funds for capital improvement projects—for the bricks and mortar that infrastructure needs. With few exceptions, bonds are not sold to finance the normal, everyday operating expenses of government, such as employees' salaries and benefits. States and local governmental units—such as counties, municipalities (which include cities), and school districts—issue bonds for roads, parks, courthouses, and schools. These securities are usually general obligation bonds (GOs) for which the full faith, credit, and taxing power of the issuer is pledged to and obliged to be used for the repayment of the bonds. Depending on the governmental issuer approval by voter referendum is frequently required for the issuance of GOs. The public purpose projects funded by GOs provide benefits for the common good and so are repaid by taxes on everyone who is subject to taxes in that governmental unit. There are times when it is not feasible or possible to provide a general obligation pledge, so other forms of *tax-backed* or *tax-supported bonds* have been developed to provide a financing structure. Tax-backed bonds are discussed in greater depth throughout the book.

State and local governments also sell securities for which specific revenues, not the governments' full faith, credit, and taxing power, are the source of repayment. These obligations are known as *revenue bonds*. The issuer can be the government itself or a separate authority. Revenue bonds have been issued for the construction of facilities and plants that provide electric power, water, wastewater treatment, and resource recovery and transportation. Revenues and user fees that can be pledged to the bonds include electric rates and charges, water and sewage usage fees, waste disposal and tipping fees, and tolls and landing fees.

Table 1.2 shows the average issuance in each of five broad categories of state and local governmental issuers in the 10-year period from 1989 through 1999, as a percentage of the total new-issue market, by dollar volume. Local governments, which include cities, towns, villages, counties, parishes, and districts, is the largest single category of issuer, followed by state authorities, local authorities, state governments, and public colleges.

Although municipal bonds are issued for hundreds of unique projects, they can be classified in a few broad categories. One way of analyzing the development of the market is by looking at the purposes for which bonds were issued in 1979 and comparing those to the purposes for which bonds were issued in 1999, as shown in Table 1.3. In 1979 the top two categories, "general purpose/public improvement" and "education," accounted for 31 percent of debt issuance. By 1999, the share of debt sold to support projects in these two categories had increased to 47 percent. Although there is still a

TABLE 1.2 Issuers of Long-Term Municipal Bonds, 1989–1999

Issuers	Issuance (%)
Local governments	39.5
State authorities	30.0
Local authorities	18.6
State governments	9.7
Public colleges	1.7
Total	100

Source: Thomson Financial Securities Data.
Note: Average annual issuance as a percent of dollar volume.

TABLE 1.3   Major Uses of Municipal Debt, 1979 and 1999

Use of Proceeds	1979 (%)	1999 (%)
General purpose/public improvement	19	26
Education	12	21
Healthcare	8	10
Public power	8	2
Water, sewer, and gas	8	7
Pollution control	6	4
Other	38	29
Total	100	100

Source: Thomson Financial Securities Data.

huge unmet need for infrastructure projects, these snapshots of issuance over 20 years clearly show that general governmental purposes and education have remained the dominant share of the market. This, however, does not mean that those bonds have been issued with only a traditional, general obligation security. Many of the developments in tax-backed bonds have occurred precisely to create new security structures for general governmental purposes, without a general obligation pledge.

MUNICIPAL BOND DEALERS

In order to raise money in the market, the issuer works with a municipal bond dealer. The *municipal bond dealer* is most often found in a department of a securities firm or bank that provides other financial services. Public finance investment banking, underwriting, marketing, and trading municipal securities are the jobs that are undertaken by the municipal bond departments of securities firms and banks. Some municipal bond departments are fully integrated as one department, with all the functional areas organized as one business unit. In other firms those areas are divided between a firm's fixed income division and the investment-banking division. There can also be any number of other organizational combinations. Because of the broad and regional nature of the business, there are dealers that operate solely in the municipal bond market, sometimes concentrating in one market sector. Others do mostly retail business, working with individual or household investors. Still other firms trade only for dealers; these are the municipal bond brokers or "brokers' brokers."

Public Finance

Public finance is the investment-banking arm of the municipal bond business. The investment bankers work with existing clients and develop new business with other issuers. Public finance specialists, with information from the underwriting and trading side, respond to the issuers' needs and the needs of investors with traditional and innovative financing structures. The investment bankers are responsible for coordinating and responding to the many written and oral "Requests for Proposals" (*RFPs*) that are sent to them by issuers. These RFPs, which include detailed plans and financial analyses of the issuer, form the basis of the issuer's selection of a municipal bond dealer in a negotiated underwriting (discussed in greater detail in the underwriting section). This selection of underwriters for a negotiated sale is highly competitive, as many firms vie for an issuer's business.

Public finance departments can be organized along geographic, market-sector, or product lines. Sometimes they also perform financial advisory work.

Underwriting

The underwriters set prices and yields on new issues. The two main ways that an underwriter can purchase bonds from an issuer are through a competitive sale or a negotiated sale. In a *competitive sale,* a sealed bid for the bonds is submitted to the issuer at a specific time on a specific date. Normally, more than one underwriter will submit a bid to the issuer. The bonds are awarded to the underwriter who offers to pay the issuer the lowest interest cost. Underwriters will often bid on bonds as part of a *syndicate,* a group of two or more underwriters from competing firms who agree to make a bid together to an issuer. Competitive sales are also called *advertised sales* or *sealed bid sales.*

In a *negotiated sale,* the issuer, prior to the public sale date, selects the *lead underwriter* or *senior manager,* whose job will be to coordinate and manage the financing through all of its many stages. The selection process (sometimes for one deal and sometimes for a series of deals), which usually includes completing the written RFP, often also entails an oral interview at which the public finance investment bankers, underwriters, and other key members of the firm present and defend their proposed financing strategies. The issuer often selects other managers from competing firms to act as co-managers. The managers, acting together or with more firms through a syndicate, make an offer to purchase the bonds from the issuer at a price that will both produce the lowest interest cost to the issuer and sell the bonds to investors. There is greater flexibility in structuring the bonds and in reacting to the most current market conditions in a negotiated sale. As in a competitive sale, the underwriters work closely with traders and salespeople to determine the right price for a new issue.

Trading

Traders maintain the secondary market for securities by actively buying bonds from, and selling bonds to, other dealers and investors. A good trader is familiar at all times with the bonds available in the municipal market, their credit worthiness, as well as with the overall conditions in the other fixed income markets. Typically, traders specialize either in one sector of the market, such as hospital bonds; in certain bond maturities, such as one to 10 years; or in *dollar bonds* (bonds that are quoted and traded in dollar prices rather than in terms of yield).

Sales

The salespeople develop and maintain direct contact with institutional investors. They sit in the trading room close to the underwriters and traders. In addition to selling new issues that the firm has underwritten, the salesperson is familiar with the investor's portfolio and looks for opportunities to serve the investor in the secondary market. The sales force can be organized in various ways: geographically, by client relationships, by the maturity of the bond, or by a combination of any of these.

Sales Liaison

Securities firms that have a client base with many individual investors often have a retail sales liaison force. The *sales liaison* staff is normally located in the trading room and works with the account executives (variously known as stockbrokers, registered representatives, account executives, or private client service representatives) in the firm's main and branch offices. The account executive calls the sales liaison with inquiries and orders, and the liaison works with the underwriter or trader to fill the investor's needs. Several large securities firms also have regional trading departments similar to their main office trading operations on a smaller scale. The salespeople and liaison staffs in these regional offices work in much the same way as they do in the main office.

Research and Credit

The complexity of the municipal market and the financial difficulties of some state and local governments have led municipal bond dealers to place greater emphasis on the creditworthiness of municipal issuers. Dealers have *research and credit specialists* who are responsible for reviewing and following issuers in the primary and secondary market. Research analysts may prepare a short opinion that can be distributed internally (within the firm) or externally to investors on competitive or negotiated issues coming to market, or they may write comprehensive reports on specific market sectors or on market strategy. In some firms, research and credit work extensively with the public finance investment bankers on RFPs and, once the firm is awarded the negotiated business, on credit issues and rating issues as well. Research and credit are responsible for reviewing offering statements under the disclosure rules in many firms.

The rating agencies, the bond insurers, and institutional investors also employ research and credit professionals.

Capital Markets

Capital markets blend investment banking and market expertise. They are responsible for creating financial and investment products such as derivatives, swaps, and synthetic securities that are used by both municipal issuers and investors. These products are created with information from the users and with the firm's own risk management team. They may also create financial products for the firm's own proprietary trading. A firm will often have a special, more highly rated subsidiary that enters into derivative transactions to offer the issuer the most secure counterparty structure.

Operations

Operations involves the complex processing involved in the buying and selling of municipal securities. The adoption of industry-wide requirements for orders, record keeping, and confirmations has significantly standardized the functions of the operations group. Its duties include processing orders and payments, verifying and delivering securities, issuing confirmations, and maintaining customer accounts and other required documentation. These operations rules of the Municipal Securities Rulemaking Board (MSRB, a self-regulatory organization) are discussed in detail throughout this book.

BOND BROKERS

Municipal bond brokers, or *brokers' brokers,* trade only for municipal bond dealers and dealer banks; they do not work directly with either institutional or individual investors. Brokers are able to facilitate trades in a more efficient way than if the dealers did the trades themselves. For example, dealers often try to sell bonds in their inventories through brokers by asking a broker to seek bids from other dealers. This is known as the *bid-wanted* business. In other cases, a dealer may be looking for particular bonds for a customer and tells the bond broker the specified yield or price at which he or she would be willing to buy the securities. In this instance, the broker will seek these bonds from other dealers.

THE LAWYERS

Bond Counsel

Essentially every municipal security is accompanied by an opinion of *bond counsel* who represents the legal interests of the bondholders. That opinion addresses the main legal issues: that the bonds constitute legal, valid, and binding obligations of the issuer, and that interest on the bonds is exempt from federal income taxation under applicable tax laws. In rendering the opinion, bond counsel (1) undertakes a review and examination of all applicable laws authorizing the issuance of securities, (2) ascertains that all required procedural steps have been completed to assure proper authorization and issuance of the securities, and (3) determines that all federal tax laws governing the issuance of the bonds. In connection with a review of laws and procedure, bond counsel assembles all relevant documentation into a *transcript of proceedings*. The transcript serves as a permanent record and reference of the steps taken to issue the bonds and of the underlying payment and security arrangements.

The Bond Buyer's Municipal Marketplace®, popularly known as *The Red Book,* is an industry-wide directory that includes listings of municipal bond dealers and attorneys, among others. The market gives greater weight to the opinion of nationally recognized bond counsel listed in the Red Book than that of one that is not included. According to the editors of the Red Book, to be eligible for inclusion a law firm must have accomplished at least one of the following during the two-year period preceding publication of that year's directory:

- Rendered a sole legal opinion in connection with the sale of state and/or municipal bonds, or
- Served as underwriter's counsel, co-counsel, or issuer's counsel for a municipal bond offering.

Underwriter's Counsel

Underwriter's counsel represents the underwriters in a negotiated issue. Underwriter's counsel conducts a thorough due diligence analysis of the issuer. *Due diligence* involves questioning the issuer and any important related parties about their financial condition, plans, reports, and other factors that are important for a purchaser to know in order to make an investment decision. At the closing, underwriter's counsel provides a 10-b-5 certificate to the underwriter stating that nothing material to the transaction has been omitted from the disclosure process and that everything material to making an investment decision has been included. Underwriter's counsel also prepares the *bond purchase agreement* or *contract*, pursuant to which the debt is sold to the underwriter.

Other Counsel

Because of the diverse and complex nature of the municipal market, some issues may require opinions in addition to those normally provided by bond counsel and underwriter's counsel. These opinions may include those of special tax counsel, bank counsel, disclosure counsel, outside bond counsel, and/or borrower's counsel. Chapter 4 discusses in detail the roles of the counsels.

FINANCIAL ADVISORS, SPECIALISTS, AND OTHER CONSULTANTS

State and local governments often seek the advice of a financial advisor and other professional experts. Financial advisors perform a variety of tasks, including (1) analyzing the financing needs of the issuer, (2) helping to choose an underwriter or organize a competitive sale, (3) structuring the issue, (4) working with the rating agencies and credit enhancers, and (5) advising on other matters related to the issuer's debt and capital plans. The scope of the advisors' work overlaps that of the underwriters, particularly in a negotiated sale. A financial advisor can act as the underwriter for an issue, although this practice is becoming increasingly rare for large issues because conflicts of interest can arise.

Capital improvement projects often require the advice of specialists in addition to that given by the financial advisor. Some consultants, for example, advise solely on the feasibility of healthcare projects; others take on the financial, engineering, and architectural aspects of airports; still other specialists evaluate toll roads or public utilities. The issuer's accountants also play a part in the financing process. The opinions of consultants are important not only for establishing the merits of a particular project but also for attracting voter approval and promoting investor acceptance and confidence in the bonds.

Municipal derivatives specialists are typically part of a larger investment-banking firm, insurer, or law firm, or they may be stand-alone organizations. They provide a wide range of services, including acting as a counterparty in an interest rate swap, municipal reinvestment, hedging strategies and other derivative services. *Arbitrage rebate specialists* also may be part or a larger organization or stand along, and they provide compliance with arbitrage regulations and with reporting services. They will work with issuers on bond rebate calculations, bond verifications, allocations of commingled funds, cash flow models, yield computations, and reporting systems.

A broker, dealer, or municipal securities firm may engage consultants on their behalves under MSRB Rule G-38. A written consultant agreement must be entered into before the consultant engages in any direct or indirect communication with an issuer on behalf of the broker, dealer, or municipal securities dealer. The use of a consultant must also be disclosed to the issuer and to the MSRB.

THE RATING AGENCIES

There are tens of thousands of municipal issuers. Because of the large number of issuers and the variety of security structures in the market, bond or debt ratings play a more prominent role in the municipal market than in the other markets where there are fewer issuers. A *rating* is an alphabetic and/or numeric symbol used to give relative indications of credit quality. A rating is considered obligatory for the sale of any major issue. Some issues may be marketed on a nonrated basis if they cannot achieve an investment-grade rating or if favorable market circumstances exist.

Underwriters or financial advisors are often involved in preparing and making presentations to rating agencies on behalf of issuers prior to a bond sale. The rating agencies also review their ratings periodically and analyze the issuer's current financial and operational information. In addition, the agencies provide a review process for municipalities seeking an *upgrade* or improvement to their ratings; lists of bonds with potential rating changes; analyses of credit trends; and other rating services.

The three dominant rating agencies for municipal securities are Moody's Investors Service, Inc., Standard & Poor's, and Fitch. All three are headquartered in New York City. Moody's has been rating municipal bonds since 1909, Standard & Poor's since 1940, and Fitch since 1913. All three rate long-term issues, short-term notes, commercial paper, and obligations secured by insurance, bank, and other credit enhancements. Although each agency has unique features in its own rating scale, triple-A is the highest rating for each one, and each scale descends down the alphabet as the opinion of creditworthiness declines. Moody's ratings within certain categories are modified by numbers (1, 2, and 3), whereas those of Standard & Poor's and Fitch are modified by "+" and "−" symbols. The lowest investment grade rating for Moody's is Baa3, and for Standard & Poor's it is BBB−.

Ratings can be classified in the general categories listed in Table 1.4.

THE CREDIT ENHANCERS

Credit enhancement is a term denoting the credit of a stronger, more highly rated entity that used to strengthen or enhance the credit of a lower-rated entity. Credit enhancement has grown substantially in the past decade for many

TABLE 1.4 Credit Ratings

Credit Quality	Moody's	Standard & Poor's	Fitch IBCA
Investment Grade			
Prime	Aaa	AAA	AAA
Excellent	Aa	AA	AA
Upper medium	A	A	A
Lower medium	Baa	BBB	BBB
Non-investment grade			
Speculative	Ba	BB	BB
Very speculative	B,Caa	B,CCC,CC	B,CCC,CC,C
Default	Ca, C	D	DDD,DD,D

Source: The Bond Market Association.

reasons, including (1) investor concerns about the credit quality of underlying issuers, (2) increasingly complex security features, (3) use in the short-term market, and (4) cost efficiency in the pricing of insurance. The major forms of credit enhancement are private bond insurance, bank letters, and lines of credit and are discussed in this section. Public forms of credit enhancement are discussed in Chapters 3 and 7. A bond is said to be *unenhanced* if it carries only its own rating and not that of private or public insurance.

Bond Insurers

Bond insurance is a legal commitment by an insurance company to make payments of principal and interest on debt in the event that the issuer is unable to make those payments on time. Generally, such payments will be made as originally scheduled, and the principal will not be accelerated (paid earlier than its scheduled date). Bond insurance typically covers the full maturity range of the bonds.

The role of municipal bond insurance in the market is threefold: (1) to reduce interest costs to issuers, (2) to provide a high level of security to investors, and (3) to furnish improved secondary-market liquidity and price support. There has been a tremendous growth in the use of bond insurance since 1980. Table 1.5 illustrates this trend. Bond insurance grew from 2.5 percent of the $46.3 billion new-issue, long-term market in 1980 to more than 46 percent of the $226.8 billion new-issue, long-term market in 1999. In the earliest years of municipal bond insurance, most of the new insured issues were general obligation bonds, whereas now most insured issues are revenue bonds.

In 1999, four major insurers accounted for 97 percent of the new-issue insured market. Bonds traded in the secondary market, municipal unit investment trusts, and private portfolios can also be insured. The major insur-

TABLE 1.5   Bond Insurance as a Percentage of the Long-Term New-Issue Market, 1980–1999

Year	Long-Term Issuance with Bond Insurance ($ billions)	Percent of Long-Term Issuance Insured	Long-Term Issuance Amount ($ billions)
1980	1.2	2.5	46.3
1981	2.4	5.3	45.6
1982	6.9	8.8	77.9
1983	12.9	15.1	85.5
1984	16.4	15.5	105.6
1985	44.8	21.6	206.9
1986	24.0	15.9	150.7
1987	19.2	18.3	105.1
1988	27.1	23.1	117.4
1989	31.0	24.8	125.0
1990	33.7	26.3	128.0
1991	52.0	30.1	172.8
1992	80.8	34.4	234.7
1993	108.1	36.9	292.5
1994	61.5	37.3	165.1
1995	68.5	42.8	160.0
1996	85.7	46.3	185.0
1997	107.5	48.7	220.6
1998	145.1	50.7	286.2
1999	104.7	46.2	226.8

Source: Thomson Financial Securities Data.

ers of municipal bonds are the Municipal Bond Investors Assurance Corporation (MBIA Corporation), successor to the Municipal Bond Insurance Association, founded in 1974; the Ambac Financial Group (AMBAC), founded in 1971; the Financial Guaranty Insurance Company (FGIC), founded in 1983; and the Financial Security Assurance Inc. (FSA) Company, founded in 1985. Standard & Poor's, Moody's, and Fitch rate all bonds insured by these four companies triple-A. Other primary insurers are Asset Guaranty and Capital Markets Assurance Corp. (CapMAC). In 1997, a new bond insurer, American Capital Access (ACA), was formed. ACA, which is rated single-A by both Standard & Poor's and Fitch, specializes in credits that are unrated or have an underlying credit quality ranging from A-rated to below investment grade.

Although bond insurance provides significant additional security to the investor, the issuers are the first source for payment of principal and interest on their bonds. For that reason (and for other technical and tax-related considerations), not all insured bonds carry identical prices and yields. The perceived strength of the insurer by the market is a major determinant of that insurer's trading value. The relative quality of insurers is evaluated by their financial strengths and by the portfolios of bonds that they have previously insured.

Banks

Bank letters and bank lines of credit are other forms of credit enhancement. *Bank letters of credit* are typically written for a much shorter term (anywhere from one to ten years) than bond insurance. A letter of credit will pay the investor principal and accrued interest if an event of default has occurred. It is stronger than a *line of credit*, which has many more conditions that must be satisfied before it will pay the investor principal and interest. Issues with bank letters of credit will receive the rating of the bank. This may be the short-term rating, the long-term rating, or both. Issues with lines of credit will not necessarily get the bank rating. Analysts look at the conditions under which the line will pay in addition to the financial condition of the issuer.

The use of letters of credit has fluctuated greatly since 1980, as shown in Table 1.6. The use of letters of credit grew from 0.2 percent of the $46.3 billion new-issue long-term market in 1980 to its peak of 18.6 percent in 1985. This usage grew during this period for a number of reasons including high long-term interest rates, which spurred the development and growth of short-term products such as variable-rate demand obligations. With these products, the investor needed to be assured of the ability of the issuer to have sufficient liquid funds on hand in case of a *put* (the ability to sell the security back to the issuer and receive 100 percent of the principal). The letter of credit provided that liquidity. In 1999, the use of letters of credit to enhance new-issue municipal bonds had declined to 5.4 percent of the $226.8 billion new-issue market. The variability in bank credit enhancement is related to many factors, including (1) the credit quality of banks, making the credit substitution less cost efficient when credit quality declines; (2) cost of the letter of credit; and (3) availability of alternative forms of credit enhancement.

THE TRUSTEES AND PAYING AGENTS

The *trustee* is responsible for carrying out the administrative functions that are required under the bond documents. These functions include establishing the accounts and holding the funds relating to the debt issue, authenticating the bonds, maintaining a list of holders of the bonds, paying principal and interest on the debt, and representing the interests of the bondholders in the event of default. There are times when a paying or fiscal agent carries out some of these functions.

The Depository Trust and Clearing Corporation (DTCC) is a securities depository and is a national clearinghouse for the clearance and settlement

TABLE 1.6 Letters of Credit as Percentage of the Long-Term New-Issue Market, 1980–1999

Date Range	Long-Term Issuance with Letters of Credit	Percentage of Long-Term Issuance with Letters of Credit	Long-Term Issuance Amount ($ billions)
1980	0.1	0.2	46.3
1981	4.8	10.6	45.6
1982	6.3	8.1	77.9
1983	6.3	7.4	85.5
1984	17.4	16.5	105.6
1985	38.4	18.6	206.9
1986	13.0	8.6	150.7
1987	14.3	13.6	105.1
1988	15.8	13.4	117.4
1989	11.8	9.4	125.0
1990	13.9	10.8	128.0
1991	10.2	5.9	172.8
1992	8.2	3.5	234.7
1993	11.1	3.8	292.5
1994	12.3	7.4	165.1
1995	11.4	7.1	160.0
1996	12.1	6.5	185.0
1997	14.7	6.7	220.6
1998	11.9	4.1	286.2
1999	12.1	5.4	226.8

Source: Thomson Financial Securities Data.

of trades in corporate and municipal securities. Members of the financial industry who are its users own it. Trustees and paying agents make a single interest and principal payment per maturity to DTCC, and DTCC distributes those payments to participating banks and securities firms for the benefit of their clients.

THE INVESTORS

Three classes of investors dominate the municipal marketplace: (1) households, consisting of individuals acting directly or through investment counsel; (2) household proxies, that is, bond funds such as managed closed-ended funds, open-ended mutual funds, money market funds, bank personal trusts, and unit investment trusts; and (3) institutions, particularly commercial banks and property and casualty insurance companies. The principal characteristic of all buyers of municipal bonds is that they are in a sufficiently high tax bracket that they can benefit from the tax exemption.

TABLE 1.7 Holdings of Municipal Bonds by Category of Investor, 1980–1999 (percent)

Category	1980	1989	1999
Households	26.2	48.2	35.0
Mutual fund totals*	1.6	15.9	33.7
Bank personal trusts	6.5	6.4	5.8
Commercial banks	37.3	11.8	7.2
Property and casualty insurance companies	20.2	11.9	13.7
Other	8.3	5.8	4.6

Source: Federal Reserve System.
*Includes mutual funds, money market funds, and closed-ended funds.

In 1980, there were $399.4 billion in bonds outstanding; by the end of 1999 that figure had grown to nearly $1.5 trillion. Table 1.7 illustrates the key trends in the holdings of municipal securities from 1980 to1999. Two changes over this time are particularly striking. First, in 1980, households both directly and through household proxies represented 34.3 percent of all municipal holdings. By 1999, they had grown to represent 74.5 percent of all holdings. Second, in 1980, commercial banks plus property and casualty companies accounted for 57.5 percent, and by 1999 their share of holdings had declined to 20.9 percent. This is mostly due to the Tax Reform Act of 1986, which removed many incentives to commercial banks for owning municipal debt.

INFORMATION AND TECHNOLOGY

Like other markets, the municipal market has been recast by the extensive and growing use of technology. The information that is now available to participants in the market allows them to manage positions, make decisions, and do their jobs better and more efficiently. Dealers, issuers, investors, and other market professionals maintain their own websites, giving up-to-date information to their clients. Both the primary and secondary markets make extensive use of technology and information, and a discussion of technology is included in Chapter 5.

THE REGULATORS

The Securities and Exchange Commission

The Securities and Exchange Commission (SEC, or the "Commission") is an independent, nonpartisan, quasi-judicial regulatory agency with responsibility for administering the federal securities laws. It was created by Congress under the Securities Exchange Act of 1934. There are five commissioners, all of whom are appointed by the President of the United States, with advice and consent of the Senate, for fixed five-year terms. The terms are staggered, with one expiring in June of each year. Not more than three members may be of the same political party. The president also designates the Commission's Chair.

The SEC enforces federal securities laws to provide protection for investors, to ensure that they have access to disclosure of material information, and to see that the securities markets operate fairly and honestly. The laws that are enforced are the

- Securities Act of 1933
- Securities Act of 1934
- Public Utility Holding Company Act of 1935
- Trust Indenture Act of 1939
- Investment Company Act of 1940
- Investment Advisors Act of 1940

The Commission also serves as advisor to federal courts in corporate reorganization proceedings under Chapter 11 of the Bankruptcy Reform Act of 1978. There are eleven regional and district offices of the SEC, staffed by lawyers, accountants, financial analysts, and other professionals.

The Municipal Securities Rulemaking Board

The Municipal Securities Rulemaking Board (MSRB) was established in 1975 by Congress to develop rules and set standards regulating securities firms and banks involved in underwriting, trading, and selling municipal securities. The MSRB is a self-regulatory organization that is subject to oversight by the SEC.

The fifteen-person board is composed of five representatives from bank dealers, five representatives from securities firms, and five representatives from the public. At least one public member must be representative of issuers and one of investors to ensure that all perspectives of the municipal securities market are represented. The MSRB has authority to make rules regulating the municipal securities activities of banks and securities firms only; it does not have authority over either issuers of municipal securities or investors.

The MSRB's rule-making authority includes the areas of professional qualification standards; fair practice; record keeping; confirmation, clearance, and settlement of transactions; the scope and frequency of compliance examinations; the nature of securities quotations; arbitration of disputes involving municipal securities transactions; and the dissemination by dealers of information supplied by issuers of new-issue securities.

One of the first rules the MSRB adopted requires that all persons involved with "any transaction" in municipal securities must pass a qualifying examination. The National Association of Securities Dealers administers the exams.

The National Association of Securities Dealers

The National Association of Securities Dealers (NASD) was established under authority granted by the 1938 Maloney Act Amendments to the Securities gulations, conducts regulatory reviews of members' business activities, and designs and operates marketplace services and facilities. The NASD has a governing board with a majority of governors chosen from outside the securities industry. Working with the governing boards of the NASD and its subsidiaries are various corporate committees, advisory boards, and standing committees that advise their respective boards regularly and make recommendations.

NASD Regulation was established in 1996 as a separate, independent subsidiary of NASD. Its creation was part of a restructuring of NASD in which the goal was to separate the regulation of the broker/dealer professional from the operation of a stock market. NASD Regulation performs many functions, including education, registration, and testing of securities professionals; field examinations of securities firms to determine their compliance with federal securities laws, the rules of the MSRB, and NASD rules and regulations; surveillance of Nasdaq markets; and other services.

Continuing Education

In 1995, the SEC approved Rule 1120 of the NASD Membership and Registration Rules, which sets the requirements for the Securities Industry Continuing Education Program. NASD, the MSRB, the American Stock Exchange, the Chicago Board Options Exchange, the New York Stock Exchange, and the Philadelphia Stock Exchange developed a two-part continuing education program that is a uniform requirement across the securities industry. NASD Regulation administers the first part, the Regulatory Element, for municipal professionals. The Regulatory Element is a computer-based training program required for all persons on the second, fifth, and tenth anniversaries of their initial securities registration. This training relates to registration and reporting requirements, ethics and sales practices, business conduct, trade and settlement practices, and securities distributions. The second part of the program is the Firm Element, in which individual firms must prepare and implement an annual training plan for registered employees. The plans focus on keeping employees current on the investment products offered by their firms. Changes to these amendments have been proposed.

OTHER PARTICIPANTS

Information Repositories

A NRMSIR is a Nationally Recognized Municipal Securities Information Repository. With amendments to SEC Rule 15c2-12, the role of the NRMSIR expanded to include not only the dissemination of final official statements but also the dissemination of secondary-market continuing disclosure information. A NRMSIR can be a private information vendor, which must meet certain conditions to be recognized by the SEC. The NRMSIR does not verify the information that is given to it by the issuer to disseminate. A SID is a state information depository which also collects and disseminates data. Disclosure requirements are more fully discussed in Chapter 9.

CUSIP

The CUSIP (Committee on Uniform Security Identification Procedures) Service Bureau was established in 1964 and is operated by Standard & Poor's for the American Bankers Association. The CUSIP Service Bureau assigns unique numbers and standardized descriptions to practically every sector of the financial markets, including the municipal market. A CUSIP number will have a combination of nine numbers and letters.

CHAPTER 2

The Basics of Municipal Securities

DESCRIPTION OF MUNICIPAL SECURITIES

The municipal market includes different types of municipal securities. Traditional *municipal bonds* are interest-bearing securities issued by state and local governments on their own behalves or on behalf of qualified entities to finance capital projects and certain cash flow needs. Because interest on most of these securities is exempt from taxation at the federal level and sometimes at state and local levels, they are also called *tax-exempt bonds*. The *par* value, *face* value, or *principal* amount is what is paid to investors when the security comes due or matures, with *interest* having been paid throughout the life of the security. Generally, when a security matures in one year or more, it is a *long-term* financial instrument and is called a *bond*. Municipal bonds usually have maturities ranging from 1 to 30 years, although some bonds have been issued with maturities ranging from 40 to 100 years. Generally, when a security has a term of less than thirteen months, it is a *short-term* instrument. Municipal short-term instruments include notes and commercial paper. *Variable-rate demand obligations (VRDOs)*, however, can have short or long-term interest rate resets, but the final maturity of the security can be the same as that of a fixed rate bond. *Zero coupon bonds* do not pay interest periodically. Rather, the interest accretes until maturity at the stated yield.

Municipal bonds are typically issued in denominations of $5,000 or integral multiples of $5,000, although some market terminology is still based on a $1,000 bond. For example, a dealer who says "one bond" is typically referring to $1,000 par value. "Twenty-five bonds" are $25,000 par value, although there may be only five bond certificates in denominations of $5,000 each. At times some municipalities have experimented with denominations as small as $100 to try to attract smaller investors, but the practice has not become widespread.

A bond or note is identified by six pieces of information:

■ *Name of issuer.* Identification of the issuing body is the first essential piece of information. When the issuer is an authority or agency issuing on behalf of another party, the name of the obligated party is also included.

■ *Coupon.* This is the interest rate stated on the bond and payable to the bondholder. Municipal bonds can pay either a fixed rate of interest throughout the life of the bond or a variable rate of interest. The rate is referred to as the *coupon* regardless of whether the bond actually has interest coupons physically attached (only so-called bearer bonds have these coupons attached). In a fixed-rate bond, the amount of interest paid semiannually (the *convention*) over the life of the bond is the same every six months and is a percentage of the face value. For example, a $1,000 bond with a coupon rate of 5 percent will pay $50 a year to the bondholder, $25 on each semiannual payment date. In a variable-rate bond, the interest paid changes on a regular basis (daily, weekly, monthly, semiannually, etc.) based on market conditions or on an index or a formula in order to keep the yield in line with the market.

■ *Maturity date.* This is the day, month, and year on which the investor will receive payment of principal, or par amount, of the bond and the final interest payment.

■ *Dated date.* This is the day, month, and year from which the bondholder is entitled to receive interest, even though the bonds may actually be sold and delivered at some other date.

■ *Yield and price.* Municipal bonds are generally quoted in terms of *yield* because of the enormous range of issues with different maturities. There are many different yields, including *current yield, yield to maturity,* and *yield to call.* Municipal bonds are generally quoted in terms of yield to maturity. Bond prices are stated as a percentage of the par value. *Par value* equals 100; a discount bond trades at a price below 100—at 99.5, for instance, which is $995 for a bond with a par value of $1,000; a premium bond trades at a price above 100—at 102, for instance, or $1,020 for a bond with a $1,000 par value.

■ *CUSIP number.* The CUSIP number is a unique identifier of a bond or commercial paper. It consists of nine characters: a base number of six digits known as the *issuer number* (the fourth, fifth, and/or sixth digit of which may be alpha or numeric) and a two-character suffix. This suffix is alpha, numeric or both, and is the *issue number.* The ninth digit is a check number.

Applying these six pieces of information, a typical municipal bond quotation, as indicated in Figure 2.1 (which is from a Bloomberg screen) would be as follows: "State of California, G.O. Bonds, dated 4/01/2000, 5.625 percent due May 1, 2026 at 5.74 percent." The quotation reflects that the bonds were originally priced at 98.455, making them discount bonds, with a yield

Figure 2.1 Listing of the Bond Offering and then the Bond Description

```
130629XFO Muni DES                                    N224 Muni   DES
Enter 66 <GO> to Msg DES.
           MUNICIPAL  BOND  DESCRIPTION Page 1/ 4
CALIFORNIA ST                                  CUSIP:130629XF(0)
G.O. BDS
TICKER: CAS    CPN: 5⁵/₈    MATURING: 5/01/2026 DATED: 4/01/2000 STATE:CA
┌─────────────────────────────────┬──────────────────────────────────┐
│ 5) TDH MSRB Trades              │        TRADING INFORMATION       │
│      SECURITY INFORMATION       │1ST SETTLE DATE          4/27/2000│
│ISSUE TYPE   GENERAL OBLIGATION UNLTD│NEXT SETTLEMENT DATE (T+3)  7/14/2000│
│MATURITY TYPE  1) CALL, 3) SINK  │INTEREST ACCRUAL DATE    4/01/2000│
│COUPON TYPE   FIXED, OID         │1ST COUPON DATE          11/01/2000│
│PRICE/YIELD @ ISSUE  98.455/ 5.740│NEXT PREMIUM CALL  5/01/2010 @ 101│
│COUPON FREQ.  SEMI-ANNUAL        │NEXT PAR CALL DATE  5/01/2011     │
│TAX PROVISION FED & ST TAX-EXEMPT│NEXT SINK DATE      5/01/2023 @ 100│
│FORM         BOOK-ENTRY          │                    FOR $  15965M │
│           RATINGS               │SALE DATE                4/19/2000│
│MOODYS      Aa3                  │INTEREST COST            TIC:5.4900│
│S&P         AA-                  │NOTES:  Personal  Office   Firm   │
│FITCH       AA                   │        24) NOT  25) ONTS  26) FNTS│
│                                 │11) RFD Request for Documents     │
│                                 │29) http://www.state.ca.us        │
└─────────────────────────────────┴──────────────────────────────────┘
```

to maturity of 5.74 percent. The bond description also shows that the coupons are paid on a semiannual basis, and that the bonds are exempt from federal and state taxes and are in book-entry form. The Moody's, Standard & Poor's, and Fitch ratings are listed, as is trading information.

YIELD AND PRICE

There is a direct relationship between price and yield in all fixed-income securities, including municipal bonds. Municipal bonds fluctuate in yield for the same economic reasons that other bonds do (see Chapter 8). General shifts in interest rates due to Federal Reserve monetary policy or to changing expectations about inflation, for example, affect municipal interest rates as well as other interest rates. Many other factors can also cause fluctuations in yield: short-term swings in the demand for municipal bonds on the part of investors, the perceived creditworthiness of a particular bond issuer, and the total volume of municipal bonds issued, for example. When the coupon interest payment is fixed, the price of the bond itself must change in order to keep the yield in line with the yields of bonds issued in the primary market as well as bonds trading in the secondary market.

Current Yield

Assume that a bond is issued with a 5 percent coupon at par. The formula for current yield would be

$$CY = \frac{C}{P}$$

where CY is current yield, C is coupon, and P is price.

The current yield is

$$CY = \frac{50}{1,000}$$

or 5 percent. Then, if the current yield goes up, from 5 percent to 5.05 percent, the price of the bond goes down. Shown as a formula, this is

$$5.05\% = \frac{50}{P}$$

where 50 is the annual coupon payment, P is the price of the bond, and 5.05 percent is the new current yield. Solving for P, the new bond price is 990.

Conversely, when the yield goes down from 5 percent to 4.95 percent, the price of the bond goes up. Shown as a formula, this is

$$4.95 = \frac{50}{P}$$

where 50 is the annual coupon payment, P is the price of the bond, and 4.95 percent is the new current yield. Solving for P the new bond price is $1,010. When the interest rate is variable, the yield also adjusts to the current market, and the price hovers at par.

Therefore, investors who pay less than par for a bond with a 5 percent coupon receive, in effect, more than 5 percent in yield; that is, they receive $50 of interest each year on an investment of less than $1,000. Investors who pay more than par for the same bond would receive a yield of less than 5 percent.

Consider another example of how the price and yield of older issues must adjust in order to be competitive with new issues. Assume a bond was issued early in 1990 with a coupon of 6 percent and a 16-year maturity. Six years later, a new bond of similar creditworthiness with a 10-year maturity is issued carrying a coupon of 7 percent. Both bonds are due to mature in 2006. Therefore, the bond with the 6 percent coupon must fall in price so that its yield will approximate the yield on the new, 7 percent bond. Ignoring the effects of taxes on pricing, sellers would not find a buyer for the older bond until its price fell to $92.89, the point where the yield would be competitive with the yield of the new bond.

Yield to Maturity

Current yield does not take into the time value of money. Yield to maturity does take into account the time value of money in a way similar to the concept of the internal rate of return. The formula for yield to maturity is as follows:

$$P = \sum_{t=1}^{n} \frac{C_t}{(1 + \text{YTM})^t} + \frac{M}{(1 + \text{YTM})^n}$$

where P = price, C = coupon, n = years to maturity, t = index of period, M = maturity value of the bond, and YTM = yield to maturity.

Years to maturity and the index of the period in this formula are yearly measurements. Most coupon payments are semiannual and interest is compounded semiannually, so the actual calculation would reflect that. One makes an initial estimate of YTM, and through a series of trial and error calculations, or iterations, the value of YTM is found. This is a very difficult and time-consuming formula to solve by hand. Yield to maturity, which years ago was calculated using a basis book (see Appendix for a page from a basis book) is now easily calculated on computers and pocket and bond calculators.

Another important concept involves calculating the value of the .05 or, even more specifically, the .01. Yields on municipal bonds are usually quoted in terms of basis points, with one basis point equal to one one-hundredth of 1 percent. The value of a .05 is the amount that the dollar price changes with each move of five basis points in the market. The value of the .01 is the amount the dollar price changes with each move of one basis point in the market. The values of both the .05 and the .01 change as you go out farther along the yield curve.

Look at an example of the change in the .01. Assume a new bond is issued at 5 percent, due December 1, 2007 at par. If interest rates go up in the secondary market to 5.01 percent, the dollar price of that bond will fall to $99.925, because as rates go up, dollar prices fall. The value of the .01 in this case, where the market moved one basis point up, is 7.5 cents. If that 5 percent bond had a maturity of December 1, 2007, or 30 years longer, and the market moved up one basis point, the bonds would fall in price to $99.844, a drop of 15.6 cents. One can see that the value of the .01 is more volatile farther out on the yield curve.

Conversely, if that same 5 percent bond due in December 1, 2007 dropped in yield by one basis point to 4.99 percent, the bonds would rise in price to $100.075, an increase of 7.5 cents. The .01 of a 5 percent bond due in December 1, 2037 would be 15.6 cents, making the dollar price $100.156. It becomes apparent that the ability to measure and manage the value of the .01 is key in trading.

TYPES OF YIELDS

Yield to maturity is used to describe bonds trading in the market because it takes into account the time value of money. Municipal bonds are bought and sold in the market on the basis of yield to maturity. In simplest terms, yield to maturity is the internal rate of return, compounded semiannually, that an investor would earn from all interest and principal payments over the life of the bond. One important assumption in yield to maturity calculations is that all interest payments are reinvested at the same rate as the bond yield. If an investor knows that this will not be the case, adjustments can and should be made to the calculations to get a truer internal rate of return.

The yield to maturity of a bond with a 5 percent coupon bought at par is 5 percent. If the bond is bought at a discount or a premium, however, the calculation gets more complicated. For example, in the case of bonds which are priced at 99.5 (an original issue discount), the yield to maturity of 5.05 percent takes into account the value of that discount.

Current yield is a quick and simple method of calculating the current income on a bond. The current yield is equal to the coupon interest payment divided by the current *price* of the bond. Current yield is of limited use because it does not take into account the time value of money and the accrual of interest-on-interest, which yield to maturity does. Municipal bonds are not sold on the basis of current yield.

Yield to call is the annual return, compounded semiannually, that an investor would earn from payments of principal and interest, assuming the bonds are redeemed at the call date. If the bonds are redeemed at a premium, the premium price is reflected in the yield.

Yield to worst is the lowest possible yield that the bond can have, given all of its parameters. If a bond can be called before maturity, the yield to call and yield to maturity will be calculated. The lower of the two, the yield to worst, will reflect the more conservative price of possible outcomes. This yield must be quoted to customers under current MSRB rules. Some extraordinary cases are unpredictable and cannot be accurately priced into the bond's yield. In the event of an extraordinary call the broker must inform the client of this under MSRB rules.

Appendix A includes MSRB Rule G-33, which details standard bond calculations. The Appendix also includes, for historical reference, a page from a basis book, which is a compilation of tables. Before computers and bond calculators were in widespread use, yields and prices were found by looking them up in a *basis book*. If three of the four components—yield to maturity, coupon, bond maturity, and price—were known, the fourth could be determined by looking at the table.

Under current federal tax laws, any capital gains earned by selling tax-exempt bonds at a price higher than the purchase price, or by redeeming bonds at par that were bought at a discount, are subject to federal income taxes. This will affect both the yield to maturity after taxes and the way the bonds are priced in the market.

TAX EXEMPTION OF MUNICIPAL BONDS

Federal Tax Exemption

The principal characteristic that has traditionally set municipal securities apart from all other capital market securities is the federal tax exemption. The interest income on municipal bonds has historically not been subject to federal income tax. Evidence of the significance of this characteristic is reflected by the fact that municipal securities are also commonly referred to simply as *tax-exempt bonds*. And, as discussed in this and later chapters, the federal tax status of interest and related tax consequences on municipal securities greatly influences the nature, type, and level of investor interest.

As discussed in detail in Chapter 9, the basis of the federal income tax exemption for municipal securities and was originally premised upon Supreme Court decisions predating the ratification of the Sixteenth Amendment to the U.S. Constitution in 1913, which authorized Congress to pass federal income tax laws. Since that ratification, all such tax laws, including the Internal Revenue Code of 1986, have provided for municipal securities' tax exemption. However, federal tax laws, including particularly the 1986 Code, have increasingly imposed significant restrictions and limitations on the types and amounts of tax-exempt municipal securities that can be issued. In addition, such tax laws as the alternative minimum tax (AMT) provisions of the 1986 Tax Code and amendments to the Social Security Act enacted in 1983 reduced the tax exemption applicable to certain types of bonds and to certain taxpayers. The taxable municipal securities market that developed, in part, because of such federal tax limitations and restrictions is described later in this chapter. The savings that the tax exemption affords to state and local issuers became obvious soon after the first federal income tax was initiated. Before 1913, interest rates on municipal securities were about the same as rates on corporate bonds, since neither was subject to federal income taxation. After 1913, the rates on tax-exempt municipal securities fell sharply relative to taxable corporate bond rates.

The Tax-Exempt/Taxable Yield Equivalent Formula

Investors are willing to accept lower yields because they gain advantages from the tax exemption; the higher the investor's tax bracket, the greater the advantage. The municipal bond industry's standard way of demonstrating to investors the relative advantages of tax-exempt bonds is represented by the tax-exempt versus taxable yield equivalent formula. The essential variable in computing equivalent yields is the investor's federal marginal tax rate. (Since federal income tax rates increase with additional dollars earned, the mar-

FIGURE 2.2   Tax-Exempt/Taxable Equivalent Yield Rate (2000 tax year)

TAX-EXEMPT/TAXABLE YIELD EQUIVALENTS
2000 TAX YEAR

HOW TO USE THIS CHART		TAXABLE INCOME*					
1. *Find the appropriate return (single or joint).*	**SINGLE RETURN**	$0– $26,250	$26,251– $63,550	$63,551– $132,600	$132,601– $288,350	$288,351 & OVER	SAMPLE EFFECTIVE MARGINAL RATE FOR CERTAIN HIGH-INCOME TAXPAYERS
2. *Determine your tax bracket by locating the*	**JOINT RETURN**	$0– $43,850	$43,851– $105,950	$105,951– $161,450	$161,451– $288,350	$288,351 & OVER	
taxable income category that you fall into.	**TAX BRACKET**	15%	28%	31%	36%	39.6%	41%**
Taxable income is income after appropriate	TAX-EXEMPT YIELDS (%)	TAXABLE YIELD EQUIVALENTS (%)					
exemptions and deductions are taken. (The	2.0%	2.35%	2.78%	2.90%	3.12%	3.31%	3.39%
table does not account for special provisions	2.5	2.94	3.47	3.62	3.91	4.14	4.24
affecting federal tax rates, such as the alter-	3.0	3.53	4.17	4.35	4.69	4.97	5.08
native minimum tax.)	3.5	4.12	4.86	5.07	5.47	5.79	5.93
3. *The numbers in the column under your tax*	4.0	4.71	5.56	5.80	6.25	6.62	6.78
bracket give you the approximate taxable	4.5	5.29	6.25	6.52	7.03	7.45	7.63
yield equivalent for each of the tax-exempt yields	5.0	5.88	6.94	7.25	7.81	8.28	8.47
in the near left column.	5.5	6.47	7.64	7.97	8.59	9.11	9.32
Example: If you are single and have a tax-	6.0	7.06	8.33	8.70	9.37	9.93	10.17
able income of $65,000 ($110,000 if married),	6.5	7.65	9.03	9.42	10.16	10.76	11.02
you would fall into the 31% tax bracket.	7.0	8.24	9.72	10.14	10.94	11.59	11.86
According to the table, you would need to earn	7.5	8.82	10.42	10.87	11.72	12.42	12.71
7.25% on a taxable security to match a 5.0% yield from a tax-exempt security.	8.0	9.41	11.11	11.59	12.50	13.25	13.56

*   The income brackets to which the tax rates apply are adjusted annually for inflation. Those listed above are estimated for 2000.

** The Internal Revenue Code phases out the personal exemption deduction for taxpayers with adjusted gross income in excess of $193,400 (married, filing jointly) and $128,950 (single taxpayers). In addition, certain itemized deductions are reduced for taxpayers with adjusted gross income in excess of $128,950. In general, the limit on itemized deductions will increase the effective marginal tax rate by 1%, and the personal exemption phaseout will increase the effective marginal tax rate by 0.8% for each exemption claimed.

Source: The Bond Market Association.

ginal tax rate is the rate that would be applied to any additional income earned.)

Marginal tax rates for 2000 are listed in Figure 2.2. For example, a married couple filing a joint return on a taxable income of $106,000 for the 2000 tax year would pay taxes at an effective rate of 31 percent on any additional income. For every additional $1,000 of taxable income they would have to pay an additional $310 in tax. Thus, this couple would have to earn only $690 in interest on a tax-exempt bond to do as well as they would if they earned $1,000 in interest on a taxable bond. The formula below calculates exactly what a taxable bond would have to yield in order to equal the yield earned on a tax-free municipal bond:

$$\frac{\text{tax-free yield}}{100\% - \text{marginal tax rate}} = \text{taxable equivalent yield}$$

For the couple who earned \$106,000 and bought a tax-exempt bond yielding 5 percent, the taxable yield equivalent was 7.25 percent, as follows:

$$\frac{5\%}{1-.31} = \frac{5\%}{.69} = 7.25\%$$

At the same time, an investor in the 39.6 percent marginal tax bracket would have had to earn 8.28 percent on a taxable bond to earn the net equivalent of earnings on a 5 percent municipal bond.

The Bond Market Association maintains a calculator on its website, *www.investinginbonds.com*. This calculator allows an investor to find the taxable equivalent yield of a tax-exempt bond by inputting his or her state, income, and tax filing status into a series of drop-down menus.

State Taxation of Municipal Bonds

The relative advantage of tax-exempt bonds can be even greater for the investor living in a state that imposes state and local income taxes, because, frequently, municipal bonds are exempt from these taxes as well. Many states exempt interest income only on bonds issued within their own boundaries. Other states do not exempt interest income on bonds issued in their own state. For example, in 2000 a married couple residing in New Jersey with a combined taxable income of \$106,000 would be in the 31 percent federal tax bracket and would be subject to a state income tax of 5.53 percent. That is a total of 36.53 percent. Note, however, that state (and, if applicable, local) income tax payments are deductible on the federal tax return under current law. If this couple itemizes deductions, the effect of the state and local taxes must therefore be offset by the amount gained back from the deduction on the federal return. Thus, the total effective income tax rate for that individual is not 36.53 percent, but is $31 + 5.53/(1 - 0.31)$, or 34.81 percent.

A 5 percent return on a municipal bond issued within the state for that couple, therefore, has the same after-tax benefit as a 7.67 percent taxable bond, since $7.67 = 5/(1 - .3481)$. Table 2.1 shows each state's taxation of municipal bonds for individuals and for corporations.

Restrictions on Tax-Exempt Bond Issuance

The types of municipal securities, the purposes for which they may be issued, the taxes and other sources that may be pledged to their payment, and the

TABLE 2.1 State Taxation of Municipal Bonds for Individuals and Corporations

State		In-State Municipal or State	Other State Bonds	U.S. Bond Interest
Alabama		Exempt	Taxable	Exempt
Alaska		Exempt	Exempt	Exempt
Arizona		Exempt	Taxable	Exempt
Arkansas		Exempt	Taxable	Exempt
California	FI:	Taxable	Taxable	Taxable[a]
	CI:	Exempt	Taxable	Exempt
	PI:	Exempt	Taxable	Exempt
Colorado		Exempt[b]	Taxable	Exempt
Connecticut	CI:	Taxable	Taxable	Taxable[a]
	PI:	Exempt	Taxable	Exempt
Delaware		Exempt	Taxable	Exempt
District of Columbia		Exempt	Taxable	Exempt
Florida		Taxable	Taxable	Taxable
		(No personal income tax)		
Georgia		Exempt	Taxable	Exempt
Hawaii		Exempt	Taxable	Exempt
Idaho		Exempt	Taxable	Exempt
Illinois		Taxable with exceptions[c]	Taxable	Exempt
Indiana		Exempt	Exempt	Exempt
Iowa		Taxable[d]	Taxable	Exempt
Kansas		Exempt	Taxable	Exempt
Kentucky		Exempt	Taxable	Exempt
Louisiana		Exempt	Taxable	Exempt
Maine		Exempt	Taxable	Exempt
Maryland		Exempt	Taxable	Exempt
Massachusetts	CI:	Taxable	Taxable	Taxable[a]
	PI:	Exempt	Taxable	Exempt
Michigan		Exempt	Taxable	Exempt
Minnesota	CI:	Taxable	Taxable	Taxable[a]
	PI:	Exempt	Taxable	Exempt
Mississippi		Exempt	Taxable	Exempt
Missouri		Exempt	Taxable	Exempt
Montana	CI:	Taxable[e]	Taxable	Taxable[a]
	PI:	Exempt	Taxable	Exempt
Nebraska		Exempt	Taxable	Exempt
Nevada		(No personal or corporate income tax)		
New Hampshire		Exempt	Exempt	Exempt
New Jersey	CI:	Taxable	Taxable	Taxable[a]
	I:	Exempt	Taxable	Exempt
New Mexico		Exempt	Taxable	Exempt
New York	CI:	Taxable	Taxable	Taxable[a]
	PI:	Exempt	Taxable	Exempt

TABLE 2.1   (Continued)

North Carolina	Exempt	Taxable	Exempt
North Dakota	Exempt	Taxable	Exempt
Ohio	Exempt	Exempt	Exempt
Oklahoma	Exempt[f]	Taxable	Exempt
Oregon	CI: Taxable	Taxable	Taxable[a]
	PI: Exempt	Taxable	Exempt
Pennsylvania	CI: Exempt	Exempt	Exempt
	PI: Exempt	Taxable	Exempt
Rhode Island	Exempt	Taxable	Exempt
South Carolina	Exempt	Taxable	Exempt
South Dakota	Taxable	Taxable	Taxable[a]
	(No personal income tax)		
Tennessee	Exempt	Taxable	Taxable
Texas	Exempt	Exempt	Exempt
Utah	Taxable[g]	Taxable	Exempt7
Vermont	Exempt	Taxable	Exempt
Virginia	Exempt	Taxable	Exempt
Washington	(No personal or corporate income tax)		
West Virginia	CI: Taxable	Taxable	Exempt
	PI: Exempt	Taxable	Exempt
Wisconsin	CI: Taxable	Taxable	Exempt
	FI: Taxable	Taxable	Taxable
	PI: Taxable[h]	Taxable	Exempt
Wyoming	(No personal or corporate income tax)		

Source: Reproduced with permission from State Tax Guide, published and copyrighted by CCH Incorporated, 4025 W. Peterson Ave., Chicago, IL 60646

FI = franchise tax, CI = corporate income tax, PI = personal income tax.

[a]Nondiscriminatory franchise tax.

[b]Interest income on obligations of Colorado or a political subdivision thereof issued on or after May 1, 1980 is exempt. Interest from obligations issued prior therein is exempt only if specifically made exempt by statute.

[c]Income from obligations of the Land Bank Fund, Illinois Sports Authority Facility, Distressed City Assistance Program, and college savings bonds is exempt from taxation.

[d]Income from certain qualifying Iowa municipal bonds is exempt: if not specially exempt, the interest must be included in Iowa taxable income.

[e]Interest income from Montana coal severance bonds and agriculture authority bonds is exempt from corporate franchise tax (latter also exempt from personal income tax).

[f]Interest on local government obligations issued after June 6, 2000 for purposes other than to provide financing for nonprofit corporations is exempt.

[g]For corporate income tax purposes, a partial tax credit is allowed for interest from Utah and federal obligations. Interest on state highway construction and repair bonds is subject to corporation (franchise) tax only.

[h]For personal income tax purposes, interest on state obligations, including those of Wisconsin, is fully taxable unless expressly exempted by Wisconsin law. Interest received on certain bonds issued by local exposition districts, local cultural arts districts, local professional football stadium districts, or the Wisconsin Housing and Economic Development Authority is exempt from taxation.

manner in which such securities may be issued and sold are all subject to state and local law. Consequently, applicable state and local statutes must be carefully examined in connection with structuring and issuing municipal securities. In addition, as covered in Chapter 9, federal tax legislation significantly affects the manner in which, and the purposes for which, municipal securities may be issued. For example, both the Tax Reform Act of 1984 and the Tax Reform Act of 1986 have curbed the issuance of bonds characterized as "private activity bonds," "exempt facility bonds," and "501(c)(3) bonds." There are different limits, including volume caps by state, for certain housing and private-activity bonds. There are also rules on the number of times that an issuer can refinance debt on a specific issue.

Taxable Bonds and Alternative Minimum Tax Bonds

Certain types of municipal bonds are taxable, and certain types are subject to the *alternative minimum tax (AMT)*. Issuance of traditional, fully tax-exempt bonds is now only 82.9 percent of all municipal issuance, because there have been shifts recently to the taxable municipal bond. Table 2.2 shows that AMT bonds have fluctuated greatly, ranging from a low of 4.6 per-

TABLE 2.2 Issuance of Long-Term, Tax-Exempt, Taxable, and AMT Securities, 1985–1999

Year	Long-Term Issuance ($ billions)	Tax-Exempt Percentage of Long-Term	Taxable Percentage of Long-Term	AMT Percentage of Long-Term
1985	206.9	99.8	0.16	0.00
1986	150.7	91.0	2.68	6.35
1987	105.1	84.5	2.77	12.74
1988	117.4	79.4	2.17	18.41
1989	125.0	83.6	2.81	13.56
1990	128.0	82.0	2.52	15.48
1991	172.8	89.4	2.80	7.76
1992	234.7	90.9	2.42	6.68
1993	292.5	92.2	3.21	4.58
1994	165.1	84.5	5.31	10.23
1995	160.0	81.7	6.75	11.59
1996	185.0	83.5	5.31	11.19
1997	220.6	82.7	6.38	10.89
1998	286.2	85.8	5.57	8.62
1999	226.8	82.9	6.77	10.31

Note: AMT is alternative minimum tax.
Source: Thomson Financial Securities Data.

cent in 1993 to a high of 18.4 percent in 1988. Since 1994, when taxable securities first reached 5 percent of the new-issue long-term market, their percentage has fluctuated between 5 and 7 percent, with nearly $75 billion issued from 1994 to 1999.

TYPES OF MUNICIPAL BONDS

The municipal market is recognized for the diverse purposes that the bonds finance and for the different security features that are offered to investors. Municipal bonds and municipal short-term securities are generally broken down into two major categories: general obligation bonds and revenue bonds.

The security for the *general obligation bonds (GOs)* is the general credit and the taxing power of the state or local government issuing the bonds. Most municipal governments depend largely on *ad valorem* (Latin meaning "to the value added"), or value-based, property taxes for their revenues. State governments, on the other hand, usually do not levy real estate taxes but rely mostly on sales and income taxes. The full faith and credit backing of a GO bond implies that all sources of revenue, unless specifically dedicated to other purposes, will be used to pay debt service on the bonds.

Revenue bonds are those that are generally issued to finance a specific revenue-generating project and, unless backed by a third-party guarantee, they are usually secured solely by the revenues from that project. Revenue bonds have enabled state and local governments to finance a wide range of capital improvements. Toll-generating bridges, airports, water and sewage treatment facilities, healthcare facilities, and state and local housing projects have generally been financed by revenue bonds. Typically, these bonds are payable from specific sources of revenues and are not backed by the full faith and credit of the issuer.

There are times when specific revenues of an enterprise are additionally backed by a general obligation pledge. These hybrid obligations are called *double-barreled bonds* because of the two revenue pledges.

Other types of municipal securities that do not fall exactly into the general obligation or revenue bond categories are special tax bonds, securitized revenue bonds, and moral obligation bonds. General obligation bonds, revenue bonds, and other types of municipal securities will be discussed in greater detail in Chapter 3.

SHORT-TERM SECURITIES

State and local governments use short-term financing to bridge the gap between the time when expenses occur and when revenues become available from incoming tax revenues, grants, other revenue sources or new issues of bonds. Municipal short-term securities, often called *anticipation notes,* usually represent maturity of 13 months or less. Interest on notes is usually paid when they mature. Some municipalities, however, issue notes at a discount, to their value at maturity, much like Treasury bills.

Notes

The issuance of short-term securities by state and local governments and the issuance of housing project notes represented a very high percentage of all new issues in the early 1970s. After New York City's fiscal crisis in the 1970s, the use by state and local governments of short-term debt declined. Beginning in 1979, as interest rates rose and the issuance of *project notes* (short-term, tax-exempt securities issued to fund housing and urban renewal projects and secured by the project's revenue and the U.S. government) accelerated, short-term debt increased again. With the elimination of project notes by Congress in 1984, together with a decline in intermediate- and long-term interest rates, the rapid rise of overall long-term financing, and increased use of alternative forms of financing such as variable-rate demand bonds, there was a reduction in the percentage of short-term municipal securities. The issuance of short-term securities now tends to fluctuate with the economic cycle. In 1999, short-term securities accounted for 14.1 percent of all new issues. Table 2.3 shows note issuance as a percentage of the total new issuance market from 1975 to 1999.

State and local governments frequently issue the following types of notes:

- *Tax anticipation notes.* Known in the market as TANs, they are issued in anticipation of tax receipts (usually property taxes) and are payable from those receipts.
- *Revenue anticipation notes.* RANs are issued in anticipation of other sources of future revenue, typically either from state or federal sources. Notes issued in anticipation of both tax receipts and other revenues are known as TRANs.
- *Bond anticipation notes.* BANs provide a means of interim financing in anticipation of a future bond offering. Unless they are otherwise secured, they are dependent upon the local government's ability to issue those bonds and are viewed as the least secure type of note.
- *Grant anticipation notes.* GANS are issued in anticipation of grants and are payable when those grants are received.
- *General obligation notes.* Some state and local governments will issue notes for a variety of purposes, backed by the full credit of the issuer.

TABLE 2.3 Short-Term Issuance as Percentage of All-New Municipal Issuance, 1975–1999

Year	Short-Term Issuance ($ billions)	Percentage Short-Term of Total Issuance
1975	0.6	2.4
1976	0.3	0.8
1977	0.3	0.7
1978	0.2	0.4
1979	0.1	0.2
1980	9.0	16.3
1981	14.2	23.7
1982	16.6	17.6
1983	19.3	18.4
1984	23.4	18.2
1985	22.4	9.8
1986	22.2	12.9
1987	20.8	16.5
1988	23.9	17.0
1989	30.0	19.4
1990	35.3	21.7
1991	44.7	20.6
1992	43.4	15.6
1993	47.8	14.1
1994	40.6	19.8
1995	38.5	19.4
1996	42.2	18.6
1997	46.3	17.3
1998	34.8	10.8
1999	37.1	14.1

Source: Thomson Financial Securities Data, March 9, 2000.

Tax-Exempt Commercial Paper

Commercial paper is a short-term promissory note issued for periods up to 270 days, with maturities commonly at 30, 60, and 90 days. It is often used for the same purposes as BANs, TANs, RANs, and general obligation notes. Its advantage is that it offers greater flexibility in both setting maturities and determining rates. Bank lines or letters of credit are often used to provide liquidity for maturing commercial paper. The strongest issuers of commercial paper, such as universities with large endowments, have financial assets substantial enough to enable them to provide their own liquidity without having to use an outside source.

Variable-Rate Demand Obligations

Before 1980, the phrase "short-term municipal" referred only to notes and short-term municipal bonds. However, the highly dynamic interest rate movements of the late 1970s and early 1980s and the emergence and growth of tax-exempt money funds fostered one of the most significant developments in the tax-exempt market during that period: a much broader class of short-term municipal securities. These short-term municipal securities were investment vehicles that evolved to meet issuer and investor concerns about the effect of interest rates. Investors were concerned about fluctuations in the value of their portfolios while issuers were concerned about the high cost of borrowing.

These short-term municipals, generically known as demand obligations or *variable-rate demand obligations (VRDOs),* are bonds with traditional, long-dated nominal maturities that also have short-term demand features. VRDOs offer the investor the assurance of the preservation of principal and offer the issuer a means of borrowing at a significantly lower rate. Table 2.4

TABLE 2.4   Variable-Rate Demand Obligations (VRDO) Issuance as a Percentage of the Long-Term Market, 1980–1999

Year	VRDO Issuance ($ billions)	VRDO as Percentage of Total Issuance
1980	0.5	1.2
1981	3.6	7.8
1982	4.2	5.4
1983	6.5	7.6
1984	29.7	28.1
1985	76.8	37.1
1986	31.4	20.8
1987	17.8	16.9
1988	24.0	20.4
1989	15.0	12.0
1990	16.2	12.7
1991	16.5	9.5
1992	19.6	8.3
1993	26.5	9.1
1994	18.3	11.1
1995	22.0	13.8
1996	21.9	11.8
1997	30.7	13.9
1998	29.6	10.3
1999	30.0	13.2

Source: Thomson Financial Securities Data.

shows the volume of VRDO issuance over the past 15 years. VRDOs' market share is calculated as a percentage only of the long-term market because they have a nominal long-term maturity.

With VRDOs, the municipal issuer sells long-term bonds that have yields determined or set as if they were short-term notes. The reason that the yields are like those of short-term notes is that the holders of the bonds are entitled to demand repurchase of their bonds at par, plus accrued interest, on a regular basis. From a bondholder's point of view, a bond subject to such repurchase is similar to a bond that matures on the date the bondholder is entitled to demand purchase. Therefore, a bond entitling the holder to demand payment every seven days carries the same yield as if it matured in a week. Similarly, an annual demand bond is priced as if it matured in one year. Although bonds with daily, weekly, or monthly demand periods are the most common, some bonds have quarterly, semiannual, or annual demand periods. From the issuers' point of view, this structure offers flexibility by enabling them to take advantage of rates at the short end of the yield curve without having to reissue and reauthorize the debt constantly.

For most of these issues, the coupon rate may change only at a point when the holder can demand interest. Since this market evolved over several years, various names, such as "floaters," "lower floaters," or "put" bonds, may all refer to the same security structure. As the market in these securities emerged, certain structures have become more common than others. Nevertheless, the structure of these transactions typically has four primary components, as follows.

Demand feature. The demand feature of the VRDO is the key element that allows for the short-term interest rate. Modern VRDOs allow for flexible demand features, with daily, weekly, or monthly demand intervals as the most common. The demand feature works in the following way: The holder of a VRDO must give notice to a tender agent in the transaction a few days prior to the date that the bond will be tendered for purchase at a price of par plus accrued interest. The tender agent then notifies the *remarketing agent* (generally a municipal bond dealer), who will use his or her best efforts to sell the tendered bonds to another purchaser. Since most VRDOs are usually sold through a negotiated sale, the remarketing agent is most often one of the municipal bond dealers who managed the financing.

Variable interest rate. Just as VRDOs have a demand interval, they also reset the interest rate at the same interval as the demand feature. As a general rule, each time the interest rate is reset, holders are allowed to tender their bonds for par purchase. The opposite, however, is not true; that is, the interest rate reset may be less frequent than the demand for payment. Current structures permit the remarketing agent to determine the new interest rate based upon prevailing market conditions.

Liquidity and/or credit support. Because VRDOs allow the holder to demand purchase upon specified notice, the issuer must have some form of liquidity or credit support in order to meet a demand. The most common forms of liquidity support are lines of credit, standby purchase agreements, or letters of credit issued by a financial institution. There are conditions under which the bank will not be obliged to advance funds in lines of credit and in standby purchase agreements. Letters of credit, which are irrevocable, fully support the bond and there are no conditions under which the bank will not honor draws for liquidity or credit needs. As a practical matter, in most circumstances, the VRDO holder demanding payment is paid from the remarketing of the security to a new buyer through the efforts of the remarketing agent. However, if a holder demands payment and no new purchasers can be arranged by the remarketing agent, then the liquidity support is available to meet the demand. Issuers with particularly strong credit may use their own financial resources to provide liquidity. This is called *self-liquidity*.

Conversion to a fixed rate. Most VRDOs allow the issuer to convert the security to a fixed interest rate structure under specified conditions and procedures. If, for example, long-term interest rates decline significantly, then the issuer may want to lock in a fixed rate of interest while rates are favorable. In order to convert a VRDO to a fixed-rate structure, the trustee notifies all holders of the issuer's intent. The notice generally requires that the holders tender either their VRDOs as of the specified fixed-rate date or expressly waive such tender. This mandatory tender requirement serves to protect the bondholder against a change in the security of the issue since, commonly, the liquidity or credit support expires at conversion.

Dutch Auction Securities

Dutch auction securities are another form of a variable rate bond. The major difference between a traditional VRDO and a Dutch auction security is that a VRDO generally requires a liquidity facility, while a Dutch auction security does not. Dutch auction bonds are often used as the floating rate component of a floater/inverse-floater bond (where the interest payable is based on a formula that has a ceiling rate, less the specified floating rate index or bond). The liquidity for the security is created through the Dutch auction rate-setting procedure.

At a Dutch auction, the rate is set at the lowest interest rate at which buyers are willing to purchase all of the securities of potential sellers. The current holder of the security can submit one of three orders to an auction agent: hold, bid, or sell. A *hold order* means than the holders wants to keep the security through the next rate period, regardless of the new rate that will be set. A *bid order* means that the holder wants to buy securities if the rate is equal to or greater than the one specified in the bid and also indicates that the holder wants to sell the securities if the interest rate is less than the one stated in the bid. A *sell order* means that the holder of the securities wants to sell the securities no matter what the interest rate is.

Investors who do not currently hold the securities but would like to purchase them can only submit bid orders. The rate on the Dutch auction securities for the next reset period (which is most often, but not always, every 35 days, versus a 7-day reset or a daily reset) is the lowest bid rate that clears the auction. If not enough bids clear the auction (a failed auction), the rate is set by a formula, and would be considered the penalty rate that is disclosed in the official statement.

The issuer does not pay for a credit facility in the same way as a VRDO. In addition, there is no risk that the liquidity facility will be downgraded, because there is no external liquidity facility. There is also no renewal of and repricing risk of any external bank line or letter of credit.

Tender Option Certificates

Tender option certificates or bonds are a kind of short-term security. Tender option certificates are considered a secondary derivative product, meaning that the certificate is not issued directly by a governmental issuer. The key difference between a traditional VRDN and a tender option certificate is that the right to tender the bonds is conditional, versus an unconditional tender in a VRDN with a letter of credit. The right to tender must be conditional to comply with Federal tax rules.

OTHER CHARACTERISTICS OF MUNICIPAL BONDS

Other important features and practices distinguish municipal securities from other kinds of securities. Knowledge of these characteristics is necessary to any understanding of the fundamentals of municipal securities. A summary of the most important of them follows.

Size of the Primary and Secondary Markets

The municipal securities primary market differs from other fixed income securities in that it has many smaller issues. Table 2.5 shows the number of bond issues in 1999 with par amounts less than and more than $10 million. There were 9,392 issues with par amounts less than $10 million, but this accounted for only $32.6 billion, or 14.3 percent of the total new issue volume for the year.

The municipal secondary market, or after market, is distinct other sec-

TABLE 2.5　Long-Term Issue Size, 1999

Par Amount	Total Dollar Amount ($ billions)	Percentage of New-Issue Volume	Percentage of Issues	Percentage of New Issues
Less than $10,000,000	32	14.3	9,392	70.3
$10,000,000 and over	195	85.7	3,966	29.7
Total	228		13,358	

Source: Thomson Financial Securities Data.
Note: Total principal amount and number of issues may differ from their actual sums due to database allocation of data.

ondary markets in several important ways. One major distinguishing characteristic of the municipal market is that the vast majority of trading is done over the counter. At this point in time the majority of trades in municipal securities are still made on a so-called dealer basis. That is, the dealers who trade municipal securities for investors own, if only temporarily, the securities they buy from one investor and sell to another or keep for their own inventory. The difference between the price for which they can sell the securities and the price at which they bought them is known as the spread. This traditional method of trading securities is changing as the markets take advantage of technology. There are online electronic trading systems that are beginning to be organized as centralized exchanges. Alternative online electronic trading systems are expected to reduce costs and to create better pricing.

The municipal secondary market is significantly different from other markets because of the sheer number and variety of issues. While overall a great deal of trading is done, trading in any one individual municipal issue may be infrequent.

Legal Opinion

An important characteristic unique to municipal bonds is the bond counsel opinion. In order to be marketable, municipal bonds must be accompanied by a legal opinion. The opinion addresses two principal areas: first, that the bonds are legal and binding obligations of the issuer under applicable state and local laws, and second, that the interest on the bonds is exempt under applicable federal and state tax laws.

The opinion requirement grew out of widespread defaults in the late nineteenth century on municipal bonds that had been issued to finance railroad construction. When such defaults occurred, some issuers successfully avoided their payment obligation on the basis that the bonds had not been duly authorized or properly issued under applicable laws. In order to restore marketplace confidence, issuers and underwriters began the practice of obtaining bond counsel opinions at the time bonds were initially issued. The increased complexity of financial structures and of federal tax restrictions has further resulted in a broadening of the traditional bond counsel role.

Official Statement

Municipal securities are exempt in most instances from SEC registration requirements. Nonetheless, an offering document, known as an official statement, is usually prepared in connection with the initial (or primary) offering of municipal securities. This is the municipal counterpart of a corporate prospectus. Underwriters are required by MSRB Rule G-32 to send official statements, if prepared for a new issue of municipal securities, to each investor in those securities. Moreover, as discussed in Chapter 9, SEC Rule 15c2-12 requires underwriters of a municipal securities offering $1 million or more in aggregate principal amount to obtain and review an official statement before bidding on or purchasing the offering, unless the offering is exempt from the requirements of the Rule. Although the Rule applies directly to underwriters, its effect is to require issuers seeking access to the public securities market to provide official statements in connection with the primary offering of municipal securities. Without such statements, underwriters would not be able to comply with the Rule. In addition, MSRB Rule G-36 requires underwriters to send copies of official statements to the MSRB.

Continuing Disclosure

The SEC-approved amendments to Rule 15c2-12 in November 1994 (effective generally for issues sold after July 3, 1995), require an underwriter to determine, as a condition to underwriting a new issue of municipal securities subject to the Rule, that the issuer or one or more persons obligated with respect to payment of debt service on the issue has committed contractually to provide ongoing disclosure with respect to the issue. In general, obligated persons with more than $10,000,000 of nonexempt securities outstanding must commit to the annual updating of financial information and operating data of the type included in the official statement for the primary offering and to provide notice of 11 specified material events. More limited requirements apply if no obligated person with respect to an issue has more than $10,000,000 of nonexempt securities outstanding or if the new issue has a maturity that does not exceed 18 months. The continuing disclosure requirement is the municipal securities market counterpart of the reporting requirement imposed on corporations subject to the Securities Exchange Act of 1934. Continuing disclosure requirements are discussed in greater detail in Chapter 9.

Serial and Term Bonds

Unlike most other types of fixed-income securities, municipal bond issues traditionally include serial maturities. A typical offering is made up of as many as 20 or more different maturities, which are called serial bonds. This structure helps the issuer to spread out debt service and stay within the legal restrictions of some states that require a bond issue to contain substantially equal annual debt service or maturities. Typically, a certain number of bonds fall due each year from, say, 1 to 20 years from their date of issue. Generally, the longer the maturity, the higher will be the interest rate offered. A representative maturity service schedule for $500,000,000 State of California General Obligation Bonds is shown in Chart 3.6. This is not a maturity schedule for all bonds of the State of California, but just for this one issue. A comprehensive debt service schedule, with principal and interest due each year, for the State is found in its annual audited financial statements.

In this example, serial bonds and term bonds are included in the issue. The serial bonds mature from May 1, 2001 to May 1, 2022. The two term bonds are as follows: $63,860,000 bonds with a 5.625 percent coupon due May 1, 2026, and $63,860,000 bonds with a 5.75 percent coupon due May 1, 2030. Unlike serial bonds, term bonds are due at only one maturity. They usually carry a sinking fund requirement with reserves set aside by the issuer to redeem term bonds to provide for their retirement. Except for being tax exempt, term bonds are very similar to traditional corporate debt. Municipal issues can include one or several term bonds. They are usually quoted by price rather than by yield.

Zero-Coupon Bonds

Term bonds that pay no periodic interest and have a coupon rate of zero interest are known as *zero-coupon bonds*. They are sold and purchased at a deep discount, with no coupons attached. Interest is not paid to the investor on a semiannual basis. Instead, at maturity, an amount equal to the principal invested plus the interest earned, compounded semiannually, at the stated yield is paid. This amount is usually par. For example, a bond with a face amount of $20,000, maturing in 20 years, may be purchased for roughly $6,757. At the end of the 20 years, the investor will receive $20,000. The difference between $20,000 and $6,757 represents the interest. This example is

TABLE 2.6 Estimated Future Value of a Twenty-Year, 5.5 Percent Zero-Coupon Municipal Bond Purchased for $6,757.04 on January 1, 1997

Year	Value ($)
2002	8,862.88
2007	11,625.01
2012	15,147.96
2017	20,000.00

Source: The Bond Market Association.

based on an interest rate of 5.5 percent, which compounds until the bond matures as shown in Table 2.6.

Convertible-coupon bonds are a variation of zero-coupon bonds. They start out as zeros (albeit not with as deep a discount) and accrete interest for a number of years. Then they convert to traditional, semiannual, interest-bearing bonds until their final maturity. These bonds are aimed at investors who want both growth and income from their bonds at different times in their investment horizon (for example, parents saving for a child's college tuition).

Another variation of zero-coupon bonds is *stripped bonds*. Municipal bonds that pay interest semiannually can be stripped (that is, separated) into the corpus, or principal and the coupons, or interest. The coupons' cash flow, which is all the interest payments due over the life of the bond, is repackaged and sold to investors interested in current income while the stripped municipal bond is sold as a zero-coupon security with maturities ranging from six months to 30 years. Stripped municipals are also issued at a deep discount.

Call Provisions

Call provisions are standard features of most tax-exempt issues. They give the issuer the option to retire all or a portion of the bonds before the stated maturity date and at a set price- usually at a premium to par. The call provisions are described in the bond resolution and official statement and are set forth in the bonds. The call option is a benefit to the issuer, which gains the flexibility to retire an outstanding bond issue prior to its stated maturity date and thus reduce debt costs. If interest rates have fallen since the original bond offering, the issuer can refund the older, high-interest issue and offer a new issue at lower rates. Table 2.7 shows the redemption features of the State of California issue.

An *optional* call allows the issuer to redeem bonds usually on a certain, earliest possible date after the date of issue. A series of call dates are specified for a period after this first call date. If the bonds are to be called on the first call date at a premium to par, bonds called on subsequent call dates will gen-

TABLE 2.7 Sample Redemption Features

Redemption Provisions

Optional Redemption

The Bonds maturing on or before May 1, 2010, are not subject to optional redemption prior to their respective stated maturities. The bonds maturing on and after May 1, 2011, are subject to optional redemption prior to their respective stated maturity dates, in whole or in part, in such order of maturity as may be designated by the State Treasurer and by lot within any maturity, on any date on and after May 1, 2010, at the redemption prices stated below, plus accrued interest to the date fixed for redemption:

Redemption Dates	Redemption Price (as percentage of principal amount redeemed)
May 1, 2010, through April 30, 2011	101
May 1, 2011, and thereafter	100

Sinking Fund Redemption

Certain bonds maturing on a single date (the "Term Bonds") are subject to redemption prior to their respective stated maturity dates, in part, by lot, from sinking fund payments made by the state, at a redemption price of one hundred percent (100%) of the principal amount thereof, without premium, on May 1 of the years, and in the amounts, shown below:

Term Bonds Due May 1, 2026

Sinking Fund Payment Date (May 1)	Principal Amount Redeemed ($)
2023	15,965,000
2024	15,965,000
2025	15,965,000
2026*	15,965,000

Term Bonds Due May 1, 2030

Sinking Fund Payment Date (May 1)	Principal Amount Redeemed ($)
2027	15,965,000
2028	15,965,000
2029	15,965,000
2030*	15,965,000

If a Term Bond is called for optional redemption in part (see "Optional Redemption" above), the remaining sinking fund installments for such Term Bond shall be adjusted as determined by the State Treasurer.

*Maturity date.
Source: $500,000,000 State of California General Obligation Bonds, Official Statement Dated April 19, 2000.

erally be redeemed at descending prices. For example, bonds might be callable ten years from the date of issue at, for example, 101 percent of par. In the 11th year, they would be callable at a lower price, and at later dates at prices declining to par. The first call date and the premium are determined by issuers, to maximize their own flexibility and to maximize the bond's marketability. This applies to all types of calls.

A *mandatory* call requires the issuer to retire bonds before their stated maturity date. In the example of the State of California, each term bond has its own mandatory redemption schedule, which in this case are called sinking funds. Specific amounts, set out in the offering documents, are called, in this case, at par. Sinking funds can be used to help the issuer manage these mandatory call cash flows.

Sinking funds are reserves set aside yearly by the issuer to redeem term bonds over a specified period prior to the stated maturity date. Just as serial maturities help issuers spread their financial charges evenly, so do sinking funds help even out payments on term bonds. Instead of paying off the entire issue at maturity, the issuer pays a set amount annually into a sinking fund from which bonds are redeemed on a set schedule. Sinking funds, therefore, add a measure of security to the bonds.

Sinking fund retirements can be optional or mandatory. A provision might require or permit the issuer to redeem a certain principal amount of bonds beginning in ten years, or to buy bonds in that principal amount in the open market. If the bonds are redeemed, the price is always at par or higher, though sometimes the bonds can be bought below par in the open market. If interest rates have risen over the period, creating a downward pressure on bond prices, the possibility of early redemption by operation of the sinking fund will tend to keep the price of the bonds up. On the other hand, if falling interest rates tend to push prices above par, the sinking fund provisions can keep a lid on prices. The bonds to be retired are usually chosen at random, by lot. The procedure should be spelled out clearly in the official statement.

A *super sinker* is a fund that functions much like a conventional sinking fund. Super sinkers are attached to single-family mortgage revenue bond issues. These bonds have a specifically identified maturity date, and all mortgage prepayments are applied to the fund so that bonds can be retired before maturity. Such bonds typically carry a long-term maturity date (20 to 30 years, for example) but have a much shorter actual life (usually between four and six years), depending on the issuer's prepayment expectations.

Changes have evolved in call features to accommodate the needs of particular types of bond issues. For example, single-family housing revenue bonds typically contain a provision allowing the issuer to call the bonds at par at any time, using funds from unexpended bond proceeds or prepayments. This provision clearly benefits the issuer. If all the mortgage money is not loaned to mortgagees (perhaps because the interest rate was not competitive with that of less restrictive, conventional financing or because there were fewer mortgage applicants than predicted), the bonds can be called at par in as little as one year from date of issue. Also, if considerable mortgage prepayments are made, owing to a fall in conventional mortgage rates, a par call can be made at any time. Healthcare issuers have provisions in their documents that allow a call at any time if there are changes in their ownership that make outstanding bond covenants onerous.

Even if an issue carries conventional call features such as the 10-year optional call protection, however, the potential for capital gains is limited. Further, if the bonds are called, the investor is usually left with the principal to be reinvested at a lower interest rate. A yield to call, therefore, is commonly computed for callable bonds, especially those selling at a premium. It is simply the yield to maturity calculated to the call price and first call date. When buying and selling these bonds, dealers will customarily tell investors both the yield to call and the yield to maturity. The MSRB has adopted a rule requiring in a transaction effected on a yield basis that the dollar price be calculated to the lower of price to call or price to maturity and be disclosed in confirmations of transactions to investors and other dealers.

Bearer Bonds versus Registered Bonds

Under federal tax laws enacted in 1982 and with limited exceptions, all municipal bonds issued on and after July 1, 1983 must be registered as to principal and interest. Investors who purchase a fully registered bond will receive the interest payments, as well as the principal when due, without having to clip coupons. Until 1982 it was traditional for most municipalities to issue bearer bonds, which are negotiable by anyone who holds them and can prove ownership. Attached to bearer bonds are coupons representing interest due, which the bondholder must clip and deposit in a bank for collection from the issuer's paying agent. While their numbers have decreased greatly, there are still some bearer bonds are outstanding and available in the secondary market.

The use of registered bonds led to the development of *book-entry* securities for municipals patterned after the way the U.S. government securities market operated. With book-entry only, issuers deposit a single global certificate for each maturity of an issue at a central clearinghouse, the Depository Trust Company Corporation (DTCC). Ownership positions and transactions in each security, including purchases, sales, and interest or principal payments, are initially reflected in DTCC's records and thereafter in the records of thousands of participating banks and brokers nationwide. The investor does not receive a physical certificate representing bond ownership, as all records are kept electronically. Table 2.8 shows the growth in book-entry

TABLE 2.8   Book-Entry-Only Form as Percent of Total Long-Term
New-Issue Market, 1989–1999

Year	Book-Entry as Percentage of Long-Term Issues, by Volume
1989	40.0
1990	45.3
1991	53.8
1992	65.2
1993	69.4
1994	69.2
1995	70.4
1996	79.8
1997	81.3
1998	86.0
1999	90.5

Sources: Depository Trust and Clearing Corporation; The Bond
Market Association.

only, from 40.0 percent of the long-term, new-issue market in 1989 to 90.5
percent in 1999.

Collecting the Interest

As stated previously, interest on fixed-rate municipal bonds is generally paid
semiannually, usually on the 1st or 15th of the designated month. Holders of
book-entry bonds and registered bonds receive their interest payments automatically. Holders of bearer bonds must clip each coupon, which is num-
bered and dated, and present it to the issuer (usually to a bank that serves as
the paying agent) in order to receive the interest.

The bondholder is entitled to accrued interest, beginning at a specified
date on the bonds, known as the *dated date,* although the bonds are often actually sold or delivered at a different date. A so-called short coupon results
when the time between the dated date and the first coupon date is less than
six months. A long coupon results when the first coupon date is more than
six months away from the dated date.

Trading Plus Accrued Interest

Because most trading of municipal bonds takes place between interest payment dates, it is necessary to allocate interest between buyers and sellers. The
investor who sells bonds is entitled to the interest due since the last interest
payment date. The convention in the industry is that the buyer of the bonds

must pay the seller any interest due when the bonds are purchased. If the settlement date for an investor's bond sale is March, 1, for example, and the last coupon date was January 1, the seller is entitled to two months' interest from the buyer. Municipal bonds, then, trade *plus accrued interest*. That is, the interest due is added to the price of the bonds. The buyer, in turn, will collect and keep the full six months of interest due on the next interest payment date.

CHAPTER 3

The Issuers

INTRODUCTION

The history of municipal debt predates that of corporate debt by several centuries: during the Renaissance, Italian city-states borrowed money from the major merchant banking families. Although borrowing by some American cities dates back to the seventeenth century, careful records of U.S. municipal bond issues were begun only in the early 1800s. The first officially recorded municipal bond was a general obligation bond issued by New York City for a canal in 1812. By the 1840s, many U.S. cities were in the debt market, and by 1843 cities had about $25 million in outstanding debt. The following two decades of rapid urban development saw a correspondingly explosive growth in municipal debt, which was used to finance both urban improvements and a burgeoning system of free public education.

For a few years after the Civil War, a great deal of local debt was issued to build railroads. Because railroads were private corporations, these bond issues were very similar to today's industrial revenue bonds. In 1873 excessive construction costs on one of the largest transcontinental railroads, the Northern Pacific, closed down access to new capital. The country's largest bank, which was owned by the same investor as by Northern Pacific, collapsed because of this, as did smaller firms and the stock market. The Panic of 1873 and the several years of depression that followed put an abrupt, if temporary, halt to the rapid growth of municipal debt. In response to the widespread defaults that jolted the municipal bond market of the day, new state statutes were passed that restricted the issuance of local debt. Some states even wrote these restrictions into their constitutions. The legality of the railroad bonds was widely challenged, giving rise to the market-wide demand that an opinion of qualified bond counsel accompany each new issue.

Once the U.S. economy started to move forward again, municipal debt resumed its momentum, which it maintained well into the early part of the twentieth century. The Great Depression of the 1930s halted its growth, although defaults were not as severe as in the 1870s. The amount of municipal debt outstanding then fell during World War II as resources were devoted to the military. After the war, municipal debt burst into a new period of rapid growth for an ever-increasing variety of uses. Just after World War II, state and local debt was $145 per capita. By 1998, according to the U.S. Census, state debt was $1,791 per capita. Local per capita debt in 1996, the most current Census data available, was $2,704. Federal debt was $20,374 per capita at the end of 1998.

In addition to the 50 states and their local governments (including cities, counties, villages, and school districts), the District of Columbia and U.S. territories and possessions (American Samoa, the Commonwealth of Puerto Rico, Guam, the Northern Mariana Islands, and the U.S. Virgin Islands) can and do issue municipal bonds. Another important category of municipal bond issuers includes authorities and special districts, which have grown in number and variety in recent years.

AUTHORITIES AND SPECIAL DISTRICTS

In the early part of the twentieth century, state and local governments began to create debt-issuing entities called *authorities* and *special districts*. Sometimes they were formed to serve a geographic area that encompassed or crossed several political boundaries; sometimes they were formed in order to raise money for a single project whose purpose and use were not necessarily limited to one state, county, or city. Two prominent early authorities were the Port of New York Authority, formed in 1921 and renamed Port Authority of New York and New Jersey in 1972, and the Triborough Bridge Authority (now the Triborough Bridge and Tunnel Authority), formed in 1933. The debt issues of these two authorities are exempt from federal, state, and local taxes.

Today, authorities and special districts of all kinds are found across the country. The majority of states, for example, have housing authorities, which issue bonds. In addition, special district bonds are commonly issued to finance water, sewer, and utility services where user charges are involved. Indeed, bond-issuing authorities have been created to finance and construct a wide variety of public projects: surface transportation facilities including toll and non-toll roads; airports, docking facilities, and mass-transit systems; government-owned sports arenas and convention centers; resource-recovery systems; educational facilities; and hospitals.

The U.S. Bureau of the Census categorizes the nation's governmental units into seven groups. According to census figures for 1997, there were 87,504 units of government. Table 3.1 shows the distribution of governmental units in 1997, 1992, 1987, and 1977 and the percentage increase or decrease in each category.

The 87,453 local governments reported in 1997 were 2,498 more than were reported for the 1992 census, an overall increase of 2.9%. Most of the

TABLE 3.1 Type of Governmental Unit

	1997	1992	1987	1977	Percentage Change 1997–92	Percentage Change 1992–87	Percentage Change 1987–77
Federal	1	1	1	1	0.0	0.0	0.0
State	50	50	50	50	0.0	0.0	0.0
County	3,043	3,043	3,042	3,042	0.0	0.0	0.0
Municipal	19,372	19,279	19,200	18,862	0.5	0.4	1.8
Town/township	16,629	16,656	16,691	16,822	–0.2	–0.2	–0.8
School district	13,726	14,422	14,721	15,174	–4.8	–2.0	–3.0
Special district	34,683	31,555	29,532	25,962	9.9	6.9	13.8
Total local	87,453	84,955	83,186	79,862	2.9	2.1	4.2
Total overall	87,504	85,006	83,237	79,913	2.9	2.1	4.2

Source: U.S. Bureau of the Census.

increase was in special district governments, which increased 9.9% over the five-year period on top of a 6.9% rise between 1987 and 1992. This increase in special district governments reflects the increased demand for services not performed directly by the existing state and local governments. Towns, townships, and school districts decreased, indicating that there were some consolidations in these units.

THE THEORY OF MUNICIPAL DEBT: PAY-AS-YOU-USE VERSUS PAY-AS-YOU-GO

Corporations borrow to build facilities or to make other investments that will improve their profits and returns on equity. The cash flow from their businesses and investments is used to repay the debt. Most state and local governments do not have the same profit motive as privately held corporations. They borrow for public purposes that better the lives of the people who live in the community or of those who use the services of municipal enterprises and certain not-for-profit organizations. The decisions as to what kind of debt to issue, along with who will repay the debt and in what way, tend to depend on the political and economic climate of the community.

Proponents of debt financing argue that new facilities should be paid for over time by all of the people who benefit from them—the *pay-as-you-use* approach. According to this argument, a community that pays for a new water system immediately assumes a burden that should be shared by future users, who will also benefit from the water system. Furthermore, it is argued, a growing city will be better able to afford the debt payments over time—and new projects today may be necessary for the municipality's growth tomorrow. With this in mind, policy makers often want the repayment schedule for municipal debt incurred to finance a project to coincide with the minimum useful life of that project.

The theory behind municipal revenue bonds is, in part, an extension of this pay-as-you-use philosophy. Revenue bonds are repaid with revenues generated by the particular project being financed. The beneficiaries of the project—the customers or users—pay off the debt, not the community as a whole.

At a time when debt financing has become the norm for corporations, municipalities, and consumers alike, theoretical justifications for borrowing may seem unnecessary. However, there may be political or economic circumstances under which governmental officials or the taxpayers or ratepayers may favor a pay-as-you-go approach. In *pay-as-you-go,* the capital projects are fully funded at the time of construction in cash from current revenues or accumulated cash. The advantages of pay-as-you-go include no interest costs, no issuance costs, no debt covenants, no overissuance of debt, and no burdening of future generations with debt.

Political pressure as well as economic circumstances can also affect the issuance of municipal debt. One way to limit tax increases and the issuance of debt is through changes to a state's constitution. In 1978, California voters approved Proposition 13, which amended the state's constitution to limiting the real estate tax to 1% of full value of the property tax base. This dramatically limited property tax increases and substantially slowed the issuance of general obligation debt in the state. In 1982, Proposition 2½, which limited overall debt to 2.5% of property values, was passed by the voters of Massachusetts. In 1996, Californians passed Proposition 218, a constitutional amendment aimed at tightening loopholes in previous tax-restriction initiatives.

Another way to limit the issuance of debt is through voter rejection of general obligation bond issues. It is interesting to examine the percentage of general obligation municipal bonds that are approved at elections. Table 3.2 shows the percentage of bonds approved at selected elections held in the years since 1947. The five years since 1947 with the highest approval rates and the five years with the lowest approval rates are presented.

The postwar years, with their low interest rates and great economic confidence, had the highest approval rates of municipal bond issues over the past 50 years. The more politically turbulent times of the late 1960s and early 1970s had the lowest approval rates. It is safe to conclude that the willingness of voters to have their governments issue bonds and debt for capital improvements fluctuates with both the health of the national economy and the political climate of the times.

The effect of property-tax limitations and swings in the approval rates for general obligation bond issues can be seen in the changing composition of state and local governmental units shown in Chart 3.1. Debt and tax lim-

TABLE 3.2 Municipal Bond Approval Rates, All Elections

Year	Percentage Approved
Highest five years	
1947	91.9
1951	88.2
1956	87.5
1946	87.4
1960	85.4
Lowest five years	
1973	52.1
1994	41.7
1969	39.6
1971	34.9
1975	29.3

Source: The Bond Buyer Securities Data Company 1999 Yearbook.

itations on traditional governments are further stimulants for creating special districts for financing operating and capital expenditures. However, these transformations are concentrated in a relatively small number of states. For example, more than half of the special districts in the United States are located in nine states, with California at 2,797 districts and Illinois at 2,920 being the two largest.

THE USES OF MUNICIPAL DEBT

Municipal bonds are issued for many purposes. The basic infrastructure needs of state and local governmental units, together with many other uses that provide public benefits, have led to a diverse market. Municipal bonds generally finance capital projects, those that will be of long-term use. The day-to-day operating expenses of state and local governments are paid for out of taxes and other current revenues.

The major purposes for which municipal debt has been issued in selected years are shown in Table 3.3.

Thirty-one percent of debt issuance in 1979 was for other, primarily general governmental purposes and education, the top two categories. By 1999, 52% of debt was issued for these two purposes. Changes in tax law and public policy have at times diminished the issuance of industrial development bonds, multifamily housing bonds, and other categories. The largest municipal issues have in most cases been for general governmental purposes, utilities, and transportation. The first $1 billion issue in the municipal market was for the Municipal Assistance Corporation for the City of New York in 1975.

TABLE 3.3 Major Purposes of Short- and Long-Term Municipal Debt, 1979, 1989, and 1999

General Use of Proceeds	January 1, 1999–December 31, 1999		January 1, 1989–December 31, 1989		January 1, 1979–December 31, 1979	
	Principal Amount ($millions)	Market Share (%)	Amount Principal ($ millions)	Share Market (%)	Principal Amount ($ millions)	Market Share (%)
Airports	6,231.9	2.4	2,747.9	1.8	675.9	1.6
Combined utilities	1,071.2	0.4	2,267.0	1.5	1,087.0	2.6
Economic development	3,999.1	1.5	2,434.0	1.6	0.4	0.0
Education	58,588.9	22.2	21,485.5	13.9	4,999.7	12.1
Healthcare	22,754.8	8.6	14,375.3	9.3	3,415.3	8.3
Industrial development	5,112.1	1.9	3,335.6	2.2	1,658.5	4.0
Multifamily housing	6,958.4	2.6	3,255.5	2.1	2,990.7	7.2
Nursing homes/life care	5,286.7	2.0	1,612.6	1.0	57.5	0.1
Other miscellaneous	79,341.6	30.0	58,098.3	37.6	7,723.3	18.7
Pollution control	9,048.9	3.4	2,328.4	1.5	2,617.9	6.3
Public power	7,099.5	2.7	8,199.7	5.3	3,414.5	8.3
Single family housing	16,182.7	6.1	8,602.4	5.6	7,541.2	18.3
Solid waste/resource recovery	1,195.4	0.5	3,193.3	2.1	54.0	0.1
Student loans	5,467.3	2.1	1,963.6	1.3	144.1	0.4
Transportation	17,230.9	6.5	7,992.9	5.2	1,441.3	3.5
Water,sewer, and gas	17,396.1	6.6	12,076.7	7.8	3,376.4	8.2
Waterfront/seaports	1,205.7	0.5	650.1	0.4	126.5	0.3
Industry Totals	264,171.2	100.0	154,618.6	100.0	41,324.0	100.0

Source: Thomson Financial Securities Data.

TABLE 3.4 Largest Long-Term Municipal Issues 1947–1999

Sale Date		Rank and Issuer	State	Par Amount ($ millions)
5/13/98	1	Long Island Power Authority	NY	3,424.5
6/26/97	2	New Jersey Economic Development Authority	NJ	2,803.0
11/21/85	3	New Jersey Turnpike Authority	NJ	2,000.0
12/18/92	4	New Jersey, general obligations	NJ	1,804.6
11/22/91	5	New Jersey Turnpike Authority	NJ	1,618.9
1/15/93	6	North Carolina Eastern Municipal Power Authority	NC	1,614.6
7/16/99	7	Foothill/Eastern Transportation Corridor/Orange County	CA	1,588.1
4/2/87	8	Puerto Rico general obligations	PR	1,546.6
9/26/97	9	San Joaquin Hills Trans Corridor, Orange County	CA	1,448.3
2/19/92	10	California, general obligations	CA	1,390.0

Source: Thomson Financial Securities Data.

Since then, there have been dozens of issues exceeding $1 billion. Table 3.4 lists the 10 single largest municipal issues that had been sold through the end of 1999.

THE SECURITY FOR MUNICIPAL BONDS

With the increased diversification of governmental units and of the purposes for which bonds are issued, there has been increased diversification in the security structures provided to bondholders. In the most general terms, securities can be categorized as general obligation (GO) or revenue bonds. Table 3.5 shows the issuance of GOs and revenue bonds, each as a percentage of the total new-issue market, from 1975 to 1999. Within these two broad categories, there are dozens of variations of security features. This next section offers a brief discussion of the diverse security features of GO and revenue bonds.

Tax-Backed Bonds

General Obligation Bonds. In recent years, the terms *tax-backed* and *tax-supported* bonds have been used to encompass both some of the most traditional and some of the most innovative forms of municipal securities. The security for GO bonds is the general creditworthiness and the taxing power of the state or local government issuing the bonds. Most municipal governments depend largely on *ad valorem* (to the value added), or value-based, property taxes for their revenues. State governments, however, usually do not levy real estate taxes but rely mostly on sales and income taxes. The *full-faith-and-credit* backing of a GO bond implies that all sources of revenue, unless

TABLE 3.5 Long-Term General Obligation and Revenue Bond Issuance, 1975–1999

| | General Obligation | | Revenue | | |
Year	Principal Amount ($ billions)	Percent of Total	Principal Amount ($ billions)	Percent of Total	Total Volume ($ billions)
1975	13.5	53.2	11.9	46.8	25.3
1976	16.2	48.7	17.0	51.3	33.2
1977	15.1	35.6	27.2	64.4	42.3
1978	15.0	32.3	31.4	67.7	46.3
1979	10.2	24.6	31.1	75.4	41.2
1980	13.7	29.6	32.6	70.4	46.3
1981	12.3	27.0	33.3	73.0	45.6
1982	20.1	25.8	57.8	74.2	77.9
1983	18.9	22.1	66.6	77.9	85.5
1984	22.3	21.1	83.3	78.9	105.6
1985	39.7	19.2	167.2	80.8	206.9
1986	45.0	29.8	105.7	70.2	150.7
1987	30.5	29.1	74.5	70.9	105.1
1988	30.9	26.3	86.5	73.7	117.4
1989	38.4	30.7	86.6	69.3	125.0
1990	40.3	31.5	87.7	68.5	128.0
1991	57.2	33.1	115.6	66.9	172.8
1992	80.4	34.3	154.3	65.7	234.7
1993	91.6	31.3	201.0	68.7	292.5
1994	55.8	33.8	109.3	66.2	165.1
1995	60.4	37.7	99.6	62.3	160.0
1996	64.4	34.8	120.7	65.2	185.0
1997	72.3	32.8	148.3	67.2	220.6
1998	93.5	32.7	192.7	67.3	286.2
1999	70.2	31.0	156.6	69.0	226.8

Source: Thomson Financial Securities Data, March 13, 2000.

specifically limited, will be used to pay debt service on the bonds. There are exceptions to this, as some issuers sell GO bonds backed by the "faith and credit" as opposed to "full faith and credit."

Unlimited tax bonds are GO securities that are backed by the full faith and credit of the state or local government. This means that the taxing power of the issuer in support of the payment of the securities is not limited as to rate or amount.

Conversely, *limited tax bonds* are used when the taxing power of the governmental issuer in support of the municipal security is specifically limited by their constitution or by statutes. The tax rate on assessed property value, for example, or the assessment rate itself may have a ceiling.

Other Tax-Backed Bonds. *Moral obligation bonds* are securities with a governmental guarantor who does not have a legal obligation to repay the debt. The pledge is used most often to enhance the credit of an agency that issues revenue bonds (e.g., housing agencies). When revenues are insufficient to cover debt service, the debt service reserve fund is used to make the necessary payments. Such a fund usually holds six months to one year in principal and interest payments. The moral obligation mechanism then calls for notification to the legislature or other governing body to replenish the reserve fund before the next interest payment date, if the legislature so desires.

Government credit-enhancement bonds encompass programs that range from partial to total credit substitution of a stronger governmental entity for a weaker one. An example of this security is state school bond credit-enhancement programs, the structures for which vary considerably from state to state. A common form of enhancement is the *state-aid intercept mechanism*, whereby a state withholds state-aid payments otherwise due a school district that has defaulted, or is expected to default, on a debt-service payment. The state then forwards the intercepted state-aid payments to the bond trustee to be used to pay debt service. The extent to which the state credit substitutes for that of the school district will depend on the specific rules and procedures of each program. Some states directly guarantee the bonds of the participating school districts; in these cases, the school bonds enjoy the same rating as the state. Other states use intercept mechanisms to enhance the credit of school district bonds; in these cases, the districts' ratings will be lower than those of the states. Other government credit-enhancement programs include annual appropriations by a state to the issuer of the bonds.

Leases and appropriation-backed obligations may be used if the issuer is constitutionally prohibited from using general obligation debt or if voter approval for general obligations is considered unlikely. Rental payments are made to the governmental entity (such as a town or a school district), to a lessor (this can be a not-for-profit financing corporation or other governmental unit) for a specific asset, such as an office building or a school. The rental payments are derived from taxes or other revenues, and most municipal leases require an annual appropriation for principal and interest. This inherently makes them less creditworthy than GO bonds. The certificates of participation structure is widely used by governments for lease-backed financing property and equipment.

A *certificate of participation (COP)* is an arrangement in which investors buy certificates that entitle them to receive a participation, or share, in the lease payments from a particular project. The lease payments are passed through the lessor to the certificate holders with the tax advantages intact. The lessor typically assigns the lease and lease payments to a trustee, who then distributes the lease payments to the certificate holders.

The government lessee commits to making future payments without incurring "debt" by using a lease that must either contain an acceptance or rent abatement clause or be renewable subject to appropriation risk. The abatement clause provides that if a property cannot be utilized (e.g., because of damage by earthquake or construction delays) the lessee cannot be compelled to make the lease payments. This clause makes the lease payments "fees for services" rather than debt, but the obligation to make payments remains a long-term obligation. Insurance provisions are generally included to protect against abatement risk. A nonappropriation clause allows the government to terminate the lease if its appropriating body does not allocate the necessary funds. Other important considerations in a COP financing are the sources of funds for repayment and the useful life of the item being financed.

Special-purpose district bonds and *special-assessment bonds* are part of one of the most rapidly growing areas of tax-backed financings. This is because only those who directly benefit from the bond-financed improvements are obligated to pay special taxes or special assessments on property for the repayment of the bonds.

Special-tax bonds are hybrid securities that combine elements of general obligation and revenue bonds. For example, specific but broad-based taxes such as motor fuel taxes may be used as part of a security package for a transportation financing.

Tax-increment bonds or *tax-allocation bonds* are used to finance improvements in developing and redeveloping areas. A base year for property assessment is set by a redevelopment agency. Taxes that are levied on the incremental growth in assessed valuation in the redevelopment district are used for debt repayment.

Tax-based notes, including TANS, RANS, BANS, general obligation notes, and certain forms of commercial paper, are also tax-backed securities.

Revenue Bonds

Revenue bonds are payable from a specific stream or streams of revenues other than property taxes and are not backed by the full-faith-and-credit taxing power of the issuer. Revenue bonds offer an advantage to the issuer in that they do not usually require electoral approval or constitute debt within the meaning of applicable constitutional or statutory limitations. They are issued to finance specific enterprises or projects and are usually secured solely by the revenues from those projects. In addition, the issuers may offer related covenants to assure the adequacy of the pledged revenue sources. Sometimes there will be a mortgage on the facilities financed by the revenue bonds, although this security feature has been used less often in recent years. There are times when an issuer will pledge its taxing power to offer additional security for its revenue bonds; these hybrid obligations are called *double-barreled bonds.*

The revenue bond issuer may be the state or local government itself, or the issuer may be an authority, as explained above. Revenue bonds can be grouped in six general categories: utilities; health care, higher education, and other not-for-profits; housing; transportation; and industrial development; and securitized revenue bonds. Of course, the types of revenues that can be used to back the bonds are related to the categories of the bonds. Chapter 7 delves more deeply into how to analyze the credit quality of different types of revenue bonds.

Utilities.   Revenue bonds are used to finance electric power, gas, water, wastewater, and solid waste systems. Utilities that provide electric power and are owned by a local governmental unit or authority are also called *public power*. These agencies may (1) generate their own electricity, (2) distribute electricity, (3) both generate and distribute electricity, or (4) engage in joint action, in which two or more governmental units or authorities combine to finance one of these three options. Independent power producers and rural electric cooperatives also issue revenue bonds. Examples of public power issuers are the Washington Public Power Supply System, the Puerto Rico Electric Power Authority, and the Omaha Public Power District.

Water systems, wastewater systems, and combined systems are steady issuers of revenue bonds. Among the issuers is the municipality itself, for which the water and wastewater systems are accounted in separate enterprise funds. Examples of this type of issuer are the City of Detroit Sewer Disposal System and the City of Detroit Water Supply System. The issuer can also be a separate municipal authority, such as the New York City Municipal Water Finance Authority. Although these systems have traditionally been financed at the local level, special state issuers called *revolving funds* have been established to assist localities in building facilities that will enable them to comply with environmental regulations; the New York State Environmental Facilities Corporation is an example. Gas systems can be financed under a city's name or as part of a combined utility system, such as the City of San Antonio Electric and Gas Systems. Solid waste and resource-recovery plants are often financed with revenue bonds, such as those of the Palm Beach County Solid Waste Authority in Florida.

Health Care, Higher Education, and Other Not-for-Profit.   Revenue bonds are used to finance hospitals, other health-care providers, public and private colleges and universities, private elementary and secondary schools, museums, and other not-for-profit institutions. State legislatures have not only created health, educational, dormitory, and cultural authorities but they have also authorized units of local governments to issue bonds on behalf of not-for-profit entities (which are not in themselves municipalities) and public colleges. Not-for-profit entities are also often referred to as 501c(3)'s, based on the section of the Internal Revenue Service Code under which they derive their tax exemption.

Bonds can be issued for medical facilities such as stand-alone hospitals, multihospital systems, and academic medical centers. Nursing homes, assisted living facilities, continuing care retirement communities, rehabilitation centers, and other healthcare related faciliites are also financed wth bonds. The issuer in these examples is a state or local authority, acting as a conduit for the obligated party, which is the organization that will actually benefit from the bonds (i.e., the hospital). Examples of hospitals financed with bonds include: The Johns Hopkins Hospital, The Cleveland Clinic, and The Sisters of Mercy Health System.

Private colleges and universities can also issue revenue bonds through an authority for construction of educational facilities. Examples of this are the Dormitory Authority of New York, issuing on behalf of Cornell University, and the Connecticut Health and Educational Facility Authority, acting for Yale University. Public universities such as the Regents of the University of California also issue bonds. Private elementary and secondary schools that have investment-grade ratings or that have been able to arrange credit enhancement have become greater issuers of bonds. Museums, such as the Getty Museum, and cultural institutions, such as Carnegie Hall, have issued bonds for capital projects. Other kinds of not-for-profit organizations that have issued bonds include social service providers, membership organization headquarters, federations, and biomedical research institutes.

The revenues generated from these organizations are used to repay the bonds. These revenues include, but are certainly not limited to, inpatient and outpatient charges and managed care contracts for hospitals; tuition, student, dormitory, and other fees for universities; and entrance fees, ticket sales, and membership dues for museums, cultural institutions, and other not-for-profits.

Housing. Revenue bonds are used to finance multifamily housing for low- or moderate-income families, single-family housing for first-time homebuyers, and housing for the aged and veterans. State or local housing finance agencies issue these bonds. Housing bonds are structured in a variety of ways, in part because they are subject to significant restriction and regulation under federal tax laws. State housing agencies often administer a wide range of programs that most closely meets the needs of the people of the state. Most states have a housing finance authority; examples of agencies that have multiple programs include the California Housing Finance Agency and the Pennsylvania Housing Finance Agency. Local housing finance agencies also issue bonds for single family, multifamily, and other housing purposes.

Housing bonds are payable from rents, mortgage payments, and various subsidies received under federal programs. A more detailed discussion of these revenues can be found in Chapter 7.

Transportation.   Revenue bonds are used to finance highways, turnpikes, airports, ports, bridges, tunnels, and mass-transportation facilities. The issuer can be a state or local authority or the governmental unit itself. Transportation revenue bonds and the projects that they finance are often cited in reference to specific municipal revenue bonds; for example, a road or bridge that collects tolls from users is an example of an entity that uses a portion of its revenues to repay the debt incurred to construct the specific revenue-generating project.

Each transportation project can have its own unique security structure, depending on the scope of the project and its community and political support. Surface transportation facilities such as highways and turnpikes may use tolls or specific taxes to repay bonds. Bridges, airports, tunnels, mass-transportation facilities, and similar projects that are financed by revenue bonds raise funds through tolls, fares, concessions, and direct fees. Tolls are collected on bridges, for example, and car rental companies pay concession fees for use of space at airports.

Industrial Development, Pollution Control, and Other Exempt Facility Bonds.   *Industrial development bonds (IDBs)* and municipal securities issued for other types of exempt facilities are revenue bonds where the credit and repayment source is the private entity for which the facilities are financed. The term *exempt facilities* refers to specific types of privately owned or privately used facilities for which bonds can be issued on a tax-exempt basis under the Internal Revenue Code. Principal categories of exempt facilities for which, subject to restrictions and volume limitations, bonds can be issued under the 1986 code include governmentally owned airports; docks, wharves, and mass-commuting facilities; water-supply systems; sewage facilities; certain solid waste–disposal facilities; qualified hazardous waste facilities; qualified residential rental projects; and facilities for local furnishing of electric energy or gas and local district heating or cooling facilities. In addition, IDBs may be issued to finance qualified projects for manufacturing, certain farming purposes, and qualified student loans and qualified redevelopment projects.

Typically, these bonds are issued by a local governmental unit to finance facilities that are then leased to the private-entity user at a rent equal to debt service on the bonds and for a term equal to the maturity of the securities. Alternatively, in some jurisdictions, the issuer loans the proceeds of the IDBs directly to the private-entity user on repayment terms equal to the terms on the IDBs. The advantage to the private-entity user is to obtain financing at tax-exempt rates in return for making a capital investment that contributes to

enumerated public purposes of the issuer, such as job creation, the enhancement of air or water quality, or increase of the tax base.

Securitized Revenue Bonds. *Securitized revenue bonds* are a relatively new
structure in the municipal market. They have the characteristics of revenue
bonds, with a specific revenue stream pledged to the repayment of the debt.
They also have characteristics of asset-backed bonds, with the focus on the financial performance of specific assets. These assets can be tax liens, other
taxes, governmental grants, tobacco settlements, or other sources with an
identifiable cash flow. The structures for securitized revenue bonds are evolving and developing. The focus has been on making securitized bonds more
legally isolated and bankruptcy remote from the issuer. The issuer aims for a
higher rating based on the legal protections and cash flow of the assets that
are being securitized.

THE FINANCING PROCESS

Capital Improvement Plan

The first step in the financing process is for the issuer to assess its capital and
operational needs, taking into account current needs and new policy man-
dates. Depending on the issuer, this may involve studying population growth,
patterns of commutation, business growth, utility usage, or the healthcare
needs of a community. A 5- to 10-year *capital improvement plan (CIP)* is then
developed, detailing the uses and sources of funds. The needs, such as additional schools, roads, housing or healthcare facilities, or expanded power
generation, are quantified into dollars. Bonds may also be used for debt repayment. The sources of funds, including current and additional taxes or revenue, grants, and notes or bonds, are estimated over the same time period.
For revenue bond issuers, the capital improvement plan usually contains projections of their income and balance sheets.

Political Factors

In addition to developing a CIP, the issuer must also shepherd the prospective
financing through public scrutiny and the political process. Bond issues need-
ing voter approval must be included in elections. For bond issues to pass, the
potential users of and payers for the project should be knowledgeable about
the costs and benefits. Community support is also important in the location
of controversial or sensitive projects, such as sewage treatment plants and
solid waste facilities.

There may be instances in which enabling legislation must be passed to
create a new authority. An example of this is the establishment of the *Transi-*

tional Finance Authority (TFA) in New York City in 1997. The City has an extensive and ongoing capital improvement plan, funded from a variety of sources, including general obligation bonds. In the mid-1990s New York City was close to its general obligation debt limit, meaning that traditional new bonds could not be sold to continue the multiyear program. The New York State Legislature passed a law creating the Transitional Finance Authority, whose bonds, secured by a portion of the city income tax, would be used for the city's capital purposes. As TFA bonds are not general obligations of the city, they are exempt from the debt limits embodied in the state constitution.

Selecting the Financing Team

The issuer identifies the professional services that are required to assemble and sell the bond issue. These professionals include legal counsel, financial advisor, and underwriter. The issuer also increasingly has its own investor relations professionals, who are available to answer questions and provide information to investors during the sale of the bonds and after.

Bond Counsel. Bond counsel performs many functions and is often selected very early in the process, because expert legal advice is needed in interpreting existing legislation and state and local finance laws. If new legislation is needed, bond counsel is instrumental in its drafting. Because tax-exempt issues are not marketable without an opinion from a nationally recognized bond counsel, the selection of such a counsel is a critical first decision in the financing process. Those involved in the search for such professional help should be aware that bond counsel has the following responsibilities:

1. Affirms the issuer's conformity with all legal requirements and authorization of the bond offering
2. Prepares and supervises bond proceedings
3. Obtains necessary approvals from governmental authorities
4. Attests to the validity and enforceability of the bonds
5. Confirms tax-exempt status of offering
6. Discloses and examines litigation that may jeopardize the validity of the offering
7. Interprets arbitrage regulations and tax law and provides guidance in structuring the issue
8. Drafts key financing documents

Financial Advisor. When the issuer is large enough to have a financial staff experienced in handling the details of bond transactions it is not necessary to hire a financial advisor. However, both large, sophisticated issuers and smaller, less knowledgeable issuers employ financial advisors to work with them during all phases of their financings. This work includes the following areas:

1. Determining financing needs and preparing analyses and plans
2. Evaluating financing options (e.g., long-term versus short-term debt) and different types of securities under different scenarios
3. Recommending negotiated or competitive sales
4. Assisting in underwriter selection for negotiated sale
5. Assisting in preparation of documents (official statement and notice of sale) for competitive bond sales
6. Preparing for and participating in rating agency presentations
7. Giving advice during pricing and sale of bonds

The Underwriter: Negotiated versus Competitive Sales. The issuer's decision to sell bonds either by competitive or by negotiated sale is often governed by state law. Certain types of municipal securities, particularly GO bonds, may be required by law to be offered pursuant to advertised sale or competitive bidding. Even where there are no such requirements, issuers who benefit from competitive bids include the frequent or well-known issuer with a simple bond structure and a higher-quality credit. The issuer usually receives at least two sealed bids, and that may assure local officials that the bonds have been correctly priced. For complicated offerings or lesser-known issuers, a negotiated sale may offer a better alternative. In a negotiated sale, the underwriter markets the bonds more extensively by providing investors with detailed information about the issue. In addition, there is flexibility in the timing of negotiated offerings, enabling the underwriter to take advantage of market conditions and steer through volatile market periods, as well as to develop a structure that suits current market conditions. There is often an underwriter's counsel who represents the interests of the underwriter.

The trend in the market over the past 25 years has been the increased use of negotiated sales. In 1975, 34% of the new-issue market was negotiated, while by 1999, it had grown to 74%. Chapter 4, *The Primary Market*, includes several charts on negotiated and competitive sales.

Private placements occur when the investment banker offers the securities directly to investors, without a public underwriting. Typically, the placement agent (the term for the underwriter in this type of transaction) contacts one or more institutional investors. The investor has the ability to negotiate favorable covenants with the issuer and to have greater influence over how the deal is structured. An issuers may want to do a private placement if its credit is new, of lower grade, or unrated. An advantage of a private placement is that information on the issuer would remain contained and controlled and would not be disseminated outside of the immediate circle of investors. Investors often will sign *investor letters,* which delineate the allowable secondary-market activity.

THE FINANCING DOCUMENTS

The issuer, together with the bond counsel, the financial advisor, and, if the issue is to be sold on a negotiated basis, the underwriter and its counsel, develop the financing documents that are the backbone of the deal. Working group meetings are held so that all the parties become conversant with the basic terms of the financings. Strategic decisions about security, size, and maturity of the issue are made, using market barometers, relevant legislation, and the issuer's own planning tools, such as the capital improvement plan. It is more common than not for the structure to evolve and change many times before the closing. The financing documents that are drafted may include many of those described in this section, again depending on the individual deal structure and state law.

Web sites for working groups on new issues have been created by private data vendors. The working groups can set up secure sites on the Internet, where all phases of the issue—from the initial draft of the preliminary official statement to the final draft of the bond purchase agreement—can be accessed and shared by all members of the group. Because access to the site can be tracked, all members of the group can always know the working status of any document in progress.

Authorizing Resolution

The governing board of the issuer authorizes the sale of debt through a resolution. The authorizing resolution will state the general terms of the financing, such as the maturity schedule, the size of debt (limited to a not-to-exceed amount), and the maximum interest cost allowable. The legal basis for the debt, be it a local ordinance or state legislation, is also cited.

Bond Resolution, Indenture, and Trust Agreement

The bond resolution, the indenture, and the trust agreement are the heart of the issue's legal structure. The key agreements between the issuer and the bondholders are written into these documents. It is common for a general obligation bond issue or a note issue to be accompanied by a bond or note resolution. Revenue bond issues have either a bond resolution or an indenture. Leases or certificates of participation generally use a trust agreement. Master trust indentures or master resolutions, with supplemental or series resolutions, have been used for cases in which many series of bonds over a period of time have been issued for the same ultimate borrower.

All these documents cover the mechanics of the issue, including the principal and interest payment dates, method and place of payment, and for variable rate bonds, the terms of how the interest rate will be set. They also establish key bond funds such as the construction fund, the debt-service fund, and required reserves. Redemption provisions, if any, are delineated. Other key sections of the indenture include the pledge of revenues and the order in which those funds are applied (called the *flow of funds*); key financial, operating, and tax covenants; and a description of the investments that the issuer is permitted to make with the monies held in the various bond funds. The importance of this is discussed further in Chapter 7. The indenture describes what the events of default are and the remedies that bondholders have, along with methods of defeasance and the rights of the credit enhancer, if any.

Lease Agreement

A lease agreement is used when the financing includes lease revenue bonds or certificates of participation. The agreement spells out the terms between the lessee (the governmental unit that uses the facility) and the lessor (a municipal authority or corporation or a not-for-profit corporation created by the governmental unit to act as the financing unit). The lease agreement includes sections relating to the maintenance of the property and to lease payments, just as would be found in a non-financing lease. It will also include the length of the lease (most often corresponding to the maturity schedule of the bonds) and what happens with prepayments (provisions should correspond to the trust agreement or indenture). The basic security, be it an annual appropriation of the lessee or, in some states, a covenant to budget and appropriate, is stated. The rights of the bondholders, as assigned to the trustee, are stated, including the ability of the trustee to repossess the property for non-appropriation of rentals.

Official Statement

The *official statement (OS)* is the issuer's offering document for publicly sold securities. The *preliminary official statement (POS)*, distributed either by the underwriter (in a negotiated issue) or by the issuer or financial advisor (in a competitive sale), is used to inform potential investors about the issuer and about the preliminary terms of the bonds being offered. The preliminary official statement is also called a *red herring* because along the side of the prospectus, printed in red ink, are statements that the information contained in the POS is subject to completion or amendment and that the POS is not an offer to sell the securities. A *deemed final official statement* is, for all practical purposes the same as a preliminary official statement. A final official statement includes the final terms of the issue, including the total principal amount, a list of serial and term bonds with their corresponding interest rates and maturities, and the sources and uses of the bond proceeds.

There is no list of mandatory information that must be included in the official statement. The SEC, in adopting amendments to Rule 15c2-12, recognized in its Interpretive Release "the extensive voluntary guidelines issued by the Government Finance Officer's Association (GFOA) and the industry-specific guidelines published by groups such as the National Federation of Municipal Analysts." The SEC encourages market participants to refer to those voluntary guidelines and the Interpretive Release in preparing disclosure documents. These are for general guidance only. According to the SEC, the GFOA, in its pamphlet *Disclosure Guidelines for State and Local Government Securities* (January 1991), calls for the following guidelines:

1. An introduction to serve as a guide to the official statement
2. A description of the securities being offered, including complete information regarding the purposes of the offering, the plan of financing, the security and sources of repayment, and the priority of the securities, as well as structural characteristics such as call provisions, tender options, original-issue or deep discount, variable rates, and lease-purchase agreements
3. Information regarding the nature and extent of any credit enhancement and financial and business information about the issuer of the enhancement
4. A description of the government issuer or enterprise, including information about the issuer's range or level of service, capacity, and demographic factors, and in the case of revenue-supported offerings, information on the enterprise's organization, management, revenue structure, results of operations, and operating plan
5. With respect to the obligations of private, profit-making, and nonprofit conduit issuers, information regarding the business or other activity, including the enterprise's form of organization and management, rate-making or pricing policies, and historical operations and plan or operation
6. A description of the issuer's outstanding debt, including the authority to incur debt, limitations on debt, and the prospective debt burden and rate of its retirement
7. A description of the basic documentation, such as indentures, trust agreements, and resolutions authorizing the issuance and establishing the rights of the parties
8. Financial information, including summary information regarding the issuer's or obligor's financial practices and results of operations and finan-

cial statements, all prepared in conformity with generally accepted accounting principles and audited in accordance with generally accepted
auditing standards

9. Discussion of legal matters, such as pending judicial, administrative, or
   regulatory proceedings that may significantly affect the securities offered, legal opinions, and tax considerations

10. Discussion of miscellaneous matters, including ratings and their descrip-
    tions and meanings, underwriting arrangements, arrangements with fi-
    nancial advisors, interests of named experts, pending legislation, and the
    availability of additional information and documentation

The cover page of an official statement gives a summary of the terms and
features of the securities. Below are The Bond Market Association's recommendations for the information that should be included on the front cover of
an official statement (if there is insufficient space available on the front cover,
this information should be included in the summary statement). A sample
cover page is shown in Figure 3.1 with the items in the following list indicated
by number.

1. Dollar amount and name of the bond issue.
2. Name of issuer (if not contained within the name of the issue), conduit
   transactions, and identification of the underlying obligor.
3. Interest rate or rates, together with the maturity date, the interest-
   payment date or dates, and the serial and term maturity amounts. Identification of variable-rate formula for determining the rate and frequency
   of rate changes, the date from which interest is paid, and identification
   of any special-interest payment features (e.g., zero coupon, limited interest, variable rate, etc.).
4. The dated date of the bonds and (if different) the date interest begins to
   accrue, together with the terms of interest and principal payments, including dates and manner of payment.
5. Summary of bond counsel's tax opinion.
6. Brief description of sources of payment for the bonds.
7. Identification of credit enhancement, if any.
8. Purpose and authority for the bond issue.
9. Name and location of trustee and/or paying agent.
10. Authorized denominations and registration provisions.
11. Whether bonds are subject to redemption.
12. Initial offering prices and/or yields.
13. Ratings, if desired.
14. Date and location of expected delivery of bonds.
15. Name of counsel providing opinions.
16. Any other special terms or provisions.

FIGURE 3.1   Sample Front Cover of Official Statement

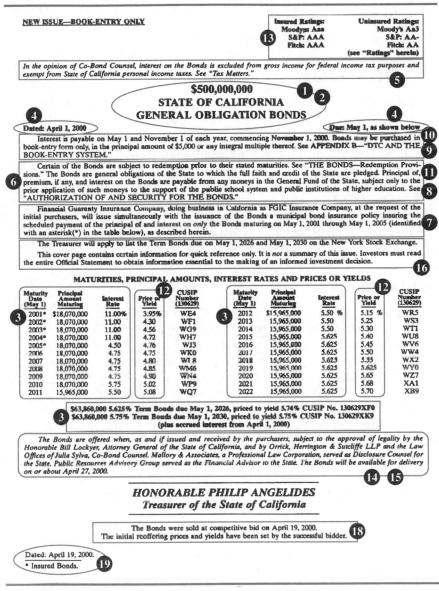

Insured Ratings:	Uninsured Ratings:
Moody's: Aaa	Moody's Aa3
S&P: AAA	S&P: AA-
Fitch: AAA	Fitch: AA
	(see "Ratings" herein)

In the opinion of Co-Bond Counsel, interest on the Bonds is excluded from gross income for federal income tax purposes and exempt from State of California personal income taxes. See "Tax Matters."

$500,000,000

STATE OF CALIFORNIA

GENERAL OBLIGATION BONDS

Dated: April 1, 2000   Due: May 1, as shown below

Interest is payable on May 1 and November 1 of each year, commencing November 1, 2000. Bonds may be purchased in book-entry form only, in the principal amount of $5,000 or any integral multiple thereof. See APPENDIX B—"DTC AND THE BOOK-ENTRY SYSTEM."

Certain of the Bonds are subject to redemption prior to their stated maturities. See "THE BONDS—Redemption Provisions." The Bonds are general obligations of the State to which the full faith and credit of the State are pledged. Principal of, premium, if any, and interest on the Bonds are payable from any moneys in the General Fund of the State, subject only to the prior application of such moneys to the support of the public school system and public institutions of higher education. See "AUTHORIZATION OF AND SECURITY FOR THE BONDS."

Financial Guaranty Insurance Company, doing business in California as FGIC Insurance Company, at the request of the initial purchasers, will issue simultaneously with the issuance of the Bonds a municipal bond insurance policy insuring the scheduled payment of the principal of and interest on *only* the Bonds maturing on May 1, 2001 through May 1, 2005 (identified with an asterisk(*) in the table below), as described herein.

The Treasurer will apply to list the Term Bonds due on May 1, 2026 and May 1, 2030 on the New York Stock Exchange.

This cover page contains certain information for quick reference only. It is *not* a summary of this issue. Investors must read the entire Official Statement to obtain information essential to the making of an informed investment decision.

MATURITIES, PRINCIPAL AMOUNTS, INTEREST RATES AND PRICES OR YIELDS

Maturity Date (May 1)	Principal Amount Maturing	Interest Rate	Price or Yield	CUSIP Number (130629)	Maturity Date (May 1)	Principal Amount Maturing	Interest Rate	Price or Yield	CUSIP Number (130629)
2001*	$18,070,000	11.00%	3.95%	WE4	2012	$15,965,000	5.50 %	5.15 %	WR5
2002*	18,070,000	11.00	4.30	WF1	2013	15,965,000	5.50	5.25	WS3
2003*	18,070,000	11.00	4.55	WG9	2014	15,965,000	5.50	5.30	WT1
2004*	18,070,000	11.00	4.72	WH7	2015	15,965,000	5.625	5.40	WU8
2005*	18,070,000	4.50	4.76	WJ3	2016	15,965,000	5.625	5.45	WV6
2006	18,070,000	4.75	4.75	WK0	2017	15,965,000	5.625	5.50	WW4
2007	18,070,000	4.75	4.80	WL8	2018	15,965,000	5.625	5.55	WX2
2008	18,070,000	4.75	4.85	WM6	2019	15,965,000	5.625	5.625	WY0
2009	18,070,000	4.75	4.90	WN4	2020	15,965,000	5.625	5.65	WZ7
2010	18,070,000	5.75	5.02	WP9	2021	15,965,000	5.625	5.68	XA1
2011	15,965,000	5.50	5.08	WQ7	2022	15,965,000	5.625	5.70	XB9

$63,860,000 5.625% Term Bonds due May 1, 2026, priced to yield 5.74% CUSIP No. 130629XF0
$63,860,000 5.75% Term Bonds due May 1, 2030, priced to yield 5.75% CUSIP No. 130629XK9
(plus accrued interest from April 1, 2000)

The Bonds are offered when, as and if issued and received by the purchasers, subject to the approval of legality by the Honorable Bill Lockyer, Attorney General of the State of California, and by Orrick, Herrington & Sutcliffe LLP and the Law Offices of Julia Sylva, Co-Bond Counsel. Mallory & Associates, a Professional Law Corporation, served as Disclosure Counsel for the State. Public Resources Advisory Group served as the Financial Advisor to the State. The Bonds will be available for delivery on or about April 27, 2000.

HONORABLE PHILIP ANGELIDES
Treasurer of the State of California

The Bonds were sold at competitive bid on April 19, 2000.
The initial reoffering prices and yields have been set by the successful bidder.

Dated: April 19, 2000.
* Insured Bonds.

17. If competitive sale, any bidding specifications.
18. If negotiated sale, names of managing underwriters (if competitive so indicate).
19. Date of the offering document.

Opinion of Bond Counsel

Even though the bond counsel's opinion is addressed to the issuer, the bondholders rely on this opinion to provide comfort about the legality of the issue. Overwhelmingly they insist that the opinion be unqualified. Buyers also want the opinion to be from a nationally recognized bond counsel.

The legal opinion covers three major areas: (1) whether the bonds are valid and binding obligations of the issuer; (2) information on the security and sources of payment for the bonds; and (3) exemption of the issue from federal, state, and local income taxes.

Figure 3.2 is the National Association of Bond Lawyers' model bond opinion for general obligation bonds.

Other Legal Opinions

In addition to the opinion of bond counsel, other legal opinions are asked for and given as part of the financing documents in more complex financings. A tax opinion, given by bond counsel or a special tax counsel, gives comfort that the issuer has complied with the applicable arbitrage regulations. Bond counsel is responsible for filing the proper public notices that bonds are to be sold. Counsel for credit enhancers, particularly for banks providing letters of credit, may be asked to provide opinions regarding preference in a bankruptcy. Underwriter's counsel provides the underwriter with an opinion that the transaction complies with the applicable securities laws—this is called a *10(b)(5) opinion.*

Credit-Enhancement Documents

When the issue carries credit enhancement, additional financing documents must be drafted. Credit enhancers have input into the indenture, and they try to write the strongest (from their point of view) covenants. Credit enhancers are concerned with, among other things, their security lien positions, rate covenants, and additional debt tests.

With a letter-of-credit financing, key documents include the letter of credit itself and the reimbursement agreement, which spells out how the issuer will pay back the bank in the event the letter is drawn upon. When the issue uses a line of credit, the document will include the definitions of events of default and the remedies that the bank can use if any of the named defaults occur.

FIGURE 3.2 Sample Bond Counsel Opinion

GENERAL OBLIGATION BONDS

MODEL OPINION

(Letterhead of Bond Counsel)
(Date)

(Addressee)

(Salutation)

(Caption)

We have acted as bond counsel [to _____] in connection with the issuance by (Name of Issuer) (the "Issuer") of $____(Title of Bonds)____ Bonds dated _____ (the "Bonds"). In such capacity, we have examined such law and such certified proceedings and other documents as we have deemed necessary to render this opinion.

As to questions of fact material to our opinion, we have relied upon the certified proceedings and other certifications of public officials and others furnished to us without undertaking to verify the same by independent investigation.

Based on the foregoing, we are of the opinion that, under existing law:

1. The Bonds are valid and binding general obligations of the Issuer.

2. All taxable property in the territory of the Issuer is subject to *ad valorem* taxation without limitation as to rate or amount to pay the Bonds. The Issuer is required by law to include in its annual tax levy the principal and interest coming due on the Bonds to the extent the necessary funds are not provided from other sources.

3. Interest on the Bonds is excluded from gross income for federal income tax purposes and is not an item of tax preference for purposes of the federal alternative minimum tax imposed on individuals and corporations; it should be noted, however, that, for the purpose of computing the alternative minimum tax imposed on certain corporations (as defined for federal income tax purposes), such interest is taken into account in determining adjusted current earnings. The opinion set forth in the preceding sentence is subject to the condition that the Issuer comply with all requirements of the Internal Revenue Code of 1986 as amended, that must be satisfied subsequent to the issuance of the Bonds in order that interest thereon be, or continue to be, excluded from gross income for federal income tax purposes. The Issuer has covenanted to comply with all such requirements. Failure to comply with certain of such requirements may cause interest on the Bonds to be included in gross income for federal income tax purposes retroactive to the date of issuance of the Bonds. We express no opinion regarding other federal tax consequences arising with respect to the Bonds.

4.   [Opinion regarding state tax exemption, if any.]

It is to be understood that the rights of the owners of the Bonds and the enforceability of the Bonds may be limited by bankruptcy, insolvency, reorganization, moratorium and other similar laws affecting creditors' rights generally and by equitable principles, whether considered at law or in equity.

We express no opinion herein as to the accuracy, adequacy or completeness of the Official Statement relating to the Bonds.

[This opinion is given as of the date hereof and we assume no obligation to [update] [revise] or supplement this opinion to reflect any changes or circumstances that may hereafter come to our attention or any changes in law that may hereafter occur.]

Very truly yours,

Source: Copyright National Association of Bond Lawyers. Reprinted with permission.

Bond Purchase Agreement/Purchase Contract

In a negotiated sale, the purchase contract between the issuer and the under-writer is called the *bond purchase agreement (BPA)*. The BPA includes the purchase price of the bonds, the principal amount of each maturity, the interest rates, and other specifics of the deal. It also includes an estimate of the closing date, the representations and warranties that the issuer makes to the under-writer, and the conditions under which the underwriter would or would not have to pick up the bond. The underwriter's counsel prepares this document.

For a competitive sale, the purchase contract is essentially made up of the notice of sale, the winning bid, and the issuer's acceptance of the bid. The winning bidder signs the purchase contract without the input of any under-writer's counsel.

Continuing Disclosure Agreement

The continuing disclosure agreement is between the underwriter and the is-suer. See Chapter 9 for a more in-depth discussion.

Other Documents

The *closing documents* are coordinated and handled by the bond counsel. They include executed (signed) copies of the major documents, title searches, and opinions of other counsel. In a refunding issue, the escrow documents re-lating to the securities used to pay off the old bonds are also prepared.

ASSESSING THE IMPACT OF THE DEBT

The issuer makes many decisions relating to the financial structure of the debt in the course of the financing. These decisions include the way the debt ser-vice schedule is structured, the inclusion or exclusion of call provisions, the use of premium or discount bonds, the method of calculating the interest cost, the use of bond insurance or other credit enhancements, and the use of financial products such as derivatives. These decisions are made in the con-text of the issuer's legal constraints, its policies and political constraints, and the market demand for the issuer's bonds at the time of sale.

Debt Repayment Schedules

There are three kinds of debt service schedules. In a *level debt* service sched-ule, the total of principal and interest repaid each year is generally level, or the same, throughout the life of the bond issue, with the principal amount of the serial maturities increasing each year. In a *level principal* or *declining debt* service schedule, the dollar amount of the annual serial maturities is the same each year throughout the life of the bond, and thus the interest portion of the debt service declines each year. In an *ascending debt* service schedule, the greatest principal payments are in the future, with little or no amortization of principal in the early years of the debt. Term bonds are usually structured with sinking funds redemptions that mimic serial maturities.

The arrangement of serial bond schedules can provide great flexibility to financial officers concerned with meeting annual budgets. For example, serial maturities can be constructed to dovetail with expected revenues and expenditures in a given year. Another area where serial maturities are advantageous is in large revenue bond projects, where local officials may want to ease the burden of rapidly increasing water or power rates. An ascending debt service schedule may be used to push the debt payments further out into the future in the belief that natural growth may be expected to pay off the debt. This strategy could be a negative factor in the rating or the issuer's ability to obtain credit enhancement, so the issuer has to weigh the positives and negatives carefully. Term maturities with all principal payments coming due 15 to 30 years after issuance can provide a useful financing option.

Indeed, marketability is an important factor in the choice of maturities. For many issues, particularly large ones, a maturity schedule incorporating short serial bonds and term bonds will usually broaden the appeal of an issue, attracting a variety of investors. The level of interest rates will also influence decisions concerning maturities. For example, if short-term interest rates are considered unusually low or if demand for short-term issues is strong, an issue weighted more heavily toward shorter-maturity serial bonds can be constructed. The bonds may also be more marketable at a given time if the issue includes *premium bonds,* which are priced initially greater than par, or *discount bonds,* which are priced below par. *Original issue discount (OID)* bonds can be used by an underwriter to create interest and demand in a specific term maturity of an issue. (OIDs are discussed in greater detail in Chapter 6.)

Redemption Provisions

The cost to an issuer of having a *call privilege* or *protection* can be a higher interest rate on the issue. Investors will often demand a higher yield for a security with a call provision because the potential for price appreciation and capital gain on a callable bond is limited. Also, if the issuer calls the bonds before they mature, the investors may be left to reinvest the principal at a lower interest rate. The question the issuer must consider, therefore, is whether the advantages of the call privilege outweigh the higher interest rate that must be offered to investors. When interest rates in general are high and volatile, a call provision is clearly most desirable, as it enables the issuer to refund an issue when interest rates are lower. Both the call premium and the amount of time that the investor has call protection have been changing markedly. Investors are highly cognizant of the importance of the call option to their portfolios, and they look for issues for which the call protection is the longest and the call premiums are the highest. Issuers, also cognizant of the value of the call option, may look to reduce the call premium and shorten the number of years of call protection they give the investor, all in order to give themselves as much flexibility as possible.

The issuers of callable bonds usually notify investors 30 days before the bonds are due to be called through an actual notice to bondholders or an advertisement in a financial publication. The notice or advertisement will state which bonds are being redeemed and how the bondholder will receive payment. The call provision normally states in which order bonds will be called (which typically has been described in the official statement).

Refundings

A considerable portion of the municipal market involves the issuance of new bonds to refund old bonds. Table 3.6 details the volume of refunding bonds from 1980 through 1999.

In a refunding, the proceeds of the new bonds are used to pay the principal, interest, and any call premium of an outstanding bond issue, to either the maturity or the call date. Issuers, with the help of financial advisors and investment bankers, regularly evaluate the feasibility of refunding outstanding debt with new bonds.

The issuer considers refunding outstanding bonds under several conditions, which include the opportunity to achieve interest rate savings, the need to extinguish old debt and thus remove or change outdated or unwanted covenants, the ability to make a favorable change in the debt service schedule, and the potential to garner other economic benefits. The issuer monitors rates in both the municipal market and in the Treasury market to see when the refunding is economical and if interest rate savings targets can be met. This is because the proceeds from the refunding bonds are used to purchase permitted securities under the bond indenture that are often special *state and local government securities (SLGSs)*, which are issued by the Treasury, and open-market Treasuries. The interest on the SLGS is then used to service the old debt. There are many federal tax laws that govern the issuance of refunding bonds and the amount of arbitrage that can be earned. *Arbitrage* in the municipal market is the difference between the interest paid on tax-exempt bonds and the interest earned on normally higher-yielding taxable securities. Moreover, federal tax law restricts the yield that can be earned on the investment in taxable bonds (the arbitrage yield).

TABLE 3.6   LONG-TERM REFUNDING BOND ISSUANCE, 1980–1999

Year	Principal Amount ($ billions)	Percent of Total Issuance	All Long-Term Issuance ($ billions)
1980	1.7	3.6	46.3
1981	1.5	3.4	45.6
1982	3.6	4.6	77.9
1983	16.2	18.9	85.5
1984	17.2	16.2	105.6
1985	71.3	34.5	206.9
1986	65.5	43.5	150.7
1987	46.0	43.8	105.1
1988	37.0	31.5	117.4
1989	35.6	28.5	125.0
1990	25.8	20.1	128.0
1991	54.7	31.7	172.8
1992	123.4	52.6	234.7
1993	195.6	66.9	292.5
1994	50.4	30.6	165.1
1995	48.3	30.2	160.0
1996	61.2	33.1	185.0
1997	82.9	37.6	220.6
1998	126.0	44.0	286.2
1999	68.1	30.0	226.8

Source: Thomson Financial Securities Data, June 21, 2000.

Three characteristics are common to refunding bonds—escrow, timing, and level of interest rates. When refunding bond proceeds are deposited in an escrow account, and those proceeds can be used solely to pay principal and interest on the original maturity dates of the old bonds, the old bonds are said to be *escrowed to maturity (ETM)*. When the refunding and proceeds are escrowed and can be used to pay principal, interest, and the call premium up to the call date of the old bonds, the old bonds are said to be *prerefunded*. The rights of the old bondholders are usually terminated, with a refunding when payment provisions have been made.

Market timing determines whether the bonds can be current or advance refunded. In a *current refunding*, the old bonds are called or mature within 90 days of the issuance of the new refunding bonds. If the old bonds are called or mature more than 90 days after the issuance of new bonds, the old bonds are said to be *advance refunded*. U.S. Treasury concerns regarding what was perceived as overissuance of tax-exempt bonds have led to restrictions on issuer's ability to do advance refundings.

The level of interest rates determines whether the refunding is *high to low* or *low to high*. With a high-to-low refunding, high-coupon bonds are refunded with low-coupon bonds; this is generally done for interest rate savings. When low-coupon bonds are refunded with high-coupon bonds (a low-to-high refunding), covenant changes, rather than interest rate savings, are generally at work.

In addition to the characteristics of refundings that have been described there are three major classifications of refundings—net cash, crossover, and full cash—that need explanation. In a *net cash* refunding, the principal, interest, and call premium of the old bonds are paid from the proceeds and investment earnings of the refunding bonds. Most advance refundings follow the net cash model. In a *crossover refunding,* the debt service on the old bond is paid by the original revenue stream until the call date, when the revenue stream crosses over and is used to pay the debt service on the new refunding bonds. The refunding escrow pays debt service on the new bonds until the crossover date, when the escrow pays the principal and call premium on the old bonds. In this instance, the old bonds are not extinguished at the time of the refunding. A third type of refunding is a *full cash* or *gross refunding.* Here, the refunding issue itself is large enough to pay principal and interest on the old bonds. There are two series of full cash securities: refunding bonds, which pay debt service on the old bonds, and special obligation securities, which pay a portion of the debt service on the refunding bonds without reliance on investment earnings or escrowed securities. There have not been many full cash refundings in recent years.

True Interest Cost and Net Interest Cost

In a competitive sale, the issuer must decide on what basis competing syndicates will calculate their bids for the bonds. In most sales, the issuer looks to the true interest cost (TIC), which is also sometimes called the Canadian interest cost. TIC is the rate that will discount all future cash payments so the sum of the present value of all cash flows will equal the bond proceeds. This calculation takes into account the time value of money, producing a more accurate indication of the true interest cost of an issue, particularly ones that contain serial bonds. The formula for the TIC is

$$B = \sum_{n=e}^{f} \left(\sum_{t=1}^{n} \frac{C_t}{(1+\text{TIC})^t} + \frac{M}{(1+\text{TIC})^n} \right)$$

where B = price of the issue, e = number of periods to earliest bond maturity, f = number of periods to last bond maturity, n = years to maturity, t = index of period, C = Coupon, M = maturity value of the bond, and TIC = True Interest Cost.

An older, simpler arithmetic calculation used before the widespread use of computers is the net interest cost (NIC). The formula for the NIC is

$$\text{NIC} = \frac{\text{total interest payments plus discount (or minus premium)}}{\text{Bond year dollars}}$$

Although NIC is rarely used anymore, the formula contains the important concept of *bond years*. Bond years alone are the number of bonds outstanding (in $1,000 denominations) multiplied by the number of years outstanding. For example, one bond year is one $1,000 bond outstanding for one year. A $25,000 bond due in one year would have 25 bond years. Bond-year dollars are the number of bond years multiplied by $1,000 for each bond. The $25,000 bond due in one year would have 25,000 bond-year dollars. Another important concept is the *average life*. This is the number of bond years divided by the total number of bonds in an issue. For example, if an issue contains 250,000 bond years, with 25,000 bonds the average life of the issue is ten years.

Considering Financial Products

The use of financial products by municipal issuers has become an integral and recognized part of the issuer's financial management. This is discussed in Chapter 10.

Considering Insurance

A major decision that the issuer must make is whether to use some form of credit enhancement. Bond insurance represents a legal commitment by a third party (the insurance company), to make timely payments of principal and interest in the event that the issuer of the debt is unable to do so. Generally, the issuer will see to it that such payments are made as originally scheduled and that the principal will not be accelerated.

The role of municipal bond insurance in the tax-exempt market is threefold: to reduce interest costs to issuers, to provide a high level of security to investors, and to furnish improved secondary-market liquidity and price support. With nearly half of the new-issue market in 1999 using bond insurance, many issuers have found that their total borrowing costs, including the insurance premium, can be lowered by using bond insurance. The issuer, in making this evaluation, will compare the rates on an insured scale with the scale for its own credit. If the issuer is not yet rated, the financial advisor should be able to approximate the rating. The issuer compares the TIC on the insured scale (which incorporates the cost of the insurance) with the TIC on the uninsured scale and then makes the decision whether to use bond insurance.

In addition to cost savings, an issuer may consider insurance for a new issue, especially if the underwriter or financial advisor has determined that the best market reception would be for an insured issue. Still, the issuer may be constrained by the bond insurer's credit capacity for that issuer's name, state, region, or type of credit.

STATE AND LOCAL GOVERNMENT ACCOUNTING

Government accounting necessarily differs in several important ways from business accounting. Business accounting is ultimately concerned with the profits of the owners; governments have no such clear-cut measure of success. Businesses must match sales to the expenses incurred in making those sales; governments must be certain that resources are sufficient to meet outlays. Businesses try to maximize profits; governments must meet the annual budget. To the owner of a business, the consolidation of all business expenses and revenues, no matter how diversified, makes sense. Sources of revenue for certain government services, however, often have little to do with revenues raised for other purposes, so that segregated accounts are usually more appropriate and, indeed, are often legally mandated.

Such differences have resulted in a separate set of accounting principles for government, originally developed by the *National Council on Governmental Accounting (NCGA)*. The NCGA began to formulate these principles in 1934. In 1984, through an agreement between the Financial Accounting Foundation, which sets business accounting standards; the American Institute of Certified Public Accountants; and the NCGA, the latter was replaced by the *Governmental Accounting Standards Board (GASB)*, which now sets standards of accounting and financial reporting for state and local governments.

Fund Accounting

To account for the diverse activities of state and local governments, accounts are divided into separate funds. As noted previously, statutes and regulations often require that government resources and expenditures be accounted for separately, by area of expenditure. This is called *fund accounting*, which, government officials argue, makes good sense because it gives a clearer picture of how the government's various sources of revenue are used to finance different kinds of expenditures.

Each fund includes a set of accounts to record the revenues, expenses, assets, liabilities, and fund balances (or equity) of the activities of that fund. The GASB specifies seven major types of funds, which fall into three categories: (1) governmental, (2) proprietary, and (3) fiduciary. A governmental unit may require one or several funds of a single type or, in contrast, may require fewer than seven funds. Six of the seven types of funds are described in the following section. The other fund type is the *internal service fund*, categorized as a proprietary type of fund.

Governmental Funds.   Most typical government functions are financed through the following funds:

- *The general fund*. This is normally the largest of the funds. It essentially accounts for all financial resources other than those accounted for in any other fund. Most current operations of the government are recorded here. Such revenue sources as property, income, and sales taxes will typically be recorded in the general fund.
- *Special revenue fund*. This fund records proceeds from specific sources that are usually earmarked for specific purposes, such as the care of parks, museums, or highways. Major capital projects and expendable trusts are recorded in other funds.
- *Capital projects fund*. Any resources used for the acquisition and construction of capital facilities are accounted for here. Exceptions are those projects financed by enterprise funds. The capital projects fund was created because so many capital projects are no longer funded with bonds but from other sources, such as direct revenues and grants. Separate capital projects funds are commonly set up for individual projects.
- *Debt service fund*. This fund records the payment of interest and principal on long-term general obligation debt as well as the accumulation of resources to pay off the debt.

Proprietary Funds.   These funds account for government operations that are similar to those of business. The accounting principles for such funds are generally the same as those for business.

Enterprise fund. This is essentially the fund in which ongoing activities that are operated like those of a business are recorded. Public utilities financed by user charges are one example of such activities. Proceeds from revenue bond issues and their dispositions are usually accounted for here.

Internal service fund. This is a proprietary fund.

Fiduciary Funds.   These are *trust and agency funds*. They account for money or property that is being held by the governmental unit as a trustee, guardian, or agent for individuals, government entities, or nonpublic organizations. For example, pension funds and investment trust funds are recorded here.

Cash versus Accrual Basis of Accounting

One of the major sources of controversy in government accounting is the question of when to record expenditures and revenues. Businesses do their accounting on an *accrual basis*—that is, revenues are recorded when they are earned, not when the cash comes in, and expenses are recorded when they are incurred, not simply when they are paid. Most governments, on the other hand, use a modified accrual basis of accounting, and it is now required by GASB.

The *modified accrual basis* for governmental accounting is known as *generally accepted accounting principles (GAAP)*. Because a government is not trying to measure expenses against sales as a business does, GAAP requires that revenues be recognized only when they are available and measurable, whereas expenditures generally should be recognized when incurred. However, according to GAAP, interest and principal payments on debt should be recorded only when the payment is due. Other expenditures that are not normally liquidated with available expendable financial resources— and therefore are not accrued—include compensated absences, claims, and judgments.

Budgeting

Budgeting is the primary means of financial management and control for governments. The GASB requires that budgets be drawn up annually for all government funds, although there is no enforcement mechanism (e.g., GAAP) for this. The GASB also requires that comparisons between actual and budgeted revenues and expenditures be provided regularly, along with the financial statements.

Financial Reporting

The GASB requires that governmental units prepare both a comprehensive annual financial report and a report that includes a more limited set of *general-purpose financial statements*. The GASB states that the latter type is adequate for official statements as well as for widespread distribution to those not interested in greater detail. The *comprehensive annual financial report,* however, is the official annual report. The GASB also requires that independent audits be undertaken of all state and local government financial statements, although NAAP does not require this.

The GASB requires that general-purpose financial statements include the following:

1. Combined balance sheet of all types of funds and account groups
2. Combined statement of revenues, expenditures, and changes in balances of all governmental funds
3. Combined statement of revenues, expenditures, and changes in fund balances—both budget and actual—of general and special revenue funds and of similar governmental funds for which annual budgets have been legally adopted

4. Combined statement of revenues, expenses, and changes in retained earnings (or equity) of all proprietary fund types
5. Combined statement of cash flows for all proprietary funds (GASB Statement 9)
6. Notes to the financial statements

The GASB requires that the comprehensive annual financial report contain all these statements as well as considerably more detail. All the materials GASB recommends for both the comprehensive report and the general-purpose statements are listed in *Codification of Governmental Accounting and Financial Reporting Standards,* published by the GASB.

In June 1999, the GASB issued Statement 34, which established new financial reporting requirements for state and local governments. The new financial reporting is designed make it easier for users of financial statements to assess whether the government's overall financial position has improved or deteriorated. In addition, citizens should be able to evaluate the costs of providing services, understand how various programs are financed, and analyze the government's infrastructure investment. Basic financial statements and required supplementary information for general-purpose governments will consist of the following information:

1. Management's discussion and analysis. This is to be introduced before the basic financial statements. It will give an analytical overview of the government's financial activities. The analysis should include significant changes in funds and in the budget. Capital asset and long-term debt activity should be discussed, as well as any currently known conditions or facts that may have an effect on operations.
2. Basic financial statements. These include government-wide financial statements, fund financial statements, and notes to the financial statements. A major change from the old model for government-wide financial statements is that all capital assets, including infrastructure assets, will be capitalized at their actual or estimated historical cost. In general, depreciation expense will begin to be reported in the statement of activities. In addition, the government-wide statement of activities will ultimately report the change in net assets for the period. There are also new requirements for proprietary funds and fiduciary funds.
3. Required supplementary information. This includes new budgetary comparisons. The original budget will be compared to the final budget for the general fund and individual major special revenue funds.

These changes will be phased in, with larger governments implementing them for the fiscal year beginning June 2001.

CHAPTER 4

The Primary Market

ISSUANCE TRENDS IN THE PRIMARY MARKET

In 1999, $263.8 billion was raised in the municipal bond markets for state and local governments, compared with a little over $26 billion in 1975. In 1999, long-term debt issues alone amounted to $226.8 billion. Table 4.1 details short- and long-term issuance of municipal debt from 1975 to 1999. Total issuance reached a peak of $340 billion in 1993. Volume has fluctuated over this 25-year time period. Factors in increased volume at various points in time have been a low–interest rate environment, changes in legislation, and need for infrastructure improvement. Many factors were involved in a drop in issuance, including a higher-interest environment, fewer refundings, the completion of major infrastructure projects, and negative voter sentiment, which reduced the number of bond issue approvals.

One of the most important trends of the past two decades has been the dominance of negotiated underwriting. Based on dollar volume, negotiated financings first surpassed competitive sales in 1978 and have accounted for the majority of underwritings in every year since then. Table 4.2 details the volume of competitive sales and negotiated sales and their percentage of the new-issue, long-term market from 1975 through 1999.

Another defining characteristic in the municipal market over the past two decades has been the steady transition from a market of general obligation (GO) bonds to a market of revenue bonds. Based on dollar volume, revenue bonds began to constitute over half of new issues in the late 1970s. Table 3.5 in the previous chapter detailed the dollar volume of GO and revenue bonds and the percentage of the new-issue, long-term market for each category from 1975 through 1999.

In the past, it was axiomatic that GO bonds were sold through the competitive bid process and that revenue bonds were sold through the negotiated process. Based on dollar volume of general obligation bonds from 1989 to 1999, negotiated sales exceeded competitive sales by a slight margin but, in that same period, negotiated sales continued to be a far greater proportion for revenue bonds. Table 4.3 shows the volume of all negotiated and com-

TABLE 4.1 Total Short- and Long-Term Municipal Securities Issuance, with Percentage Change in Volume from the Prior Year, 1975–1999

Year	Short-Term Volume ($ billions)	Long-Term Volume ($ billions)	Total Volume ($ billions)	Percentage Change from Prior Year
1975	0.6	25.3	26.0	
1976	0.3	33.2	33.5	28.8
1977	0.3	42.3	42.6	27.3
1978	0.2	46.3	46.5	9.2
1979	0.1	41.2	41.3	−11.1
1980	9.0	46.3	55.3	33.9
1981	14.2	45.6	59.7	8.0
1982	16.6	77.9	94.4	58.1
1983	19.3	85.5	104.8	11.0
1984	23.4	105.6	129.0	23.1
1985	22.4	206.9	229.3	77.7
1986	22.2	150.7	172.7	−24.7
1987	20.8	105.1	125.6	−27.3
1988	23.9	117.4	141.1	12.3
1989	30.0	125.0	154.6	9.6
1990	35.3	128.0	162.8	5.3
1991	44.7	172.8	217.2	33.4
1992	43.4	234.7	277.7	27.9
1993	47.8	292.5	340.0	22.4
1994	40.6	165.1	205.4	−39.6
1995	38.5	160.0	198.3	−3.4
1996	42.2	185.0	226.7	14.3
1997	46.3	220.6	266.9	17.7
1998	34.8	286.2	321.0	20.2
1999	37.1	226.8	263.8	−17.8

Source: Thomson Financial Securities Data.

petitive sales from 1989 through 1999, categorized by either GO or revenue bond, and the percentage of each category in the whole market. More complex general obligation structures and large deal sizes mean that roughly the same percentage of general obligation bonds are now sold on a negotiated basis as on a competitive basis.

Based on the number of issues, this matrix is quite different. Table 4.4 shows the number of all negotiated and competitive issues from 1989 through 1999, categorized as either GO or revenue bond issues, and the percentage each category represents of the entire market. Most significantly, competitive general obligation issues accounted for 8.1 percent of the number of new issues versus 16.2 percent of the dollar volume of new issues.

TABLE 4.2 Long-Term Municipal Debt Issuance, by Competitive and Negotiated Sales, 1975–1999

Year	Competitive Sales		Negotiated Sales		Total Long-Term New-Issue Market ($ billions)
	Principal Amount ($ billions)	Percent of New-Issue Market	Principal Amount ($ billions)	Percent of New-Issue Market	
1975	16.7	66.0	8.6	33.8	25.3
1976	19.4	58.5	12.4	37.2	33.2
1977	21.7	51.3	20.0	47.3	42.3
1978	20.6	44.6	24.7	53.3	46.3
1979	17.9	43.4	22.4	54.4	41.2
1980	19.3	41.6	26.4	56.9	46.3
1981	15.7	34.3	28.8	63.1	45.6
1982	23.2	29.8	53.5	68.7	77.9
1983	21.1	24.7	62.1	72.6	85.5
1984	21.8	20.6	79.3	75.1	105.6
1985	27.8	13.4	173.6	83.9	206.9
1986	33.0	21.9	114.6	76.1	150.7
1987	23.4	22.3	77.7	74.0	105.1
1988	26.5	22.6	88.7	75.5	117.4
1989	29.7	23.7	92.1	73.7	125.0
1990	30.1	23.5	95.8	74.8	128.0
1991	40.2	23.3	129.3	74.8	172.8
1992	44.2	18.8	187.3	79.8	234.7
1993	55.6	19.0	234.3	80.1	292.5
1994	49.5	30.0	112.7	68.3	165.1
1995	40.8	25.5	115.4	72.1	160.0
1996	47.0	25.4	134.4	72.7	185.0
1997	47.8	21.7	166.4	75.4	220.6
1998	65.4	22.9	214.6	75.0	286.2
1999	52.8	23.3	166.6	73.5	226.8

Source: Thomson Financial Securities Data.

These charts provide the background for the next section, which describes negotiated and competitive underwriting

TABLE 4.3 Long-Term Municipal Debt Issuance, General Use of Proceeds, 1989–1999 (based on volume)

	Negotiated		Competitive		Total Long-Term Financings, 1989–1999 ($ millions)
	Sales ($ millions)	Percent of New-Issue Market	Sales ($ millions)	Percent of New-Issue Market	
General obligation	373,739.7	17.4	347,976.7	16.2	721,716.4
Revenue	1,275,417.8	59.3	155,219.7	7.2	1,430,637.5
Total	1,649,157.5	76.6	503,196.4	23.4	2,152,353.9

Source: Thomson Financial Securities Data.
Note: Excludes private placements.

TABLE 4.4 Long-Term Municipal Debt Issuance, General Use of Proceeds, 1989–1999 (by number of issues)

	Negotiated		Competitive		Total Financings, 1989–1999
	Number of Issues	Percent of New-Issue Market	Number of Issues	Percent of New-Issue Market	
General obligation	27,715	22.1	35,278	28.1	62,993
Revenue	52,668	42.0	9,676	7.7	62,344
Total	80,383	64.1	44,954	35.9	125,337

Source: Thomson Financial Securities Data.
Note: Excludes private placements.

THE BASICS OF UNDERWRITING

The vast number of new municipal offerings each year, originating in every region of the United States, has given rise to a large underwriting industry. The highest volume of underwriting activity is concentrated in national firms and large banks. According to *The Bond Buyer 1999 Yearbook*, the 25 leading underwriters senior managed 78 percent of the total volume of all new long-term issues in 1998. Even greater concentration exists, with 63 percent of the long-term volume senior managed by the top 10 firms. There are also small, local underwriters that primarily handle their own communities' and states' bond offerings.

The Role of Banks in Underwriting

There are four ways that commercial banks can underwrite municipal bonds: (1) through a traditional structure of a bond department within the bank registered with the Municipal Securities Rulemaking Board (MSRB), (2) through a broker dealer affiliate organized under the Bank Holding Company Act, (3) through an operating subsidiary of the bank, or (4) through a financial subsidiary of the bank.

In the past, banks generally could only underwrite general obligation bonds and certain bank eligible revenue bonds. However, the *Financial Modernization Act* has given banks new authority to underwrite revenue bonds, which were formerly restricted under the Banking Act of 1933 (the Glass-Steagall Act). The Act provides that the limitations and restrictions regarding the authority of a bank to deal in, underwrite, and purchase investment securities for the bank's own account will not apply to certain obligations issued by or on behalf of any state or political subdivision of a state or any public agency or authority of any state or political subdivision of a state.

Competitive and Negotiated Underwriting

In principle, the job of the underwriter is very straightforward. For a competitive sale, the underwriters bid against each other by submitting to the issuer on a given day at a given time a sealed bid to buy the issuer's bonds and then reoffer them to investors. The underwriter that offers to pay the lowest interest cost for the bonds will win the competitive sale. In a negotiated offering, where there is no sealed bid, the underwriter is chosen before the actual sale date through the Request for Proposal (RFP) process that was discussed in Chapter 3. Under both procedures, the underwriter functions as the quarterback of the deal by coordinating the traders, the salespeople, and all the members of the syndicate.

In recent years, issuers have routinely asked underwriters to indicate their fees in their written or oral proposals. While the fee is usually a preliminary quote, it has the practical effect of making a "negotiated issue" extremely competitive on price. The underwriter's fee from the bond sale, called the *gross spread,* is the difference between the price the underwriter pays the issuer for the bonds and the price at which the bonds are reoffered to the investing public. The gross spread is also referred to as the *underwriter's discount.* Spreads are usually quoted in terms of dollars per thousand bonds. For example, for each $1,000 the issuer borrows through a negotiated issue, the gross spread that the underwriters get may be $6.00, with the net proceeds to the issuer $994.00.

The gross spread is allocated to the various expenses that have been incurred during the financing. Typical underwriter's expenses may include, but are not limited to, the following:

1. Underwriter's counsel
2. Insurance fee

3. Investor information meetings
4. Travel
5. Advertising
6. CUSIP fee
7. MSRB fee
8. Professional salaries
9. Sales commissions
10. Overhead
11. Cost of capital (including what is called *cost of carry*, the direct costs paid to maintain a securities position)
12. Other out-of-pocket expenses

The gross spread less the sum of the expenses is the underwriter's net profit or net loss. This assumes that the bonds are sold at the issue price. Sales at other than issue price may result in a different profit or loss to the underwriter.

The issuer is responsible for certain expenses, many of which can be paid from the bond proceeds. In addition to the capital project costs and reserve funds, the issuer's expenses may include, but are not limited to, the following:

1. Financial advisory fee
2. Insurance fee
3. Rating agency fee
4. Issuer's counsel; bond counsel
5. Feasibility study/engineer's report/marketing survey
6. Printing costs

Table 4.5 details the average gross underwriting spreads for long-term issues from 1989 to 1999. Two points emerge from this data about competition in the municipal market and about competitive and negotiated prices. First, gross underwriting spreads were on a downward trend for that time period. The average long-term spread has declined 40 percent, from $11.97 per $1,000 bond in 1989 to $7.20 per $1,000 bond in 1999. Second, the spread between competitive and negotiated spreads has narrowed; in 1999, the spread between negotiated and all long-term issues had nearly disappeared.

In both negotiated and competitive sales, underwriters assume complete risk and responsibility for selling the bonds. Competitive underwriting is more risky because, when a bid is made, that bid is final. The underwriter is committed to the price, regardless of whether the market goes up or down. In a negotiated sale, the underwriter decides on price when the deal is underwritten based on how the issue is selling, not on a specific time schedule, and the underwriter can adjust the yield to respond to market conditions. Successful underwriting depends on professionals who know all aspects of

TABLE 4.5 Long-Term Municipal Debt Issuance: Average Gross Underwriting Spreads, 1989–1999 ($ amount per $1,000 bond)

Year	Negotiated Sales	Competitive Sales	All Long-Term Sales
1989	11.97	9.86	11.54
1990	11.37	10.53	11.22
1991	10.57	9.82	10.43
1992	9.39	9.49	9.40
1993	8.54	8.38	8.53
1994	8.67	8.20	8.56
1995	8.32	7.27	8.10
1996	7.83	7.53	7.79
1997	7.32	6.75	7.26
1998	7.23	6.16	7.07
1999	7.20	6.92	7.22

Source: Thomson Financial Securities Data.

the primary and secondary market and who keep in touch with what investors need and want for their portfolios at that given point in time. Successful underwriters master the delicate balance of finding the yield that produces not only the lowest borrower cost for the issuer but also the highest yield for the investor consistent with the issuer's credit and deal structure. They also generally have enough capital to carry their positions during the selling period, if the issue sells slowly.

For most sizable issues, negotiated or competitive, underwriters join in a syndicate in order to spread the risk of the sale and to gain wider access to potential investors. The composition of syndicates varies from issue to issue. One syndicate co-manager might be a major national securities firm, while the other might be a smaller dealer with a strong marketing organization in the region or state of the issuer. Another team might combine a manager specializing in institutional sales with a so-called *wire house*—that is, a firm with many branch offices and a broad clientele of individual investors.

The procedures, rules, and technicalities involved in underwriting an issue are intricate, and the pace is often very fast. Major underwriting firms may bid on and purchase dozens of issues a week while running the books as senior manager on several negotiated issues at the same time.

Advantages and Disadvantages of Competitive and Negotiated Underwriting

The choice between competitive bidding and a negotiated sale offers advantages and disadvantages to the issuer, summarized below.

Advantages of Competitive Bidding
- The lowest possible capital cost is likely to be achieved as the underwriters search for the investors with the highest offer prices.
- Historically, the gross underwriter spreads have been lower on issues sold by competitive bidding
- Competitive sales avoid the appearance of unfairness or impropriety in the selection of an underwriter.

Disadvantages of Competitive Bidding
- Bids may contain a risk premium, as bidders do not know whether they will be awarded the bonds.
- An issuer has less flexibility to change the sale date or the structure on an issue once the notice of sale has been published.
- An issuer has less control over the composition of the underwriting syndicate.
- The terms of the offering may not be the best possible terms; there may be trapped bidders (members of a syndicate who would have been willing to pay more than the winning offer price).

Advantages of Negotiated Sale
- The negotiating underwriter can perform origination tasks, eliminating the need for, and cost of, an outside advisor.
- A higher level of presale search can be conducted, thereby increasing the likelihood of an underwriter finding investors with the highest offer prices.
- There is greater flexibility to change the sale date or the structure of an issue in response to changing market conditions.
- The issuer has greater control over the composition of the underwriting syndicate.

Disadvantages of Negotiated Sale
- There is no direct competition among underwriters in setting the terms of the offering.
- It is difficult to determine whether the gross underwriter spread is appropriate, as a wider range of services is provided.
- There may be charges of favoritism toward firms that are selected to underwrite the bonds.

(Source: "An Empirical Analysis of Competitive Bid and Negotiated Offerings of Municipal Bonds, Paul A. Leonard, Municipal Finance Journal, Spring 1996, Volume 17, Number 1, takes this information from J. B. Kurish and Patricia Tigue, An Elected Official's Guide to Debt Issuance (Chicago: Government Finance Officers Association, 1993.)

The next two sections will describe in greater detail how both negotiated and competitive sales are handled, how they differ in certain aspects, and how they are similar in certain other aspects.

NEGOTIATED UNDERWRITING

Selection of Managers

Before the sale as described in Chapter 3, the issuer selects the senior manager. The issuer may also select one or more senior co-managers or one or more co-managers or may chose to let the senior manager "sole" manage the issue. For large and frequent issuers, a team of underwriters may be picked to serve for several transactions. In such cases, the senior managers may rotate their positions as each deal comes up, in much the same way as established competitive syndicates operate. When a large new credit makes its debut in the market, it is considered most prestigious to be chosen as the initial senior manager.

Financial advisors occasionally act as underwriters of an issue for which they are advisors, but this practice is becoming rare for large issues. The MSRB has adopted Rule G-23 to address potential conflicts of interest in such relationships. This rule states that a financial advisor must terminate the advisory relationship or disclose possible conflicts of interest and compensation to be earned before acting as underwriter on a negotiated issue.

Forming a Syndicate

After the issuer selects the managers, it is up to the managers to bring additional members into the syndicate, if necessary. It is the job of the senior manager to make a judgment about the size and composition of the syndicate. The senior manager may want a firm that has a particular distribution capability in the kind of credit being sold, such as health care or high-yield bonds. The issuer may also want certain firms to be in the syndicate, such as other national firms, or the issuer may want local firms that are not large enough to be managers but that have strong local and regional distribution networks. The financial advisor or issuer may believe that including or excluding certain firms for any number of reasons (legal, reputation, etc.) will add to the strength of the syndicate.

There are times when the senior manager may not want to form a syndicate at all, preferring to price and market the bonds solely with the other managers. Reasons for this may include the size of the issue, its prominence, whether or not it can be sold easily, and its potential profitability. Alternately, the issuer or financial advisors or the underwriters themselves may decide to include a *selling group,* instead of a syndicate, as part of the offering.

Selling Groups

Selling groups are formed by underwriters and syndicate managers to participate in the initial distribution of municipal bonds. In some instances, particularly in smaller offerings, a senior manager will form a selling group rather than a syndicate. Members of a selling group are brokers and dealers who are permitted by the senior manager to acquire underwritten municipal securities for resale on the same terms offered to syndicate members. However, selling group members do not share in the syndicate's net underwriting profits, nor do they assume pro rata liability for any underwriting loss or for the purchase of any unsold securities.

Agreement among Underwriters

As part of the syndicate formation, the lead manager circulates the *Agreement Among Underwriters* (AAU), which is the legal document generally used in negotiated sales. The AAU was originally developed in 1991 by The Bond Market Association and consisted of two sections: (1) instructions, terms, and acceptance and (2) standard terms and conditions. In 1997, The Bond Market Association released revisions to the original AAU by simplifying the agreement to reflect changes in market practices and legal requirements. The updated AAU contains the two sections detailed above, but unlike the 1991 version, it does not require that standard terms and conditions be circulated for each new deal. They are publicly available at The Bond Market Association's website. (www.bondmarkets.com)

It is assumed that all underwriters are familiar with the standard terms and conditions, common to most deals. The lead managers need to send syndicate members only the instructions, terms, and acceptance section of the AAU, including any supplements or modifications. Subsequent syndicate members will thus receive a seven- or eight-page document, compared to the 18 pages or more in the old AAU.

Credit and Research

In a negotiated sale, the underwriter must obtain the preliminary official statement, which has been deemed final under Rule 15c2–12, and review it in a professional manner. The underwriter is obligated to have a reasonable basis for recommending any municipal security and is responsible for reviewing in a professional manner the accuracy of the offering statements. In negotiated municipal offerings, where the underwriter is involved in the preparation of the official statement, the SEC believes that development of a reasonable basis for belief in the accuracy and completeness of the statements should involve an inquiry into the key representations in the official statement. Here too, the inquiry must be conducted in a professional manner, drawing on the underwriters' experience with the particular issuer, and other issuers, as well as their knowledge of the municipal markets. Sole reliance on the representation of the issuer does not suffice.

The continuing disclosure agreements required by the Securities and Exchange Commission (SEC) must also be in place. In some firms, the public finance bankers perform these due-diligence and underwriting tasks; in other firms, the credit and research professionals have that responsibility. Chapter 9 contains an extensive discussion of securities law and disclosure.

Marketing the Bonds

One of the major advantages of a negotiated sale is that time can be devoted to presale marketing. Salespeople can concentrate more on a negotiated issue in which their firm is a senior or co-manager than on a competitive sale because they are certain that there will be an underwriting and that there will be bonds to sell. The salespeople thus work together with the public finance bankers in the early stages of a deal to develop a marketing plan for the bonds. The presale activities can take many forms, depending on the size and complexity of the issue. Often a conference call will be organized so that the issuer can make a presentation to the underwriters' institutional clients. The investors will have been sent the preliminary official statement. In 2000, the SEC authorized that electronic delivery of official statements can be a replacement for delivering printed copies. Sometimes a presentation book that highlights the key features of the deal is also delivered to investors. Investors then ask the issuer and the investment bankers questions on the credit and other aspects of the offering.

The underwriter may arrange a *road show,* where the issuer travels to meet potential investors. The Internet is used for financial road shows, which reduces the need for travel and makes the information available to a broader audience. An information meeting where the issuer makes a formal presentation may be part of the road show. A summary analysis of the key features of the deal may be distributed to salespeople with a retail clientele. Again, the purpose is to provide a forum for investors to ask as many probing questions as are needed to fully understand the financing.

Pricing the Bonds

At propitious time, the senior manager will inform the market that the deal is ready to be priced. Negotiated sales do not usually require the more formal competitive sale notice; a notice to *The Bond Buyer* or other news service is normally sufficient to alert the whole market to the deal (the syndicate has already been formed). The night before the expected pricing of the bonds, the senior manager sends a *consensus scale* over a private syndicate wire to the syndicate members. This scale is a listing by maturity of the price or yields at which a new issue will be offered. The scale is the result of many conversations among the syndicate members, their salespeople, the public finance investment banker, and the issuer. The next morning, a preliminary scale usually will be distributed to the syndicate. The manager will run the books during the *order period* (a set period of time that depend on market conditions and the issuer). The manager keeps centralized information on which maturities are oversubscribed, meaning more orders received than the par amount, and which are undersubscribed, meaning fewer orders received than the par amount. After the initial order period, the underwriter makes a decision either to extend the order period in order to get more orders or to terminate it. If the order period is extended, the scale is adjusted to market conditions to make some bonds either richer (higher dollar price, lower yield) or cheaper (lower dollar price, higher yield).

At some point during the day, the underwriter proposes a final scale and bid to the issuer. The underwriter then tells the issuer that the deal is *underwritten*. This can, and often does, happen even if all of the bonds have not yet been sold. To attract investors and react to the market, the structure may have been changed, the par amount may have been changed, and the call features may have been changed from the original scale. This flexibility usually gets the best price and structure for the issuer.

After the deal is verbally underwritten and a final pricing wire is sent to the syndicate, the final pricing information is disseminated to the rest of the market through electronic and print media. The formal purchase contract between the underwriter and the issuer, the BPA is signed. The syndicate desk then processes orders and allocates bonds, as described later in this chapter.

COMPETITIVE UNDERWRITING

Informing the Market

Once the issuer decides to issue bonds to fund its capital needs, financial advisors, if used, will provide the issuer with opinions as to the size, terms, and timing of an offering. There are several ways that an issuer can initiate a competitive sale.

The Notice of Sale. Placing an official *notice of sale* or announcement electronically and in local and national newspapers and in trade publications is the usual way to initiate a competitive sale. Notice to *The Bond Buyer* is virtually a requirement for any significant issue. News services also distribute the information electronically. This electronic notice is often called a summary notice of sale. Active issuers usually send the notice of sale directly to prospective bidders and have the preliminary official statement available on their own website. Notices are organized in a calendar format, allowing the underwriters to keep close track of all new issues that are coming to market.

The notice of sale typically includes the following information:

1. Name of issuer
2. Dollar amount of issue
3. Date, time, and place of sale
4. Purpose, authorization, and security features
5. Dollar denominations
6. Form of bond; name of registration nominee and depository
7. Bond insurance, if available
8. Name of paying agent, bond registrar, or trustee
9. Dated date of bonds
10. Interest payment dates
11. Maturity schedule and call features
12. Basis for bidding and method of award
13. Structure and restrictions on coupon rates
14. Total amount of the bid at par or better or discount if allowed
15. Required amount of good-faith deposit
16. Statement of issuer's right to reject any or all bids
17. Covenant to enter into an *undertaking*, a written agreement or contract to provide ongoing disclosure under SEC Rule 15c2–12
18. Method, approximate date, and place of settlement for the bonds
19. Conditions for delivering the *final official statement*
20. Name of bond counsel and list of opinions and documents that will be provided
21. Name of financial advisor
22. Statement on whether the issue is bank qualified

Electronic dissemination of information has reached the point where it is more the norm than not. It is expected that there will be additional growth in the number of providers and in the extent of the products that are distributed to the new-issue market. Electronic commerce in municipals is further discussed in Chapter 5.

Forming a Syndicate for a Competitive Sale

For small issues, a single dealer may bid on the entire offering. For larger issues, as explained earlier in this chapter, underwriters usually form bidding syndicates. Traditionally, underwriters stay with the group with which their firms bid on the last occasion that the issuer came to market; conversely, most firms are in different syndicates for different issuers. The composition of a syndicate can change, of course. Firms go out of business, new firms are started, and some firms may simply want to drop out of the syndicate for a particular offering.

Syndicates in municipal bonds can have as few as two members or as many as 100 or more members. There may be one manager or several co-managers, although only one of them—the senior or lead manager—actually runs the books of the account, that is, keeps track of sales and of the availability of the bonds. It is customary for the managers to rotate their positions each time the same issuer comes to market. For example, if firm A is the senior manager on a deal in March and the same issuer comes to market again in September, firm B will rotate to the co-manager, or senior manager position. If the issuer sells on a regular semiannual schedule and there are three senior co-managers, firm A will be the senior manager again in September of the next year. However, it remains within each firm's discretion to join or remain in a syndicate. If a firm decides not to be in a given syndicate, or if it wants to bid alone, it is free to do so.

Syndicate Letters and Account Structures

The syndicate members are bound together on any issue by the syndicate letter or contract. This letter specifies the terms under which the account will be managed, including the obligations of all the members. The lead manager sends the letter to each member of the account—typically two weeks before the issue is to be sold. Each member must sign and return to the manager a copy of the syndicate letter, indicating the member's acceptance of the terms. The letters vary, but they generally include the following:

1. Preliminary amount of bonds to be underwritten by each member, called the *participations*
2. Duration of the account
3. Acknowledgment that the bid and offering terms will be set by the majority of the members
4. Obligations of members as to expenses, good-faith deposit, and liability for any unsold bonds
5. Appointment of the manager as agent for the account
6. Granting of rights to the syndicate manager, including rights to borrow, advertise, pledge securities, and make the bid
7. Granting of unspecified authority to the manager where necessary for the proper performance of management functions

8. A provision that no liability is assumed by the manager except for lack of good faith
9. Priority of orders (MSRB requirement)

The most commonly used syndicate account structure is one that is undivided as to sales and liability. Members of the account pool the bonds they have to sell as well as the liability for any unsold bonds. Thus, syndicate members can sell any of the bonds in an account as long as they are available. However, the syndicate profits are divided according to the *participations* agreed on before the sale, no matter how many bonds any individual member sells. If any bonds cannot be sold, all members are liable for a proportionate share of those bonds according to the same participations.

For example, a member might have a 10 percent participation in an account but sell only 5 percent of the bonds. In this case, the member is still entitled to 10 percent of the syndicate's net underwriting profits. However, that same member may sell more than 10 percent of the bonds, while the syndicate as a whole fails to sell the entire issue. In this case, the member is still liable for 10 percent of the unsold bonds, despite its own sales record, and will still receive only 10 percent of any underwriting profits—or be assessed for 10 percent of net underwriting losses. Syndicate managers usually take the largest participations; other members take varying amounts of participation.

The undivided account structure described above was historically known as an *Eastern account* because its roots were in the major national financial centers of the Northeast. It is currently the predominant structure used for competitive bids. The divided, or *Western account,* is another type of structure whose use has declined drastically. In a divided account, members are assigned a portion of each of several groups of bonds. The bonds, for example, might be broken down into several categories (or brackets) of different maturities. However, the account is divided only as to liability, not as to sales. Thus, as in the undivided account, a firm can sell any of the bonds in the issue, according to a priority that is discussed later in this chapter. However, a member is liable for unsold bonds only if it has not sold its full participation in each bracket.

It should be emphasized that net underwriting profits are by no means the only revenues that the members of a syndicate can earn through participation in an underwriting. They receive discounts, known as concessions and takedowns, on bonds they sell or take for their own inventory. If a member can sell bonds for the offering price or at a smaller discount than the member's price, the profit on these sales is part of the firm's revenues. This is discussed more fully later in this chapter.

Credit and Research

In 1994, the SEC promulgated major amendments to Rule 15c2–12, which covers municipal securities disclosure. The changes became effective on

July 3, 1995. An extensive discussion of Rule 15c2–12 is included in Chapter 9, but it is important here to understand how these changes have added to the responsibility of the underwriter in the primary market with regard to credit review and disclosure. The SEC has written that in a normal competitive bid offering involving an established municipal issuer, a municipal underwriter generally would meet its obligation to have a reasonable basis for belief in the accuracy of the key representations in the official statement, in which it reviewed the official statement in a professional manner and received from the issuer a detailed and credible explanation concerning any aspect of the official statement that appeared on its face, or on the basis of information available to the underwriter, to be inadequate.

The job of reviewing official statements for competitive bids has in most cases been assigned to the credit and research staffs of the municipal bond dealers. The analysts also check to see that the issuer has committed, in writing, to continuing disclosure. These responsibilities come in addition to the more traditional role of the underwriter, determining through extensive research as to the relative creditworthiness of an offering. If their own research analysts are particularly confident about the financial health of a municipality, the underwriters may make a more aggressive bid for the offering. However, if a firm's municipal analysts believe that the disclosure is inadequate or that the credit is weak, the firm may not bid at all.

The rating agencies and bond insurers also review the issue before the competitive sale in anticipation of releasing a rating or an insurance commitment. This process will be discussed extensively in Chapter 7.

The Preliminary Scale

The formation of the syndicate sets in motion the actual competitive bidding process for the dealer. Typically, on the day before the bid is to be placed, the managers put out a *preliminary scale,* which is a listing by maturity of the prices or yields at which the issue will be offered. Syndicate members are also asked for their preliminary pricing ideas at this time. The preliminary scale is developed with the goal of coming up with this highest dollar bid and lowest interest cost to the issuer while still being confident of selling the bonds at a profitable spread (which is also tested at this preliminary scale). The senior manager must be careful to develop the scale in accordance with the parameters set forth in the notice of sale. This includes the basis of the bid (true interest cost or net interest cost) and whether only par and not discount bonds are allowed.

After the preliminary scale is set, the underwriters at the firms in the syndicate distribute the scale to their own traders and salespeople. This is done to gauge the interest that the market has in the issue and to see how other comparable issues have sold. The salespeople at the firms solicit orders, and frequently, some orders for the bonds have already been lined up before the actual bid.

The manager must also make arrangements for a good-faith deposit to be delivered at the time stated in the notice of sale. The good-faith deposit is a security deposit, which the issuer retains as compensation in the event that the winning bidder fails to pay for the bonds or notes on the delivery date. The amount of the good-faith requirement is established by the issuer and is stated in the notice of sale. In most cases, the winning syndicate's good-faith deposit is subtracted from the final payment for the issue at the time of delivery and final settlement. The good-faith deposit may range from 1 to 5 percent of the par value of the bonds or notes; it is normally about 2 percent. The good-faith deposits of the losing syndicates are returned to their managing underwriters immediately after the bid award has been made. Instead of the cashier's or certified check that had traditionally been used for the good-faith requirement, issuers can use a financial surety bond. The issuer's bond documents must authorize the use of the surety for the good-faith deposit.

Pricing Call on the Day of the Bid

There is a final pricing conference call usually one hour before the bid is due. The call begins with the manager announcing the proposed pricing scale and recommending the size of the spread. If any sales have been made or lined up already, they are announced at this time. The final pricing call can create tremendous tension because there is intense pressure to submit the best bid on time.

During the final pricing call, the senior manager also informs syndicate members of the latest developments in the market. The yields on other issues for sale that day are watched closely as benchmarks for determining yields on the issue being underwritten. The manager then polls the members for their opinions about the scales and the spread. Disagreements among the members often arise at this time. They tend to center on the yields for particular maturities or on the size of the spread. Members may drop out of the syndicate at any time before the bid is placed, and some do so at this time.

During this period, the salespeople at the syndicate firms are working to line up orders and to determine where on the scale demand is strong or weak. The underwriters are continuously informed as those orders are received. In an offering that is going well, some maturities may sell out before the call is over. As orders come in, the members can start to raise their bids by lowering the yields on some maturities. Conversely, the salespeople may be communicating to the underwriter why they are not getting orders. There may be pricing or credit problems or competition with other issues. If few orders come in, the syndicate may become more cautious and raise yields to sweeten the deal.

Sometimes the members decide the spread is too small and try to get the manager to widen, or increase it. Occasionally, a compromise is reached, where the spread is widened while yields on some maturities are reduced. Generally, the manager wields the most influence at the price meetings, but a big order from a member can force a sudden adjustment in the scale. The order period, which usually runs for one or two hours, is also set at the final pricing call. A few minutes before the deadline, the final scale is set and the bid is calculated.

Delivery of the Bid

The senior manager makes the arrangements to deliver the sealed bid before the deadline. The deadline is adhered to very strictly, and any irregularities will disqualify the bidder. If the bid is to be hand delivered the senior manager makes sure that someone representing the syndicate delivers the bid properly. Bids can also be made by phone or fax, with the good-faith deposit covered by a surety bond company. Electronic bid submission has becoming increasingly more common.

The good-faith deposit is submitted along with the bid form in a sealed envelope. At the time stated in the notice of sale, the bids are opened in front of all that are assembled; usually this includes the issuer, financial advisor, bond counsel, and of course, representatives of each competing syndicate. Each bid is read aloud, including the dollar amount offered and the interest cost.

The preliminary winner will be announced at the meeting, although usually the underwriters back at their offices will know who won the bid before the people at the meeting. This is because the underwriters call the competing syndicates' managers right after submitting the sealed bid to ask what they bid. Competitive sale results are disseminated immediately through the news wires and are printed in *The Bond Buyer* the following day.

The winning syndicate then immediately works to sell the bonds, although the official award of the bonds usually occurs several hours after the bid, often after the financial advisor has verified that the bid numbers are correct. The types of orders and the way that they are filled are described in the next section.

Use of the Internet for a Competitive Offering

On November 18, 1997, the City of Pittsburgh became the first issuer to use the Internet for a competitive bid. The $70 million GO issue was auctioned maturity by maturity on the MuniAuction website, which is operated by the city's financial advisor. The issue had 20 serial maturities, and the bidders could bid on individual maturities over a 30-minute auction period, as opposed to the traditional all or none, one-deadline competitive bid process. There were 26 bidders involved, and eight firms ended up buying various maturities. To date, all or none is still the preponderant practice in competitive bidding. Bidding on the Internet has now becoming increasingly common as technology has provided more venues.

Another aspect of competitive bidding on the Internet has been for qualified investors to bid directly for the issue, without an underwriter. This practice is quite controversial and has not become as common. Many questions arise when investors bid directly for bonds, including which party bears the regulatory responsibility and what kind of support the bonds will have in the secondary market from dealers.

ORDERS AND PROCEDURES

Types of Orders

There are three types of orders—*net, concession,* and *takedown.* The highest-priced order is sold to investors *at the net,* that is, at the price or yield actually shown in the reoffering scale. These prices are always the ones agreed to by the underwriting group, which retains the full spread.

However, an underwriting group or syndicate will generally give up part of its spread to get orders from dealers who are not in the syndicate. These dealers are offered what is known as a *concession,* a fractional discount from the public offering price. The concession works as follows. A typical spread might be $5 per $1,000 bond (one-half point). The concession might be $1.25 (an eighth of a point), so that a nonsyndicate dealer with a municipal bond department would be entitled to buy the bonds for $998.75 and to sell them to a customer for the full $1,000, retaining the $1.25. These bonds are said to be bought at the concession. Since most bonds are sold in lots of 100 or more, the concession can be important to each firm's profit.

Individual members of a syndicate can buy the bonds *at the takedown* for their own accounts, for sale to another dealer, or for sale directly to an investor. The takedown is the fractional discount from the public offering price at which the underwriters purchase the bonds. The concession is a part of the takedown. The takedown might amount to an additional $1.25, the total takedown coming to $2.50. Hence, a syndicate member could buy the bonds at $997.50 and sell them to a dealer outside the group for $998.75; the dealer, in turn, could sell them for $1,000. In this case, the member would keep only the $1.25 for compensation. If the member sells the bonds at the net price to an investor, the syndicate member would then keep the full $2.50 takedown. To summarize, the net is the highest price, the takedown is the lowest price, and the concession is somewhere in the middle.

Priority of Orders

The priority of the types of orders is a critical part of an underwriting. If an offering is oversubscribed, low-priority orders may not be filled. According to MSRB's rule G-11, the priority of orders must be furnished in writing to all syndicate members. The AAU specifies the priority of orders in a negotiated financing as follows:

1. *Group net orders.* These are orders taken at the net reoffering price. The spread is retained by the whole syndicate as part of its profit.
2. *Net designated orders.* These are orders from investors at the net or concession price. The commission is designated by the investor to the syndicate member.
3. *Members orders.* These orders are at the public offering price less the total takedown. They are purchases made by syndicate members for their own accounts or for sale to another dealer or investor.

Within each of these levels of priority the syndicate may grant preferences in allocation to institutional purchasers, retail purchasers, or other purchasers if such preferences are not contrary to the best interests of the syndicate.

An exception can occur in a competitive offering. The difference in designation policy is that in a negotiated issue, the issuer determines designated orders, and in a competitive sale, the buyer makes the designation.

If the issue, or certain maturities of the issue, are oversubscribed, allotments will be made according to the priority of orders, as stated earlier. If given levels of priority bonds are oversubscribed; bonds are fairly allotted to members of the syndicate by the senior manager.

Many MSRB rules relate to the primary offering of securities. The public can access the most current MSRB's rules on the MSRB website at *www. MSRB.org.*

Orders are usually confirmed by the manager of the account when the initial order period is over. However, only issues in the greatest demand are typically sold out within the one or two hours of the order period. Subsequently, orders are taken from members on a first-come, first-served basis, regardless of the type of order. When the issue is sold out, the syndicate is disbanded.

Most syndicate accounts are set up to run for 30 days. The members can then renew them, if necessary, but very few new offerings are held open for that long. When an issue proves difficult to sell, the terms of the offering are often revised. Changing the terms usually requires the majority consent of the members, with votes weighted by their respective participations.

If the issue still cannot be sold, the bonds may be distributed among the members. The members are free to sell them at whatever price they want or the bonds may be given to one or more bond brokers. The broker then puts the bonds out for the bid. Members of the syndicate also have the right to bid for the bonds, as may any other dealer. The party that produces the best bid for the group of bonds will win them, although the manager retains the right to reject all bids.

Retail Order Period

An exception to the priority of orders is a *retail order period,* during which the issuer requests that retail and smaller investors be allowed to place their orders for bonds before the institutional buyers do so. If an issuer opts to include a retail order period, orders received during that time will have the first priority. The goal is to have bonds available for both in-state and out-of-state investors and to have a fair distribution between retail and institutional investors. The retail investors generally have the ability to cancel their orders if the preliminary institutional price is increased.

After the Sale

After the issue is sold, the manager of the syndicate must undertake a number of procedures to confirm orders, deliver and pay for the bonds, and meet legal requirements. The MSRB Rule G-12 (the Board's Uniform Practice Code) describes the procedures for confirming orders to members in an underwriting. All sales of new issues are made on a "when, as, and if issued" basis. Written confirmations for "when, as, and if issued" orders must generally be sent within one business day following the trade date, according to MSRB Rule G-12(c). Rule G-15(a) establishes the requirements for confirmations to a customer.

Just after the purchase of the issue by the underwriters, the senior manager sends a letter to all members of the account, stating the terms of the issue. The letter sets forth the reoffering terms of the issue, including the spread, takedown, and concession, and confirms the price to be paid to the issuer. It also announces whether and how the issue will be advertised in the financial press, lists the participations of the members in a competitive sale, and includes other relevant information as well. The members must sign and return the letter. In most advertisements, the members of the account are listed in the order of the size of their participations.

MSRB Rule G-32 requires that before or at the time that customers are sent their final written confirmations, the underwriter must send each customer a copy of the issue's official statement in final form. In a negotiated sale, information on underwriting spreads, fees, and the offering price for each maturity must also be sent to customers; it is usually included in the final official statements. The rule requires members of the syndicate to promptly provide copies of official statements on request to dealers who have purchased the new-issue securities. It also places other requirements on managers and financial advisors to facilitate distribution of the disclosure documents.

It takes no longer than a month (and usually less) from the sale date before the bonds are actually ready to be delivered to investors. This allows time for bond counsel to prepare the final opinion and a transcript of proceedings. Up to that point, bond counsel has given only a preliminary opinion and the sale of bonds is conditional on the final opinion. The transcript typically includes a certificate stating that there is no litigation pending against the bonds and a guarantee of the signatures of the officials who signed the bonds.

The senior manager must pay for the bonds when they are available for delivery. The manager may borrow the money to finance the purchase of the bonds. The payment made is the bid price plus accrued interest less the amount of the good-faith deposit. In turn, the bonds are delivered to the members of the account according to the allotments. The members then pay for their shares of the sales. As the payments come in, the manager pays off the loan, usually within a few days.

Once the bonds are paid for and expenses totaled, the senior manager will distribute the profits to members of the syndicate. If there was a loss on the underwriting, the members are assessed for their share. The distribution is accompanied by a final statement of the member participations and the expenses and profits of the syndicate.

Depending on the issue's dated date, investors are not always entitled to the full six months' interest for the first payment period. The interest payment may be a long or short first coupon. The investor must pay the accrued interest to the seller—in this case, the issuer. The investor then receives the accrued interest from the dated date up to but not including the interest payment date. Dealers will simply add on the accrued interest to the price of the bonds.

MSRB Rules adjust to meet changing industry practices and needs. Investors, issuers and underwriters should consult the MSRB's website at *www.MSRB.org* for the most current version of the rules.

CHAPTER 5

The Secondary Market

INTRODUCTION

Secondary markets exist to provide liquidity to investors, enabling them to sell a security after its initial offering. The best-known secondary markets are for corporate equities. Because stocks are not redeemable at a specific date, investors need a secondary market, such as the New York Stock Exchange in order to convert their investments to cash. While bondholders expect to receive their principal in cash when their bonds mature, they still want the option of selling their securities before maturity.

A thriving secondary market helps to support the primary market for securities. It also serves investors by providing them with an array of different types of securities at different points in time. By having the ability to buy or sell quickly, investors can employ a variety of strategies for maximizing return within their risk constraints.

THE OVER-THE-COUNTER MARKET

Exchange versus Over-the-Counter

The two broad categories of financial markets are the *exchange market* and the *over-the-counter market*. Equities can be traded in an exchange market where publicly owned corporations meeting certain minimum capitalization and other requirements are listed. The price of the security is shown after each trade. Certain types of equities, including those of newer, smaller companies, are now commonly traded over the counter. An over-the-counter market is one where transactions are executed through dealers, not through a centralized exchange.

Municipal bonds are traded on the over the counter market, with market participants executing transactions through voice contact. The market has changed in recent years, however, as technology has allowed dealers and customers increasingly to interact through electronic media such as communication networks employing electronic messaging services. This, in turn, has led to the creation of alternative or electronic systems that allow for instantaneous execution of transactions.

Electronic trading systems developed along with the growth of the Internet, which allows for unprecedented connectivity among nearly all market participants. The minimal cost associated with this connectivity has also played a major role, allowing even the smallest individual investor access to tools and sophisticated information sources that were, until recently, the private domain of institutional investors.

The size of the secondary market in municipal securities had historically been hard to determine because there was no central listing of all trades. Beginning in 1998, The Bond Market Association began to electronically disseminate the MSRB price reports. Municipal bonds that trade four or more times on the previous trading day are included in each daily report, which will typically include about 1,000 issues out of the 1.4 million issues that are outstanding. These reports can be found on *www.investinginbonds.com*.

Figure 5.1 is the current menu of options that an investor sees when logging on to this website.

Figure 5.2 is an example of this daily report of municipal bond transaction. There were 91 municipal bond trades for Florida issues, which traded four or more times on June 21, 2000, sorted by rating. Only the first three issues are shown in this chart. Reading across, the user sees the ratings; the issue name, CUSIP number, state, coupon, maturity, call dates and prices; and high and low prices for the day and their corresponding yield to maturity. An investor can sort daily transactions on any of these criteria.

Other sources compile information on offerings available for purchase in the secondary market. One of the major traditional sources is *The Blue List*, which is published by Standard & Poor's. This is a daily listing, available both in print and electronically, of securities offered by over 700 participating broker-dealers. It typically lists 7,000 to 8,000 municipal bonds available for sale each day with a par value of $1.4 billion. There are also now many electronic trading systems that offer various types of secondary market information for both the professional investor and for the public.

E-COMMERCE, INFORMATION, AND TECHNOLOGY

The municipal market, along with all other financial markets, has been transformed by the extensive use of technology. Dealers and investors have vast amounts of information literally at their fingertips, which they employ to help them manage positions and portfolios. Large and small firms maintain their own websites and E-mail. They access specific news services with dedicated screens; they use television and radio and print media. Market professionals try to get as much information as they can to get a leg up on their competition, and technology enables them to do their jobs better.

Technology in its many forms does the following things in the municipal market:

FIGURE 5.1   www.InvestinginBonds.com (web page detail)

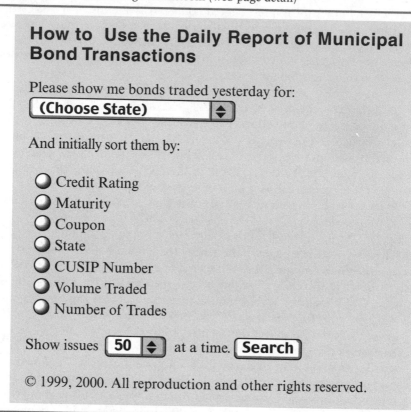

How to Use the Daily Report of Municipal Bond Transactions

Please show me bonds traded yesterday for:

(Choose State)

And initially sort them by:

- Credit Rating
- Maturity
- Coupon
- State
- CUSIP Number
- Volume Traded
- Number of Trades

Show issues **50** at a time. **Search**

Source: The Bond Market Association.

- Furnishes data and news in a timely and comprehensive manner.
- Tracks primary and secondary market activity.
- Increases trading efficiency with electronic trading platforms.
- Increases liquidity in the secondary market, as investors and dealers have greater access to information.
- Disseminates key disclosure information.
- Responds to the constantly changing demands of the market by adding new features and products.
- Offers analytical tools to the investor and dealer.

A comprehensive directory of municipal market information sources can be found at The Bond Market Association's website at *www.bondmarkets.com*.

FIGURE 5.2   MSRB Daily Price Report

►Ratings Insur.	►Issue ►CUSIP	►St	►Coupon	►Maturity Calls	Call Prices	►Hi $ Price ►Lo $ Price	►%YTM	►%YTC/P
AAA S AAA M AAA F AMBAC	ALTAMONTE SPRINGS FLA HEALTH FACS AUTH HOSP REV ADVENTIST HL 021433DK0	FL	5.375%	11/15/2023 11/15/2003 11/15/2005	102.000 100.000	97.500 93.500	5.567 5.890	

►Volume of $ 600,000 for ► 7 trades. ► Show Trade Details
►Search MuniStatements.com for official statements on this issue.

| AAA S AAA M AAA F AMBAC | LEE CNTY FLA CAP REV AMBAC - BOOK ENTRY ONLY - FITCH LT RTG A 52348LDF1 | FL | 4.800% | 10/01/2008 | | 100.000 100.000 | 4.799 4.799 | |

►Volume of $ 025,000 for ► 4 trades. ► Show Trade Details
►Search MuniStatements.com for official statements on this issue.

| AAA S AAA M AAA F AMBAC | LEE CNTY FLA CAP REV AMBAC - BOOK ENTRY ONLY - O.I.D. REOF @ 52348LBE4 | FL | 4.700% | 10/01/2007 | | 99.811 99.811 | 4.730 4.730 | |

►Volume of $ 1,095,000 for ► 7 trades. ► Show Trade Details
►Search MuniStatements.com for official statements on this issue.

Source: The Bond Market Association.

Electronic Trading Systems

The use of electronic trading systems in the municipal market is expanding rapidly because of the growth of the Internet, which has given market participants immense communication tools.

The systems that have been introduced recently are just the beginning of a threshold change in the way the secondary municipal market functions. At this point in time, systems can be classified into four distinct categories, although many vendors offer services that are included in several categories. Undoubtedly these categories will change and evolve as the market adapts and adjusts to ever-changing technology.

Dealer systems. Dealer systems allow investors to execute transactions directly with dealers through an electronic interface. The category includes single-dealer systems as well as multidealer systems that consolidate orders from two or more dealers.

Cross-matching systems. Cross-matching systems bring both dealers and institutional investors together in electronic trading networks that provide real-time or periodic cross-matching sessions.

Primary market auction systems. Auction systems permit issuers to solicit bids for new debt offerings directly from dealers and investors.

Interdealer systems. Interdealer systems allow dealers to electronically execute transactions with other dealers through the fully anonymous services of brokers' brokers.

SELLING MUNICIPAL BONDS

The secondary market provides the liquidity for the investor to sell their securities before the stated maturity date. Investors who sell may get a higher or a lower price for the bonds than they originally paid, depending on two major factors: market risk and credit risk.

Investors securities sell before maturity date for a number of reasons, including

1. Concerns about unfavorable direction of interest rates
2. More attractive investments in the municipal or other markets
3. Changed, usually lower credit quality
4. Mutual funds redemptions may create a need for cash
5. Cyclical changes in the investor's prime business may create a need for cash
6. Changes in the investor's financial circumstance
7. Heirs want to convert securities that they have inherited to cash
8. Tax law changes
9. Individual tax considerations

Market risk is the term given to the potential price fluctuations in a bond that are caused by changes in the general level of municipal interest rates. If the level of these rates has changed since the bonds were bought, the resale value of those bonds will of course reflect that shift. Thus, if interest rates are currently higher than they were when the bonds were bought, the bonds may be worth less; conversely, if interest rates have declined, bond prices generally will have risen and the bonds may be worth more.

Credit risk is associated with the individual issue and issuer. (See Chapter 7 for an extensive discussion of credit.) If the credit standing of the issuer improves, the bonds may be worth more in the market. If the issuer's credit standing weakens, the bonds may fall in value.

The management of market risk and credit risk has become an important aspect of all financial markets, including the over-the-counter municipal market. Investors and dealers alike have placed a greater emphasis on risk management. By measuring how many bonds are owned and how long they have been in an investment portfolio, and by layering the credit risk, investors and their advisors can quantify the risks involved in holding different bonds. The capacity to perform complex risk-management calculations has been spurred on by advances in information technology.

Dealers have developed analytic systems that enable traders and their

managers to see the value of a bond at any given time, along with hedging vehicles, and to see profits and losses on a daily basis. This information allows
the traders to increase or reduce their market positions as needed. Integrating
interest rate forecasts into a firm's inventory position and analyzing how
changes in rates will affect a particular bond's performance is another aspect
of risk management. Risk-management techniques will continue to evolve
with the need to control exposures to market and credit risks and with the development and accessibility of new technology.

THE BASICS OF MUNICIPAL BOND TRADING

Key Participants in the Secondary Market

The secondary market is vastly different from what it was only a few years
ago. The rapid pace of technological advancement that has affected all seg-
ments of the economy has radically elevated the complexity of trading and
has made enormous quantities of information available to the market.

Trading is a fast-paced, risky business where concise communication and
quantitative skills are highly valued. Municipal bond traders, the principal
market makers, sit on a trading floor with underwriters and salespeople.
Their long, connecting desks are crammed with telephone turrets, flashing
market screens, computers, news service terminals, bond trader calculators,
time stamps, and a *hoot and holler* or *squawk box* for internal verbal com-
munications. The traders who work for full-service securities dealers and for
many banks buy and sell securities from other dealers and from investors
both for immediate sale and to stock their own inventories. Municipal traders
must have a sense of the kinds of bonds their firms' clients want, which means
they must have clear and consistent communication with the salesforce,
which in turn must maintain open lines with the investor clients. Generally,
traders try not to be caught with inventory that is hard to sell, and they try to
hedge their positions if possible.

Firms that are often called *brokers' brokers* play a significant role in the
secondary market. This relatively small group of brokers provides anonymity
for the bond dealers and dealer banks on whose behalf they act. Some maintain full trading operations, and others specialize in certain types of securities, but for the most part, none carry inventories of bonds. They act as
agents, not as principals.

Brokers perform several services that both create markets and help them
to operate efficiently. One of these services is their involvement in the "bid
wanted" business. When dealers cannot, or do not, wish to obtain bids directly for bonds they want to sell, they may give them to a broker who will
obtain bids from other dealers. Brokers not only identify specific buyers for
bonds, they also help dealers find specific bonds from other dealers. If a

dealer has an offering that he does not want the whole dealer community to see, a broker may be able to find a buyer by making a few telephone calls. Bond brokers are also occasionally called on to obtain bids for the balance of an underwriting. Brokers are discreet; they generally do not release the identity of the dealers involved in any transactions without permission.

The brokers continuously communicate with dealers, tracking closely who owns what and who might want to sell or buy bonds. They have a good picture of the market. The anonymity they guarantee to dealers makes the latter more willing to give bond brokers information, and thus, bond brokers often have access to more information than do dealers. Brokers are paid a commission only when they trade bonds.

The firm's salespeople also actively participate in the secondary market. They are on the telephone with dozens of clients throughout the day, providing updates of developments not only in the municipal market but also in other related markets. The salesperson becomes acquainted with the bonds in the investor's portfolio and is familiar with the account's investment goals and objectives. That way, when the trader either buys bonds or has them in inventory, the salespeople can offer clients the right security to match their needs. Often, the salesperson and the trader will cross bonds between two customers. For example, Investor A holds a block of single-family housing bonds that he or she wishes to sell. The salesperson also knows that Investor B has been looking to buy bonds with those credit and maturity characteristics. With pricing assistance from the trader, the bonds will be crossed from one account to the other.

An investor who is about to circulate a *bid list* often alerts the salesperson. A bid list is a group of bonds distributed by the current bondholder in order to get a current price, or bid, on the bonds. The bondholder asks the salesperson to bid on some or all of the bonds by a specified time. The salesperson will consult with the traders and research to arrive at the best price.

MUNICIPAL BOND TRADING

A trader sells securities out of, and buys securities into, the firm's inventory and also hedges those positions if possible. Traders look at spreads within their own market, as well as the relationships between their market and the other markets. The net revenues from trading come from the relatively small price markups over the trader's initial cost, less any associated costs, which are primarily the cost of carry. The goal of a trader is to turn over their inventory quickly because the cost of carrying inventory for too long can be expensive, as dealers usually borrow funds to finance their inventories. Furthermore, holding securities always carries the inherent risk of the securities losing value if interest rates move upward quickly, as prices must then be marked down. Municipal bond trading has four distinguishing characteristics. The impact of these four distinguishing characteristics will be apparent in the following sections, which describe the factors that go into the decision to trade a bond, how the trade is actually done, and the range specialists involved in trading. The distinguishing characteristics of municipal bond trading are: (1) Most municipal bonds are traded on the basis of yield to maturity; (2) Trades are executed over the counter through dealers acting as principals; (3) There are no set trading hours; and (4) There are a vast number of outstanding secondary market issues.

Factors in a Trade

Market Spreads. Traders are constantly looking at the spread relationships among different securities markets in order to buy and sell securities at the optimal time. For example, the relationship between tax-exempts and Treasuries is monitored to determine when the municipal market is *cheap* to Treasuries and when it is *rich*. In these terms, municipals are cheap when they are trading at a yield that is a relatively high percentage of the Treasury yield, and they are rich when they are trading at a relatively low percentage of Treasuries.

In addition to looking at the spreads between markets, traders always take into account the term structure of interest rates. The shape of the yield curve (see Chapter 8, Understanding Interest Rates) is crucial to trading decisions, including those based on market spreads and the other factors described below.

Sector Spreads. Traders also look at the spreads between different sectors of the municipal market. For example, a trader may focus on the spread in basis points between *triple-B revenue bonds* and *triple-B hospital bonds*. Triple-B revenue bonds are mostly those of utilities and transportation and exclude those of hospitals. If the spread relationship changes over some period of time, the trader tries to determine why that has happened and then trade in or out of a position based on that knowledge. For example, pending legislation or variations in new bond issue supply may trigger changes in spreads between sectors.

Benchmark curves, such as that of general market insured triple-A bonds are often used as a basis to compare sectors. *General market* refers to bonds without specific state tax issues. The Bond Market Association, in conjunction with Bloomberg, produces a daily benchmark curve of triple-A-rated tax-exempt insured revenue bonds. Figure 5.3 is an example of this information in text form.

Credit Spreads. In addition to analyzing sector spreads, traders also look at credit spreads. These are similar to sector spreads, with the emphasis on ex-

FIGURE 5.3 Municipal Bond Yields (triple-A rated, tax-exempt, insured revenue bonds)

NATIONAL MUNI BOND YIELDS Triple-A Rated, Tax-Exempt Insured Revenue Bonds.							
	6/29	6/28	Change in	31% eq	6/22	6/1/00	12/30/99
Maturity	Yield	Yield	Yield	Yield	Yield	Yield	Yield
Two year	4.74%	4.76%	−0.02%	6.87%	4.71%	4.97%	4.44%
Five year	4.96%	4.98%	−0.02%	7.19%	4.96%	5.28%	4.85%
Seven year	5.06%	5.08%	−0.02%	7.33%	5.06%	5.36%	5.03%
Ten year	5.21%	5.23%	−0.02%	7.55%	5.21%	5.45%	5.28%
Fifteen year	5.56%	5.58%	−0.02%	8.06%	5.56%	5.82%	5.73%
Twenty year	5.78%	5.80%	−0.02%	8.38%	5.78%	6.06%	6.02%
Thirty year	5.90%	5.92%	−0.02%	8.55%	5.90%	6.16%	6.14%

Source: The Bond Market Association, Bloomberg L. P.

amining spreads within a sector; for example, general-market triple-A in-sured hospitals against general-market triple-B hospitals. There are times when credit spreads are wide—say, 100 or more basis points between a triple-A and a triple-B bond—and there are times when those spreads narrow to 40 or 50 basis points. When spreads are wide, there is more opportunity to make judgments about the relative value of one type of credit to another. Looking at these spreads is also valuable to issuers in the primary market as they make the decision to sell bonds with or without credit enhancement. If the cost of insurance is less than the spread between generic insured municipal bonds and triple-B municipal bonds there is a more compelling reason to issue with insurance.

Ratings Changes. Changes in ratings, either upgrades or downgrades, often stimulate trades. If a bond is downgraded, or if it is expected to be down-graded, its spread to others in its rating category and to a triple-A benchmark may widen. Conversely, if a bond is upgraded from Baa1 to A3, the yield spread to a benchmark triple-A bond will narrow. Table 5.1 shows represen-tative quarterly yields from December 1994 through February 26, 1998, on New York City GOs, 8.25s of 2006 (noncallable), versus the benchmark triple-A State of Georgia GOs 6.20s of 2006. Along with the general nar-rowing of spreads over this period, the spread between New York and the triple-A scale narrowed even more, especially in 1997. This happened for two reasons: an overall shortage of municipal bonds, and the overall view that New York City was an improving credit risk. Indeed, New York City was up-graded by Moody's on 2/24/98 from Baa1 to A3. On 2/26/96, the yield spread had narrowed to 41 basis points, its lowest in three years. The representative

TABLE 5.1   Spread Analysis of New York City General Obligation (GO) Bonds to State of Georgia GO Bonds, 1994–1998

Date	New York City vs. Triple-A GO Yield Spread	New York City GO n/c 8.25s of 2006	Georgia GOs n/c 6.20s of 2006
December 1994	100	6.88	5.88
March 1995	111	6.36	5.25
June 1995	107	6.20	5.13
September 1995	108	6.07	4.99
December 1995	120	5.88	4.68
March 1996	111	6.08	4.97
June 1996	118	6.24	5.06
September 1996	94	5.98	5.04
December 1996	91	5.69	4.78
March 1997	78	5.82	5.04
June 1997	60	5.34	4.74
September 1997	53	4.99	4.46
December 1997	54	4.83	4.29
February 1998	41	4.67	4.26

Source: Thomson Financial Municipals Group.
Note: n/c = noncallable.

Baa1 spread to triple-A GOs on that same date was 25 basis points, showing that New York City was still relatively cheap, but not as cheap as before the upgrade.

Material Events.   Material events, such as a draw on an issue's reserve fund, may cause some investors to want to trade out the bonds, while investors on the other side may view any decline in prices as a buying opportunity. Material events must be disclosed to investors under Rule 15c2-12 (see Chapter 9).

HOW A TRADE IS DONE

Municipal bond trading conforms to the normal *bid-and-offer* (or *bid-and-ask*) procedure followed in most over-the-counter markets. The listing of the yield by dealers is always the offered side of the market. Investors, however, may not care to buy the bonds at that yield and may, therefore, bid for them at a higher yield (lower price.) A bid yield of 5.25 percent and an offered yield of 5.20 percent means that a dealer is willing to buy the bonds at 5.25 percent and to sell them at 5.20 percent.

In the dialogue that constitutes a trade, the seller of the security will say, "I will sell to you the following," and then give the relevant information par value of the bonds: name of the bonds; coupon rate; maturity date; agreed yield or dollar price; concession, if any; and CUSIP number. If bonds are callable, the call date, price, and whether the bonds are priced to maturity or a call date must be made known to the buyer. The buyer will carefully go over the terms of the trade before confirming. It is common for traders to call back the seller or seller's agent immediately if there is any doubt over the terms agreed upon. A trade is consummated with precise information.

Bonds trade this way every day in this manner. The market operates in this fashion because of the dictum that "Your word is your bond." If you state that you will buy or sell at a certain price, you must honor that verbal commitment. Electronic offerings on dealer systems, cross-matching systems, and interdealer systems reduce the need for verbal commitments, but the basic ethos still applies.

Sometimes offerings are made on an all or none basis. These are known as *AON offerings,* where the offerer agrees to sell the bonds only if all the bonds on offer will be bought. *Multiples of offerings* are also common, where, for example, sellers offer bonds only in lots of 25, 50, 100, or 200 bonds of $1,000 each.

A frequent practice in the industry is the use of the option to buy. Unlike the case for most securities, this option is free. The seller is asked to make a bona fide firm offering to the prospective buyer, which will hold good for a stated time (usually from one half to a full hour). During this time, the bonds are said to be *out firm.* The prospective buyer uses this grace period to get additional information on the bonds, such as an updated credit opinion. The buyer thus has the option to get back to the seller and buy the bonds at the agreed-on yield within the set time. If the buyer does not do so, the dealer can sell the bonds elsewhere. Essentially, this procedure sets a time frame for the trade, no matter what the market does in the intervening time period. Again, this is where "your word is your bond" is particularly important, as the market can move either up or down while the bonds are out firm, and the commitment to a certain price must remain. As a rule, the option is accompanied by a recall privilege, which gives the seller the right to recall the "firm" bonds in a shorter time period. The amount of time is agreed upon beforehand.

Specialists

Some large securities dealers maintain small trading staffs in regional sales offices where municipal bond trading is particularly active. For most issues, trading decisions in these offices are often made independent of the main office, although some firms may refer large or complex trades to the specialists at the main office. There are over $1.5 trillion outstanding bonds, and because of this, there are specialists in many segments of the market. Among the important segments are:

1. *Dollar bonds.* Unlike most other securities in the municipal market, dollar bonds are traded on the basis of price, not yield. Some of the more active and competitive trading occurs in these securities because the issues are usually large and create considerable institutional investor interest. Typically, dollar bonds are the term bonds from an issue, rather than the smaller serial maturities common to the municipal market.

2. *General revenue bonds.* Particularly when they are issued by national names in utilities and transportation, general revenue bonds are the bellwethers of the market. They are closely watched to assess the trends in the market.

3. *Housing bonds.* These bonds require specialists because of the complex call features that affect their valuations. The traders look at bond prepayments to calculate the average lives of the bonds.

4. *Health care bonds.* A hospital bond trader requires up-to-date information on the financial strength of the borrower. With the continual transformation of health care, the trader must know, for example, whether a hospital is a stand-alone facility or if it has merged into a system, or if a system has merged with another system. Credit ratings range widely and can change rapidly in this sector, which is therefore more volatile than others.

5. *State-specific names.* Local issues can be the province of a trader who may be responsible, for example, for New York State municipalities or California names. Trading operations with broader geographical territories may divide their trading staff by region.

6. *High-yield bonds.* High yield bonds are those that are rated below investment grade or are not rated at all. Often these bonds are in the industrial development, health care, and energy sectors. A high-yield trader closely follows the credit stories of these bonds to assess if they are improving, deteriorating, or remaining stable, and will price and trade the bonds accordingly.

7. *Short-term products.* Firms also frequently maintain a specialist in the trading of notes and other short-term paper such as *variable-rate demand obligations* (VRDOs) and *tax-exempt commercial paper.* Notes, VRDOs, and commercial paper appeal principally to financial institutions and to money market funds, which typically trade in large denominations and desire liquidity.

8. *Odd lots.* A *round lot* in municipal trading is generally $250,000 or higher. Because of the serial maturity structure of most deals, however, there is not always a $250,000 block of bonds to trade. Odd lots are usually trades of $25,000 or less. These smaller issues generally trade at wider bid-offer spreads than do larger blocks. Since the average new-issue size is less than $16 million, there is a thin trading market for these numerous smaller issues.

MUNICIPAL FUTURES

Traders in most U.S. debt markets are able to maintain short positions. A short position is when they borrow and then sell securities that they do not own, either in anticipation of a decline in prices or to hedge against a long position in other securities. If prices fall, the traders can buy back at a lower price the securities that they sold short, return the securities to the lender with interest, and earn a profit. By going short, these dealers are able to hedge against a loss in their inventory positions that would be caused by a rise in interest rates (and a decline in prices). If prices rise, of course, the dealers cover their short positions by buying back the securities at a higher price and taking a short-term loss. However, municipal dealers are prohibited from shorting municipal securities. Municipal dealers can, however, use a municipal futures contract to hedge their trading positions.

Trading in municipal bond index futures contracts began in June 1985 on the Chicago Board of Trade (CBOT), after approval by the Commodities Futures Trading Commission. The MOB (*municipal over bond*) spread, which is the spread that is traded, measures the relative difference between the municipal bond index futures price and the U.S. Treasury bond futures price. In order to understand the muni bond futures contract, one must understand the makeup of the underlying index as well as the basics of the futures market.

The contract is based on *The Bond Buyer*'s 40-Bond Index (BBI-40) of 40 general obligation and revenue bonds. The BBI-40 is composed of long-term, investment-grade issues and is expressly designed to track the broader municipal bond market.

Each term bond must fulfill specific criteria to be included in or deleted from the BBI-40. The bonds in the index are subject to change every two weeks—on the fifteenth and the last day of each month. At that time, new bonds fulfilling the inclusion criteria are added to the index, and bonds that no longer fit these criteria or that are the least actively traded are deleted. Also at this time, the value of the index is recalculated using a continuity coefficient designed to prevent the value of the index from changing as a result of the change in the composition of the bonds included in the index.

The Chicago Board of Trade Rules and Regulations define eligibility criteria as follows:

1. *Size.* Term bond (term component only) shall have a principal value of at least $50 million ($75 million for housing issues).
2. *Ratings.* Shall be rated A– by Standard & Poor's or A3 or better by Moody's, on initial inclusion in the BBI-40.
3. *Maturity.* Have a remaining maturity of at least 19 years.
4. *Call provisions.* May or may not be callable prior to maturity. If callable, the first call shall be between seven and 16 years from date of inclusion

in the index. The callable term bond must have at least one call-at-par date prior to maturity.

5. *Par issue.* Must be reoffered at a price between 85 and 105.
6. *Trading eligibility.* Shall be reoffered out of syndicate and eligible for dealer-to-dealer-broker trading at least one business day prior to inclusion in the index, provided *The Bond Buyer* has had enough time to gather the necessary information.
7. *Private placements.* Not eligible for the index.
8. *Coupon.* Must have a fixed coupon rate with semiannual interest payments.
9. *Term bond limit.* No more than two term bonds from the same issuer may be included. If more than two are available for inclusion, the two largest will be added. If two are the same size, the term bonds with the longest maturity will be added.

Bonds will be deleted if they meet the following criteria:

1. *Call provisions.* If the official statement includes extraordinary redemption provisions and the bonds have a dollar price of 102 or higher on both of the two business days immediately preceding the revision date.
2. *Ratings.* Must meet minimum rating criteria.
3. *Term bond limit.* If a new bond is added to the BBI-40, causing the index to have more than two bonds from the same issuer, the old bonds with the lowest trading volume are deleted until the number of bonds from that issuer is not greater than two.
4. *Timeliness of bond.* Bonds that have seniority, that is, bonds that have been in the BBI-40 for 18 months or longer, if deletions are needed. Old bonds with the lowest trading volume since the last revision also fall into this category of endangered listings.

The BBI-40 is priced twice daily and reported at approximately 11:00 A.M. and 2:00 P.M. (Chicago time). Evaluations are performed by broker's-brokers. The broker's-brokers provide evaluations based on their assessment of the price at which a minimum $100,000 or higher face value of each bond could be sold in the cash market.

The Bond Buyer drops the highest and lowest prices submitted. The average of the remaining three prices is then divided by a conversion factor that equates the bond's price to a 6% yield. The index value is computed by taking the price per bond, averaging those converted prices, and then applying the continuity coefficient that is calculated bimonthly. Until August 1999, the coupon had been 8%. The CBOT changed the notional coupon to 6% from 8% to more accurately reflect the yield environment prevalent during the late 1990s. In addition, the 6% coupon has the effect of increasing duration, which makes the contract a better hedge for the long end of the curve, as further described later.

The futures contract based on this index was devised for use as a hedging instrument, to help traders and investors manage interest rate risk, and as an alternative to trading in the cash market. Municipalities may use futures to lock in a rate, thereby hedging against rising interest rates if they are anticipating a bond issue. Underwriters and dealers can use futures if they own (are *long*) bonds in the primary or secondary market and want to hedge against rising rates until the bonds are sold or traded. Funds and portfolio managers often use futures to manage duration. Professional traders such as arbitrageurs capitalize on the spread between the municipal futures and the municipal cash market, and others may capitalize on the MOB spread at times when municipals are cheap to Treasuries.

As a hedging instrument, the futures contract can be used to protect the value of a portfolio of municipals or a dealer's inventory position. For example, some dealers might want to short futures against their inventory so that if prices in the market decline, they would take a profit in their futures position that would help offset the loss of value in their cash position. They may go long the municipal contract as a substitute for municipal bonds (which is known as municipal cash) when the market prices increase.

As in all futures contracts, certain features of the municipal bond contract are standardized. For example, a contract is $1,000 times the BBI-40. Contracts are quoted in 32nds of a point (where a point is $1,000), making each 32 equal to $31.25. The daily price-change limit is three points, or $3,000. Contracts have quarterly settlement cycles, with settlements occurring in March, June, September, and December. In December 1999 the CBOT received approval from the CFTC to limit the position that anyone can hold in municipal bond index futures to 4,000 contracts during the last three days before the contract expires.

CBOT Municipal Bond Index futures differ from traditional bond futures in that, on the delivery date, no physical bonds change hands; instead, the contract is settled in cash.

For example, assume you are long one Municipal Bond Index futures contract for September settlement and that you intend to maintain this position until the last day of trading for the September contract. On that day, the closing September index futures value is automatically set to equal the cash index value for that day. Your account would be marked-to-market one final time—that is, gains or losses since the previous day's September futures close would be credited to, or debited from, your account, representing the final settlement for your September futures position.

Bids and offers on futures contracts are made openly by competitive outcry in the CBOT muni bond futures trading pit. Thus, while the futures contract is based on *The Bond Buyer* 40-BBI, the daily closing value of the contract does not necessarily coincide with the value of the index until the last day of trading for each quarterly contract settlement. On this day, the settlement value for the futures contract is set to equal the index value for that day.

For example, if BBI has a value 125-05 (125 5/32) on the close of the last day of trading, the futures contract has an underlying value of $1,000 times the index, or $125,156.25. Before that last day, the price of the futures contract is established in the marketplace.

It should be noted that an investment in a Municipal Bond Index futures contract is not an investment in a municipal bond. Profits or losses derived from transactions in Municipal Bond Index futures contracts are subject to federal tax treatment different from interest income derived from municipal bonds, which is generally free from federal income taxation.

Internal control procedures for dealers in municipal futures contracts should conform to the accounting and reporting requirements outlined in Statement No. 80 of the Financial Accounting Standards Board (FASB), "Accounting for Interest Rate Futures."

PROVIDERS OF DATA IN THE MUNICIPAL MARKET

Municipal market data can be accessed in many ways. It is distributed not only by companies that are dedicated primarily to the municipal market but also by divisions of companies that cover certain facets of many financial markets. The list below is by no means a comprehensive list because this field is rapidly evolving and changing as new providers enter the field and established providers are continuously adding new products and services.

- News, both general and financial
- Issuer websites
- Communication tools, such as syndicate messaging systems
- Broker dealer offerings
- Bond security descriptions
- NRMSIRs (Nationally Recognized Municipal Securities Information Repositories)
- SIDs
- Disclosure and material event notices
- Primary market worksheets
- Pricing and evaluation services
- Active bid-wanteds and offering

MARKET STATISTICS AND INDEXES

The Bond Buyer Indexes

The most widely watched municipal bond indexes are compiled by *The Bond Buyer*. The 20-Bond Index is composed of dealers' estimates, gathered weekly by *The Bond Buyer*, of the yield that a hypothetical 20-year GO bond would have to offer if that issue came to market during the week. The 20-Bond Index includes GO bonds of 20 actual issuers. The average of the ratings of these issuers is roughly equivalent to Aa2 from Moody's and AA– from S&P. The 11-Bond Index is composed of GO bonds of 11 of the 20 issues in the first average, but the quality rating averages Aa1 from Moody's and AA+ from S&P. The Revenue Bond Index includes bonds of 25 issuers of revenue bonds maturing in 30 years. The average rating on the bonds in this index is A1 from Moody's and A+ from S&P. The annual average 20-Bond Index and 11-Bond Index from 1975 to 1999, and the average annual Revenue Bond Index from 1979 (the year it was first published) to 1999 are shown in Table 5.2.

TABLE 5.2 Average Annual Yields, 1980–1999

Year	The Bond Buyer 20-Bond Index	The Bond Buyer 11-Bond Index	The Bond Buyer Revenue Bond Index	U.S. Treasury 30-Year Bond
1975	7.04	6.61		
1976	6.62	6.11		
1977	5.68	5.38		7.75
1978	6.03	5.72		8.49
1979	6.51	6.18	7.90	9.28
1980	8.57	8.15	9.44	11.27
1981	11.37	10.98	12.26	13.45
1982	11.64	11.26	12.48	12.76
1983	9.51	9.26	10.04	11.18
1984	10.10	9.98	10.52	12.41
1985	9.11	9.01	9.56	10.79
1986	7.33	7.21	7.76	7.78
1987	7.66	7.53	8.04	8.59
1988	7.68	7.57	8.03	8.96
1989	7.23	7.12	7.51	8.45
1990	7.27	7.13	7.53	8.61
1991	6.92	6.77	7.11	8.14
1992	6.44	6.33	6.59	7.67
1993	5.59	5.49	5.82	6.59
1994	6.19	6.10	6.45	7.37
1995	5.95	5.85	6.20	6.88
1996	5.76	5.66	6.01	6.71
1997	5.52	5.44	5.78	6.61
1998	5.09	5.02	5.32	5.58
1999	5.44	5.37	5.65	5.87

Sources: The Bond Buyer; Federal Reserve System.
Note: The Revenue Bond Index began on September 20, 1979. The 30 Year Treasury Series began in March 1977.

Since 1985, *The Bond Buyer* has been compiling its 40-Bond Index also for use as the basis for Municipal Futures contracts. As previously noted, this index is heavily weighted with revenue bonds. It is priced daily and reported in *The Bond Buyer.*

The Bond Buyer Placement Ratio and Visible Supply. *The Bond Buyer* publishes two measures of the demand for bonds that are widely followed in the industry. These are the weekly *placement ratio* and the daily *visible supply.*

Although these are indicators of the primary market, they are also bell-wethers of the demand for municipal bonds in general and good indicators of secondary market demand. A sizable inventory of unsold new issues in the primary market depresses the secondary market, while unsatisfied demand for new issues improves the secondary market.

The Bond Buyer placement ratio is compiled weekly from data as of the close of business on Friday and is reported on Monday. It represents the percentage of the dollar volume of the week's new competitive issues placed with permanent investors during the week. The minimum issue size for inclusion in the ratio is currently $10 million.

Since 1990, there have been eight years where the highest weekly placement ratio has exceeded 99 percent. Excluding weeks where there were no bond sales, the lowest percentage in this ten-year time period was 50.1 percent on October 11, 1991. Previously, the lowest percentage recorded since the initiation of the ratio was 29.2 percent on November 23, 1960, when the ratio was based on combined competitive and negotiated sales. Interestingly, the average annual placement ratio has been slowly inching upward, from 84.2 percent in 1990 to 91.3 percent in 1999. Table 5.3 shows the high and low placement ratios and their dates for each year since 1988, along with the average placement ratio for the year.

The 30-Day Visible Supply is a chart compiled each day from the "Competitive Bond Offerings" and "Negotiated Bond Offerings" tables. It shows the total dollar volume of bonds expected to reach the market in the next thirty days, including issues scheduled for sale on the publication date of the chart.

The 30-day visible supply of competitive bonds has been reported since 1927. It has ranged from a low of $928,000 on March 3, 1943, to a high of $6,107,150,000 on July 18, 1994. The 30-day visible supply of negotiated issues has been reported since 1971, ranging from a low of zero on January 4, 1971, and December 26, 1989, to a high of $9,412,589,000 on September 23, 1992. Table 5.4 lists the highs and lows of the total of competitive and negotiated issues for each year from 1990 to 1999, with the date on which the high or low occurred. In eight years during this time period the lowest date of visible supply occurred in the first or last week of the year, while the high point of supply was more evenly spread throughout the rest of the year.

TABLE 5.3   Placement Ratio, 1990–1999

	Percentage	Date
1990		
High	99.3	7/13/90
Low	56.4	1/19/90
Average	84.2	
1991		
High	97.3	12/20/91
Low	50.1	10/11/91
Average	84.8	
1992		
High	99.3	11/13/92
Low	61.0	11/6/92
Average	85.7	
1993		
High	99.3	4/16/93
Low	65.9	3/12/93
Average	87.0	
1994		
High	99.7	4/8/94
Low	62.7	9/9/94
Average	87.8	
1995		
High	98.4	12/22/95
Low	62.7	3/3/95
Average	85.1	
1996		
High	99.9	7/12/96
Low	57.2	7/5/96
Average	89.6	
1997		
High	99.7	2/14/97
Low	61.6	11/28/97
Average	89.1	
1998		
High	100.0	10/2/98
Low	64.9	4/9/98
Average	89.6	
1999		
High	99.4	7/9/99
Low	74.3	4/23/99
Average	91.3	

Source: The Bond Buyer.

TABLE 5.4 30-Day Visible Supply, 1990–1999

	Competitive ($)	Date	Negotiated ($)	Date	Total ($)	Date
1990						
High	1,921,389,800	4/3/90	3,830,801,000	12/10/90	4,728,969,000	12/10/90
Low	166,050,000	12/20/90	17,000,000	12/21/90	251,146,000	12/21/90
1991						
High	2,619,924,700	2/15/91	5,902,315,000	11/18/91	8,053,912,082	11/15/91
Low	133,933,000	12/19/91	63,220,000	12/20/91	220,187,000	12/20/91
1992						
High	4,332,526,400	2/4/92	9,412,589,000	9/23/92	10,864,557,965	9/22/92
Low	177,473,350	5/20/92	297,124,500	5/28/92	1,965,188,500	5/28/92
1993						
High	4,409,343,000	10/25/93	7,278,600,595	3/24/93	9,905,975,345	3/24/93
Low	458,230,000	12/15/93	861,161,000	9/16/93	2,014,679,000	9/2/93
1994						
High	6,107,149,758	7/18/94	4,890,320,000	1/7/94	9,066,227,758	7/15/94
Low	312,940,000	12/21/94	450,455,000	12/29/94	862,395,000	12/21/94
1995						
High	3,341,294,120	7/18/95	5,132,885,280	12/12/95	6,556,432,768	11/14/95
Low	351,040,000	12/20/95	304,055,000	1/30/95	1,313,582,000	1/3/95
1996						
High	3,084,751,000	10/22/96	6,697,930,000	3/15/96	8,228,268,600	3/15/96
Low	324,160,200	12/18/96	596,025,000	12/26/96	1,236,495,000	12/24/96
1997						
High	3,353,500,000	10/7/97	5,946,579,000	6/24/97	7,719,816,099	6/24/97
Low	449,360,000	12/19/97	706,385,000	12/24/97	1,462,400,000	12/19/97
1998						
High	5,946,579,000	2/18/98	8,022,953,000	11/18/98	11,484,037,361	11/18/98
Low	1,215,810,803	8/27/98	1,144,130,000	1/2/98	2,727,068,687	1/2/98
1999						
High	3,723,755,500	10/20/99	6,432,690,000	10/15/99	9,466,504,500	10/15/99
Low	1,001,319,171	12/17/99	710,745,000	12/28/99	1,887,764,171	12/20/99

Source: The Bond Buyer.

MSRB RECORD-KEEPING RULES

The MSRB has established several rules governing record-keeping for holding securities and for transactions with customers. Rule G-8 is the basic record-keeping rule of the MSRB. It requires every broker, dealer, and municipal securities dealer to maintain account records for each customer, showing all purchases and sales of municipal securities, all receipts and deliveries of securities, all receipts and disbursements of cash, and all other debits and credits to such account.

Subsections of Rule G-8 require that records be kept to show the following information for each security: all long and short positions carried by a municipal securities broker or dealer for its own account or for the account of a customer; the current location of all such securities held in the long position and the offsetting position to all such securities sold short; and the name or other designation of the account in which each position is carried. The securities records should also show any movement of the securities, such as whether securities have been sent out for validation or transfer.

In addition, records of each transaction, whether undertaken as a principal or an agent, must be maintained according to specific subsections of Rule G-8. Trading tickets will suffice for such records. They must show such information as the price and amount of the order as well as the time of the execution to the extent feasible. Some of the other areas covered by Rule G-8 include the types of information to be obtained from customers, customer complaints, and records for put options and repurchase agreements. By and large, the record-keeping regulations do not apply to dealers or brokers who do not do their own clearing, but Rule G-8 does provide that nonclearing dealers and brokers remain responsible for accurate maintenance and preservation of the books and records.

Uniform Practices and Confirmation of Transactions

MSRB Rule G-12 establishes uniform practices among municipal securities dealers, and Rule G-15 establishes procedures for confirmation, clearance, and settlement of transactions with customers. Many provisions of the rules are codifications of traditional practices and industry standards that were in existence before the establishment of the MSRB. The Board also has written into the rules standards and procedures to expedite the processing of transactions. For example, the rules require clearance and settlement of most interdealer transactions and most transactions with institutional customers to occur through automated systems operated by clearing agencies registered with the SEC.

The rules allow the settlement date of a transaction—the date used for computing yields and price—generally to be subject to agreement by the parties to the transaction. The rules specify, however, that the settlement date for cash transactions will be the day of trade, while for regular way trades the settlement date will be three business days after the trade date. Firms that engage in transactions that are eligible for automated trade comparison through a registered clearing agency follow the rules for such transactions.

For interdealer transactions not cleared and settled through automated systems, Rule G-12 provides standards for the contents of confirmations and procedures for verifying confirmations sent between dealers. The rule requires confirmations to be sent on the business day after the trade date and to contain certain items of information; dealers receiving confirmations with incorrect information or describing trades that they do not recognize must take specific steps to resolve the discrepancies or trades. Similarly, Rule G-15 requires certain information to be on each customer confirmation and requires the confirmation to be provided at or before the completion of the transaction (if the transaction is *delivery versus payment* or *receipt versus payment,* the confirmation must be sent not later than the day of execution). Information required to be on an interdealer or customer confirmation includes certain items that provide evidence of the contract, a description of the securities, and in the case of customer transactions, certain other items that the MSRB has deemed necessary for disclosure to customers as follows (for more information on MSRB rules, consult the MSRB website at *www.MSRB.org*).

CHAPTER **6**

Investing In Bonds

INTRODUCTION

A primary attraction that municipal bonds have for investors is that the interest income is exempt from federal income tax. Interest income from state and local issues is usually exempt from income taxes in their states, although it is generally not exempt from taxes in other states. The major investors in municipal securities have been households and household proxies (mutual funds, money market funds, closed-end funds, and bank personal trusts), property and casualty companies, and commercial banks. The demand for municipal bonds and the relative importance of each of the major categories has shifted over the years. Investors' purchasing patterns are cyclical and are dependent on factors such as interest rates, tax rates, alternative investments, and profitability.

Municipal bonds are bought and sold with specific investment objectives and goals in place. The buyer achieves these goals by structuring and managing a portfolio using the basic principles of investing in bonds.

THE BASIC PRINCIPLES OF INVESTING IN BONDS

A fundamental relationship between interest rates and price exists in all fixed-income securities. When interest rates rise, the prices of fixed-income securities in the secondary market generally fall to make their yield comparable to that of currently issued securities. When interest rates fall, the prices of outstanding fixed-income securities generally rise. Prices are also affected by the supply of and demand for bonds. The relationship between yield and price is not a straight line, but rather, it is convex, or curved like the exterior of a circle or a bow. The degree to which bond prices shift relative to interest rates is affected by several factors. When the bond is *option-free*, meaning that the bond does not contain an embedded put or call (the bond is noncallable or nonputtable), the two most important factors affecting a bond's price volatility (a statistical measure of the variance of price or yield over time) are its term to maturity and its coupon rate. For bonds containing embedded options, those redemption features constitute a third factor in the bond's price volatility.

Term to Maturity

The category of short-term securities includes different products with different terms to maturity. Short-term securities, which mature in 13 months or less, are called notes. Commercial paper matures within 270 days, although there have been issues with longer maturities. Short-term bonds, however, can have maturities from one to four years. Medium-term bonds have maturities from 5 to 12 years, while long-term bonds have maturities greater than 12 years.

The longer a bond's maturity, the wider and more volatile are the swings in its price caused by any change in interest rates. For example, a bond with a coupon of 5 percent due in one year would sell at $970 to produce an 8 percent yield to maturity, while a 5 percent bond due in 20 years would have to sell at $700 to produce the same 8 percent yield to maturity. In the first example, a $30 discount over one year is sufficient to bring the yield up to 8 percent. In the second, a $300 discount is required to generate the same yield because the gain is spread over a longer period of time. Short-term bonds will trade closer to par, because the investor will receive the full amount of the principal sooner.

Coupon Rates

Generally, the higher the coupon interest rate, the smaller the price movements will be for a given change in market interest rates. Conversely, the price volatility is greater for a bond with a lower coupon rate. For example, if interest rates fall 200 basis points from 8 percent to 6 percent on 10-year bonds the price of a par bond will rise by about 15 points, to 115. On the same drop of 200 basis points, a 6 percent, 10-year bond trading at par would rise more in value than the 8 percent bond from the first example. The price on the 6 percent bond would rise to about 116½ if interest rates fell from 6 percent to 4 percent.

Bonds trading at a discount experience wider price swings for a given shift in interest rates, while bonds trading at a premium shift proportionally less. Consider, for example, two noncallable 20-year bonds, both yielding 6.5 percent to maturity. One, a discount bond with a 2 percent coupon, is selling for 50; the other, with an 8 percent coupon, and selling for nearly 117. If interest rates increase such that the yield to maturity on both bonds becomes 7.5 percent, the price of the discount bond would fall by about 6½ points to 43½. The price of the premium bond, however, will fall by 11½ points. However, the percentage change in the price of the bonds is the key calculation. In the situation described above, the price of the discount bond will have dropped by 13 percent, whereas the price of the premium bond will have dropped by only 10 percent.

The difference in volatility between premium bonds and discount bonds is even more dramatic in the case of so-called cushion bonds—that is, callable bonds selling above the initial call price. In the case of cushion bonds, the volatility will be based on the call date rather than the maturity date, and the bonds will tend to act like shorter-maturity bonds.

Because gains earned on discount bonds are subject to federal income taxation, the prices of discount bonds will fall even lower than these calculations suggest.

Redemption Provisions

Redemption provisions describe the terms and conditions under which an issuer may redeem bonds that contain an embedded call option. Redemption provisions are also discussed in Chapter 2. Investors scrutinize the bond's structure, particularly its call features, for a number of reasons. First, when a bond is called before maturity, the duration of the bond changes, which changes the portfolio's return. Second, when bonds contain a call option, those bonds are priced to the call, which is a better statement of their value than if they were priced to maturity. However, if the bonds are called, the investors must replace the income stream generated by the first bond. If interest rates have fallen, it will be hard to replace the bond coupon with one of comparable credit quality. Thus, overall return of the portfolio may suffer. However, investors can purchase market discount bonds from active sinking funds, which are subject to par calls. Purchasing these bonds at prices substantially below par can lead to significant capital gains when the mandatory sinking fund is used to retire debt. The issue of capital gains is another reason to examine calls as bonds called before maturity may give the investor capital gains or capital losses. While the capital gain on a bond that is redeemed is taxed as ordinary income, any capital loss incurred is not deductible. Again, because bonds are priced to the call, the call provisions can limit the capital gains potential on a bond.

Bonds can be called at par, at some premium above par, or in the case of zero-coupon bonds, at the compound or straight-line accreted value. Call protection refers to the bond issuer's inability to exercise a call for some specified period of time. It also refers to the protection a specific bond maturity may enjoy over other bonds in the same issue that are called ahead of it. *First call* refers to the earliest date the issuer can execute a call. Interest accrual or compound value accretion ceases once a bond has been called.

There are three primary types of call features commonly found in municipal bond issues: *optional, mandatory sinking fund,* and *extraordinary* (or special redemptions).

The optional call feature describes the manner in which an issuer may voluntarily redeem bonds. A typical optional call provision allows the issuer to retire serial and term bonds at a price above par ten years from the issue date. After the first call dates, the call price declines each successive year until it reaches par. There are times when market circumstances allow the issuer to price a new issue so that it does not pay the investor any premium for exercising the call option and other times when investors demand a high premium. Funds for optional calls come from refunding bonds or surplus funds of the issuer.

The mandatory call feature typically describes the way the sinking fund works. The sinking fund is used to redeem term bonds on a schedule, enabling the issuer to spread the costs of retiring the term bonds over the life of the issue. Sinking funds add some measure of security on the bonds by avoiding one large payment on the term bond at its final maturity. Sinking funds can be used either to call bonds or to purchase equal face amounts in the secondary market. Open-market purchases provide price support for sinking fund bonds during periods when such bonds are selling at a discount because of rising interest rates. However, sinking fund bonds are called at par when lower interest rates would normally make such bonds worth substantially more. When bonds are called, they are selected on a random basis within each maturity.

Extraordinary or special redemptions are specifically designed to protect the issuer by allowing bonds to be retired in the event extraordinary circumstances impair the issuer's future revenue stream or ability to operate. These provisions are in bonds issued for the construction of capital projects, allowing special redemptions from unexpended monies if the project is not built by a certain time or from insurance proceeds if a catastrophe occurs and the project is damaged or destroyed. They are also found in housing bonds, permitting calls from unexpended bond proceeds, prepayment or sale of mortgage loans securing the bonds, loan insurance proceeds, or excess program revenues.

Extraordinary redemption provisions are often complex and vary considerably among bond issues. They may be mandatory or optional, they can occur at any time after the bonds are issued, and they are usually made at par (or accreted value for original-issue discount bonds). Bond redemptions are most often executed on a pro rata basis across all bond maturities in an issue. This means that the redemption funds available are applied to each bond maturity on the basis of what percentage a particular bond maturity bears to the total amount of bonds outstanding. In the case of single-family housing bonds, prepaid mortgage loans are applied to a particular term bond or bonds before any other maturity. This type of bond is known as a super sinker and provides call protection for the other term bonds in the issue. The average bond life on a super sinker is substantially shorter than for other term bonds in the same issue, but the yields tend to be only slightly less. Investors must carefully consider the possibility of such a call when evaluating the purchase of premium bonds.

The yield to call shows investors what yield will be earned if the bonds are called at the first call date. It is similar to the yield to maturity, except that it is calculated to the first call date and price. The yield to call, if lower than the yield to maturity, must be cited in written confirmations of orders. Bonds with little time left to the first call date often trade at lower prices and higher yields to maturity than equivalent bonds with ample call protection. This is especially the case when interest rates are high and are expected to fall, a condition that would make redemption likely.

MEASURES OF YIELD AND RETURN

Figuring out yield and return on a municipal bond is not solely a process of checking interest rates and tax deductibility. Professionals in the field use calculations based on finance theory to figure out the most profitable uses of their capital. Below follows a brief review of present value theory and of the measures of returns and yields.

Present Value

Present value is a concept that takes into account the time value of money. One dollar received today is worth more than one dollar tomorrow. Thus, higher value is placed on a three-year investment rather than on six-year investment, for example, even though both promise identical returns. Therefore, the timing of cash flows on an investment is important in any investment including fixed income. The formula for the present value of $1 received at the end of year n is

$$PV = \frac{1}{(1 + r)^n}$$

where PV is the present value, r is the discount rate, and n is the number of years.

The formula for the present value of $1 received in one year invested at the discount rate is

$$PV = \frac{1}{(1.05)^1} = \$0.9524$$

The present value of $1 received in two years invested at 5 percent is

$$PV = \frac{1}{(1+.05)^2} = \$0.9070$$

The present value of a series of $1 future cash flows is the sum of each year's present value, which is $1.8594, a sum that is less than the $2 face value. The discount rate and the number of years are the two variables that change the present-value calculation. Given the same number of years, a higher discount rate will generate a lower present value, and a lower discount rate will generate a higher present value. For example, if a 10 percent rate were used in the above example, the present value of the future stream of cash flows for two years would be $1.7325; and if a 3 percent rate were used, the present value of the future stream of cash flows would be $1.9135.

Internal Rate of Return

Present value theory is used in another important way. An issuer may return to an investor one dollar seven years from now on a loan of 75 cents today. Alternatively, another issuer might repay one dollar in six years on a loan of 85 cents today. To select the better investment, the investor compares the two offerings by calculating the internal rate of return. The internal rate of return is the discount rate at which the present value of the cash flow, or series of cash flows, from an investment equals its price. The internal rate of return cannot be computed as cleanly as the present value can. There is no algebraic formula for it. Rather, it is calculated by a trial and error process, where an interest rate is estimated and applied to compute the present value of each cash flow. If the total present value of the cash flows is more than the price of the investment, a higher rate must be used to recalculate the cash flows. If the total present value of the cash flows is less than the price of the investment, a lower discount rate must be used. After a series of trials and errors, when the total present value of the investment equals the price of the investment, the correct discount rate and yield will have been found.

In the above example, the internal rate of return for the 75 cent loan due in seven years is about 4 percent. The internal rate of return for the 85 cent loan due in six years in about 3 percent. Clearly, the first loan offers the investor a higher return, albeit for a longer period of time.

YIELD TO MATURITY AND PRICE

Given the coupon, current price, and time to maturity, the yield to maturity is the internal rate of return an investor earns from payments of bond interest and principal, with interest compounded semiannually. Yield to maturity assumes that interest is compounded semiannually and will be reinvested at the same rate for all present value type calculations. If an investor knows that this will not be the case, adjustments can and should be made to the calculations to get a truer internal rate of return. The formula for yield to maturity is in Chapter 2.

The price of a bond is precisely the present value of all the cash flows—interest and principal—discounted by the yield to maturity or the internal rate of return. For example, if a bond quoted at a 7 percent yield to maturity has a coupon of 6 percent and is due in three years, the price will be the sum of the present values of each semiannual interest payment of $30 plus the present value of $1,000 received in three years, all discounted by 7 percent. What is the price of the bond? The problem can be formulated as shown in the following list.

Time from the Purchase	Cash Received	Present Value at a 7% Discount Rate
6 months	$ 30.00	$ 28.99
12 months	30.00	28.01
18 months	30.00	27.06
24 months	30.00	26.14
30 months	30.00	25.26
36 months	1,030.00	837.91
Total	$1,180.00	$973.36

The total cash payments to the bondholder are $1,180.00, but the sum of the present values, which is the price of the bond, is only $973.36.

To find the yield to maturity when the price is known is the reverse of this process. A discount rate is applied to each semiannual payment to derive the present value. As in the internal rate of return, an interpolation is unavoidable if computed by hand, but is easily calculated on computers and calculators.

Total Return

One way of evaluating a portfolio's performance is to calculate its total return and then compare that total return to some benchmark index. Performance will be discussed more thoroughly after investment objectives, risks, and strategies have been explained. *Total return* is the investment performance measure over a given time period and includes coupon interest, interest on interest, and any realized or unrealized gains or losses. The aggregate or cumulative total return and the average annual total return of portfolios are often calculated. The cumulative or aggregate total return reflects the actual performance of the bond over a stated period of time. That stated period of time could be one, five, or ten years or any other time period that is defined by the investor, an investment manager, or the sponsor of a mutual fund. The average annual total return is a hypothetical rate of return that, if achieved annually, would have produced the same cumulative total return if the performance had been constant over the entire period. Note that the way this is similar to the internal rate of return and to the net present value is that the performance is assumed to be constant. Calculating the average annual total return smoothes out variations in performance and is not the same as an actual year-to-year result. Average annual total return also includes any sales charges that may be involved. Neither average annual return nor cumulative total return take into account the effect of any federal or state income taxes that may be payable when the bond is sold or the fund is redeemed.

Tax-Equivalent Yield

Yield is another measure of performance. Yield, as has been discussed in previous chapters, can be stated as yield to maturity, current yield, yield to the call, or yield to the worst or in other ways. For an investor in tax-exempts, it is important, no matter which of these yields is used, also to calculate the tax-equivalent yield. This allows investors to make a comparison between the lower yield on a tax-exempt bond and the higher yield on a comparable taxable bond, enabling then to compare equivalent yields on the two securities. The calculation for the tax-exempt/taxable yield equivalent formula is shown in Chapter 2.

INVESTMENT OBJECTIVES

Investment objectives are the goals that an investor sets in structuring and managing portfolio investments. An investor often has more than one investment objective. Sometimes those objectives complement each other, and at other times they may contradict each other. With the great diversity of municipal issues, however, it is nearly always possible to structure a portfolio that fits the investor's criteria. A summary of basic investment objectives follows.

Current Income

Current income is the periodic income stream paid on a bond. In a low–interest rate scenario, premium bonds may improve the current income. For example, a 7 percent, five-year premium bond priced at 108.75 would have a yield to maturity of 5 percent with current income of $70 for every $1,000 invested. If the investor bought a par bond at the same time with a yield to maturity of 5 percent, the current income would be only $50 per $1,000 invested. While the premium bond enhances the current income, the premium cannot be deducted as a tax loss. The taxation of premium and discount bonds are discussed in greater detail later in this chapter.

Capital Preservation

Capital preservation is the safe return to the investor of the principal amount invested. Some investors cannot tolerate any risk in losing principal; for example, they may have invested funds specifically for retirement or education purposes. There are many ways to maximize capital preservation. The longer the term of the investment vehicle, the greater its potential for price swings, so an investor interested in capital preservation would invest on the short end of the yield curve. Credit risk also plays an important part in capital preservation. All things being equal, a highly rated credit will provide greater safety of principal than a lower-rated credit.

Capital Appreciation

Capital appreciation is the expectation that the investment will be valued more in the future than in the present because current credit, market, or other risks will eventually be resolved. For example, one might purchase a bond trading cheaply compared to others of the same credit quality because of a specific current problem, such as large operating losses, with the expectation that the losses will be reversed. Another way to maximize capital appreciation is to purchase discount bonds. However, the capital gains earned on discount bonds are taxable as ordinary income. Capital gains and losses are discussed in greater detail later in this chapter. These bonds can be attractive to investors who will be in a lower tax bracket when the bonds mature. Discount bonds can meet the capital gains objective while still providing tax-exempt income before maturity.

Timing the Maturity

Investors can tailor their portfolios to meet specific cash needs at known times by purchasing bonds with specific maturities. For parents who may have children entering college in 10 years, for example, discount bonds that mature at the time the tuition is due may be appropriate. Zero-coupon bonds, which provide no semiannual income but pay out all of the tax-exempt interest in a lump sum at maturity, are one way to accumulate funds for college. Investors can also stagger bond maturities along the yield curve if there is uncertainty when the future cash needs will occur.

In-State Tax Exemption

Investors in high-tax states that levy an income tax on municipal bonds from states other than their own will generally invest in bonds issued in their own states and in U.S. territories. The interest on bonds issued in these U.S. territories—American Samoa, the Commonwealth of Puerto Rico, Guam, the Northern Mariana Islands, and the U.S. Virgin Islands—is exempt by law from all federal, state, and local income taxes. However, the yields on bonds from these specialty states may be lower than the yield on other issues because the demand for their bonds exceeds the supply of new and outstanding issues.

RISK FACTORS

Achieving investment objectives involves undertaking a certain amount of risk. Risk is a way to categorize the degree of uncertainty and the possibility of financial loss on an investment; often, an investment will carry more than one risk.

Credit Risk

Credit risk is the chance that the obligor, or issuer, on bonds will be unable to make debt service payments or will default on the loan because of a weakening of the credit. Credit risk is reflected in a bond's rating. By definition, a bond that carries less credit risk will have a better rating than a bond with more credit risk. Triple-A bonds have less credit risk than double-A credits, and so on all the way down the rating scale. Investors whose objective is preservation of capital generally are averse to credit risk. Such investors may choose to invest only in triple-A insured issues, or they may prefer only the most highly rated GO bonds.

Event and Political Risk

Event risk is the risk that an issuer's ability to make debt service payments will change because of unanticipated changes, such as a corporate restructuring, a regulatory change, or a catastrophic event. Regulatory changes, which generally take a long time to be enacted, can be included in the total risk profile of an issuer, while unforeseen events or disasters cannot. Political risk in municipal bonds is generally tied to the civic climate in a state or local governmental unit, and may be reflected by tax-limitations referendums or voter rejection of bond issues. Political risk as a subset of credit risk assesses the issuer's willingness to pay. If an investor's goal is in-state tax exemption and voter referendums with negative implications for bonds have been passed in that state, that investor could be incurring more political risk than an investor with a portfolio of national names not concentrated in any one state.

Market Risk

Interest rate risk involves the potential price fluctuations in a bond that are caused by changes in the general level of interest rates. While every fixed-income investment has some interest rate risk, the price volatility of a bond with a shorter term is lower than one with a longer term. Investors who have a low tolerance for interest rate risk should keep their investment at the short end of the yield curve. Inflation risk is the risk that a bond's value will diminish if there is greater overall inflation. Liquidity risk is the risk that an investor may not be able to buy or sell a bond because there is no market for that bond at a particular time. Liquidity problems may be macro problems, those affecting the whole market, or they may be specific to one issuer or to one type of credit. Short-term instruments, such as commercial paper and variable-rate demand bonds, usually contain highly rated bank lines of credit to provide liquidity and to reduce the risk that an issuer will not have monies available if bonds are put to them. The banks providing the liquidity may themselves have a problem if their own credit is not favorably received, and the issuers may end up paying a higher rate for liquidity than they had originally thought because the market's perception of the liquidity provider's credit has diminished.

Reinvestment Risk

Reinvestment risk is the risk that investors will not be able to invest their interest at the same rate as the original bond rate. Yield to maturity assumes that coupon interest can be reinvested at the original bond rate. When interest rates are dropping, there is a greater reinvestment risk because it is more difficult to find high-interest coupons.

INVESTOR STRATEGIES

Individuals and institutional investors use various techniques to match their investment objectives with their level of risk tolerance. These are general strategies, and each investor should consult with their own advisor as to the applicability to their own situation.

Laddering

One strategy to reduce interest rate risk is to build a *laddered portfolio,* which has maturities that are distributed over time. For example, equal principal amounts of bonds can be purchased with maturities in two, four, six, eight, and 10 years. When the two-year bonds mature, another bond with a 10-year maturity could be purchased, which will continue the ladder. A ladder portfolio reduces interest rate risk and price volatility because prices at the short end of the yield curve are not as volatile as prices at the longer end of the yield curve, but the investor does give up some yield by using this strategy. The investment objectives that can be met with this strategy are current income, capital preservation, and timing of maturities while at the same time controlling the interest rate risk.

Barbell

The *barbell strategy* is another technique to manage interest rate risk. Investors concentrate their holdings at both ends of the maturity spectrum rather than in the middle—hence the term barbell strategy. This strategy is used by investors who are uncertain about the course of interest rates. They invest equally in long-term bonds for the higher yields while at the same placing the same portion of their funds in securities with very short-term maturities. This strategy can also limit the risk of fluctuating prices when interest rates turn sharply in either direction. The investment objectives that can be met with this strategy are current income, capital preservation, and timing the maturity while at the same time controlling the interest rate risk.

Diversification

Diversification is a strategy to manage credit risk. A portfolio that contains a balanced mix of bonds from many different categories is less likely to lose value if one issue or sector is experiencing problems. Diversifying the portfolio can involve selecting general obligation and other tax-backed bonds and revenue bonds of many issuers in different states. It can mean selecting from within the broad category of revenue bonds a mix of housing, water and sewer, power, and health care bonds. Within a single state it can mean selecting issuers from levels of government that provide different services that rely on different tax and revenue streams. It can mean building a portfolio with ratings ranging from triple-A to low investment grade or even non–investment grade. It can also mean having a mix of bond insurers and banks backing bonds in a credit-enhanced portfolio. The investment objectives that can be met with this strategy are current income, capital preservation, and in-state exemption while controlling for credit, event, and political risk.

Bond Swapping

A *bond swap* is the simultaneous sale of one bond and the purchase of another with the proceeds of the sale. Swaps are used to change bond maturities, adjust portfolio credit quality, increase yield, enhance call protection, benefit from interest rate changes, and, most commonly to generate tax losses. The tax swap is done to produce a loss for tax purposes that can be used to offset capital gains or, to some extent, ordinary income.

The typical tax swap is a two-step process. First, the investor sells a bond that is currently valued below its amortized purchase price. Next, the investor simultaneously purchases a bond with similar but not identical characteristics. For example, an investor owns a $50,000, 20-year, triple-A-rated bond with a 5 percent coupon that was purchased five years earlier at par. As current interest rates have risen to 5.50 percent, the bond price has fallen to $47,500. The $2,500 capital loss incurred when the bond is sold is applied to offsetting the investor's capital gains on other investments or ordinary income. The investor then purchases, for example, a 5 percent triple-A bond from a different issuer, maturing in 15 years, which costs approximately $47,500. The yield, maturity, and bond quality are the same as before, but the unrealized loss was turned into a real loss used to offset taxable gains. It is important to note that if the replacement bond were held the full 15 years, the $2,500 gain would be taxed as ordinary income at maturity.

There are several rules about tax swaps that investors must take into consideration. Under current tax law, the maximum tax rate on long-term capital gains is lower than the maximum rate on short-term capital gains, but the investor must hold the bond a year to be eligible for the long-term capital gains rate. In addition, investors try to avoid doing a *wash sale,* which is the sale and repurchase within 30 days before or after the trade or settlement date of the same or a substantially identical security. The Internal Revenue Service will not recognize a tax loss generated from a wash sale. While the term "substantially identical" has not been explicitly defined with regard to tax swaps, two bonds have generally not been considered substantially identical if the securities have different issuers or if there are substantial differences in either maturity or coupon rate.

With a swap the investor usually wants to maintain credit quality, keep the total dollar amount of bonds the same, and maintain the same level of current income. Often, to satisfy all of these requirements, the new bond has a longer maturity than the original bond.

TAXATION OF MUNICIPAL BONDS

This section does not cover all of the possible tax consequences resulting from ownership of tax-exempt bonds and the receipt of interest thereon, and it is not intended as tax advice to any person. It addresses only beneficial owners who hold such bonds as capital assets, and does not address special classes of beneficial owners such as dealers in securities or currencies, banks, life insurance companies, persons holding such bonds as a hedge against interest rate or currency risks or as part of a straddle or conversion transaction, or beneficial owners whose functional currency is not the U.S. dollar. This section is based upon the United States federal income tax laws as currently in effect and as currently interpreted and does not include any description of the tax laws of any foreign government that might apply to a beneficial owner. Prospective purchasers of tax-exempt bonds should consult their own tax advisors concerning the application of federal and state tax laws to their particular situation.

Capital Gains and Losses

Even though the interest paid on a municipal bond is tax-exempt, a holder can recognize gain or loss that is subject to federal income tax on the sale of such a bond, just as in the case of a taxable bond. The amount of gain or loss is equal to the difference between (1) the sale price of the bond and (2) the holder's tax basis in the bond (the amount the holder paid for the bond originally, including any additions to such basis, such as OID, as discussed in the following section). Thus, if a holder purchased a $5,000 face amount municipal bond for $5,000 and then sold the bond for $5,200, the holder would have a capital gain of $200. Typically, the purchase and sale price of a municipal bond includes the dealer's markup; however, in cases where a commission is charged, it should be taken into account by the holder in computing gain or loss.

There are currently two types of capital gains: long-term and short-term. A long-term gain requires that a bond be held for more than 12 months before it is sold; a short-term gain is the result of holding a bond for 12 months or less. The maximum tax rate on long-term capital gains is 20 percent and the maximum tax rate on short-term capital gains is 39.6% (which is also the maximum tax rate on ordinary income).

When a bond is sold, an investor may also recognize a capital loss if the sale proceeds (adjusted for selling costs) are less than the holder's tax basis. In such a case, capital losses are first applied against capital gains of the same type to reduce such gains. Thus, a long-term capital loss will first reduce long-term capital gains, and a short-term capital loss will first reduce short-term capital gains. Any capital losses remaining after offsetting all available capital gains can then be used to reduce ordinary income by up to $3,000 per year, with any losses in excess of that amount available to be carried forward indefinitely to reduce capital gains or ordinary income in future years under the same procedures.

Original Issue Discount

If a tax-exempt bond is originally issued at a price less than par (as distinguished from a subsequent sale of a previously issued bond), the difference between the issue price of such a bond and the amount payable at the maturity of the bond is considered *original issue discount* (OID). For instance, if a $5,000 face amount bond (with a maturity of 10 years and a stated interest rate of 5 percent, payable semiannually) is issued for $4,628, the bond is treated for federal tax purposes as having been issued with $372 of original issue discount ($5,000 minus $4,628). From the bondholder's perspective, OID is simply additional interest that the bondholder will receive on the bond, except that it is paid at maturity instead of annually throughout the life of the bond. In the case of a tax-exempt bond, such OID is treated as tax-exempt interest.

Although the OID is treated as tax-exempt to the holder, it will increase the holder's tax basis in the bond (over the life of the bond) for purposes of calculating gain or loss if the holder disposes of the bond before maturity. In the example above, the value of the bond on the day it is issued is $4,628; at maturity, the bond will be worth $5,000 (assuming it is not in default). If interest rates remain stable, the value of the bond will increase over time from $4,628 to $5,000. If the OID did not increase the holder's tax basis during the period the bond is outstanding, a sale of the bond for an amount in excess of $4,628 would produce taxable capital gain to the bondholder, even if the increase in value arose solely as a result of the accretion of OID. In order to avoid this result, the Internal Revenue Code (the *Code*) provides that the holder's basis will increase over time based on a *constant yield to maturity* (CYM) method. Because this CYM method is also utilized for other purposes related to tax-exempt bonds, including the treatment of premium and market discount, we will calculate the CYM on the above bond to demonstrate how the holder's basis is increased.

To determine the constant yield to maturity on a bond, it is necessary to determine a constant discount rate that must be applied to each and every payment on the bond (principal and interest) in order to produce an aggregate value (as of the issue date) that is equal to the issue price of the bond. Using the above example (a bond that will pay $125 semi-annually for 10 years, with a final principal payment of $5,000 at the end of such a 10-year period), the discount rate that must be applied to each of those payments to produce a value of $4,628 is 6.00 percent, compounded semi-annually. Thus, even though the stated interest rate is 5 percent, the bond actually produces a yield to the bondholder of 6 percent due to its being issued at a discount. This 6 percent CYM will enter into the accretion of the holder's basis, and such basis will increase each year by an amount equal to the excess of the accreted issue price at the beginning of each semi-annual period multiplied by the 3 percent yield (6 percent annual yield divided by 2 to reflect semiannual interest payments), over the amount of interest actually paid on the bond during such period. For instance, assume the bondholder purchased the bond upon issuance on July 1, 2000. The holder's basis six months later on January 1, 2001 would be equal to the opening basis of $4,628 plus ($4,628 × 3 percent or $138.84) minus ($125 of interest), which will produce a basis of $4,641.84 as of January 1, 2001. Because this calculation is only necessary to determine the bondholder's basis, it need not be done by the bondholder until sale or other disposition of the bond and, if the holder holds the bond until maturity, it need never be done. The basis of a bond purchased at issuance and held to maturity will equal the principal amount of the bond at maturity.

In the case of a taxable bond, if the OID is less than one-fourth of one percent (¼ percent) of the principal amount of the bond multiplied by the number of full years until the bond's maturity, the OID is treated as de minimis and is ignored. This rule does not apply in the case of a tax-exempt bond to ensure that the full amount of OID is treated as tax-exempt interest to the holder and that the holder does not have an "artificial" gain on the sale of the bond.

Bond Premium

If a tax-exempt bond is purchased at a premium (i.e., at a price in excess of the face amount of the bond), whether at original issue or in the secondary market, the bond premium is amortized over the remaining term of the bond using the same CYM method discussed under Original Issue Discount. The amount of bond premium amortized each year is not deductible by the holder but, instead, reduces the holder's tax basis.

Amortizable bond premium can also result if a holder purchases a bond that was originally issued at a discount and the purchase price exceeds the issue price of the bond plus any accrued OID on the bond.

Market Discount

Market discount on a tax-exempt bond can arise if the bond is issued at par or at a premium and is later purchased in the secondary market at a price that is less than par or if the bond is issued at a discount and is later purchased in the secondary market at a price that is less than the original issue price plus accrued original issue discount through the date of purchase. Market discount, unlike OID, is not treated as tax-exempt interest to the holder when recognized because it arises as a result of market forces, not through the action of the issuer.

The effect of this rule is that a taxpayer who purchases a tax-exempt bond subsequent to its original issuance at a price less than its stated redemption price at maturity (or, if issued with OID, at a price less than its accreted value), either because interest rates have risen or because the obligor's credit has declined since the bond was issued, and who thereafter recognizes gain on the disposition of such bond will have part or all of the gain treated as ordinary income.

For example, if a $5,000 tax-exempt bond (issued at par on January 1, 2000) with a 20-year maturity were purchased five years after its issuance (on January 1, 2005) at a price of $4,400, the market discount would be $600. If that bond were sold on January 1, 2010, at a price of $4,700, one-third (five years of owning the bond divided by 15 years from purchase to maturity) of the market discount would have accrued. Thus, $200 (⅓ × $600) of market discount would have accrued, and that portion of the holder's $300 gain would be treated as ordinary income. The remaining $100 of the holder's gain would be taxed as long-term capital gains.

In the above example, the market discount accrued ratably over the remaining term to maturity of the bond, i.e., on a straight-line basis. Alternatively, a holder can elect to accrue market discount using the same method that is used for OID (that is, using a CYM method). In general, the effect of the election is to slightly decrease the rate at which the market discount is deemed to accrue, which will generally produce a beneficial result for the bondholder by reducing the amount of ordinary income recognized on a sale of the bond before maturity. If the bondholder retains the bond until maturity, both methods will produce the same result with the entire amount of market discount taxed as ordinary income.

If the market discount is below a certain de minimis amount, it is treated as zero. In the case of a tax-exempt bond, this is beneficial to the holder because, although the discount will be taxable when the bond matures, it will be taxed as a capital gain instead of ordinary income. Market discount is treated as de minimis if it is less than one-fourth of 1 percent (¼ percent) of the redemption amount of the bond (typically the par value) multiplied by the number of complete years until the bond matures, measured from the date it is acquired by the holder. For example, if an individual acquires in the secondary market a $10,000 face amount bond (issued at par) on January 1, 2001, for a price of $9,800, and the bond matures on January 1, 2011, the $200 market discount is de minimis. This result occurs because the face amount of the bond, $10,000, multiplied by ¼ of 1 percent, multiplied by 10 years until maturity, equals $250. Thus, any market discount less than $250 is de minimis. If the purchase price had been exactly $9,750, the market discount would not have been de minimis and would have been treated as ordinary income on maturity of the bond.

How would market discount be calculated in the case of a tax-exempt bond that was originally issued at a discount? For example, the bond that was discussed in the Section on OIDs was issued at $4,628 on July 1, 2000, had a coupon rate of 5.00 percent, and a yield to maturity of 6.00 percent. On July 1, 2001, the original holder would have accrued $28.10 in original issue discount (calculated by multiplying the issue price by 3 percent, reducing that amount for the actual interest paid, and repeating the calculation for two semi-annual periods). Thus, the *adjusted issue price* would be $4,656.10 ($4,628 plus the accrued OID). Assume the holder sells the bond for $4,456.10 ($200 less than the adjusted issue price). In that case, the new holder has $200 of market discount. The new holder will continue to accrue the tax-exempt OID at the same rate as the prior holder (and for this purpose should consult IRS Publication 1212 for the appropriate amount of OID that accrues each period). Those amounts of OID will equal, in the aggregate, $343.90 by the time the bond matures ($5,000 face amount minus the adjusted issue price of $4,656.10). When the second bondholder adds that amount to his cost basis of $4,456.10, he will have a final basis of $4,800 in the bond. If the second bondholder holds to maturity, he or she will thus recognize a gain of $200 ($5,000 proceeds on maturity minus $4,800 basis). Since this gain is wholly attributable to the market discount, the gain will be taxed as ordinary income.

What if the second holder sold the bond before maturity? In that case, he would have to determine his adjusted basis by starting with his cost basis ($4,456.10) and adding to that the amount of OID that has accrued (based on the original discount on the bond). If the holder would sell after two years, the amount of OID that would accrue in the above example would be $61.42 in those two years. Thus, the second holder's basis would increase to $4,517.52. If he sold the bond for $4,600, he would have a gain of $82.48. Part of that gain is attributable to the $200 market discount at the time he bought the bond. That market discount accrues on a straight-line basis at the rate of $200 divided by nine years or $22.22 per year. As he has held the bond for two years, $44.44 of his gain is ordinary income and the remaining $38.04 is long-term capital gain.

These calculations are very complex, and holders who purchase bonds in the secondary market should consult with their brokers and tax advisors to ensure that they have adequate information to properly calculate their tax basis, the amount of original issue discount and market discount that accrues during the period they hold the bond, and the appropriate amount of gain on sale or maturity. In many cases, the information supplied on Form-1099 (in the case of a taxable bond) or through IRS Publication 1212 may be insufficient (or inaccurate) in the case of a secondary purchaser of bonds. This will be true with respect to both tax-exempt bonds and taxable bonds. Accordingly, all secondary purchasers of bonds should ensure that they fully understand the information that is supplied to them on Forms-1099 (in the case of a taxable bond) or through Publication 1212 (for both taxable and tax-exempt bonds) so that they (or their tax advisors) can properly determine the tax consequences of holding or disposing of bonds after purchase in the secondary market.

The treatment of market discount as ordinary income applies to tax-exempt bonds purchased after April 30, 1993. Thus, if a holder bought a market discount bond in the secondary market prior to May 1, 1993, any gain realized on the eventual sale of such bond would be treated as capital gain, not ordinary income, whether or not the gain was attributable to accrued market discount.

Redemption of Bonds at a Premium

An issuer will sometimes be permitted under the terms of a bond to redeem the bond prior to its maturity date at a fixed price. Such a redemption is treated as a sale of the bond by the bondholder. Thus, the holder may recognize a capital gain or loss on such a sale. If the bond is redeemed at a price above the stated face amount of the bond, it is considered to be redeemed at a premium. For instance, assume a holder purchased at original issue a 10-year bond for $10,000 on January 1, 2000, and that the issuer was permitted to redeem the bond on January 1, 2005, for a payment of $10,300. If the issuer in fact chooses to redeem the bond at such a time, the additional $300 paid by the issuer to the holder is considered a premium and will produce a $300 long-term capital gain to the holder.

Borrowing to Buy a Tax-Exempt Bond

Taxpayers may, in some instances, claim an interest deduction for debt that is incurred to purchase or carry investments. However, a taxpayer may not deduct interest on indebtedness incurred or continue to purchase or carry obligations that are exempt from federal income tax. Without this rule (the *interest disallowance rule*), taxpayers would realize a double tax benefit from using borrowed funds to purchase or carry tax-exempt bonds, as the interest expense would be deductible while the interest income would escape federal tax.

The interest disallowance rule applies whenever a taxpayer uses borrowed funds to purchase or carry tax-exempt bonds. Thus, if borrowed funds are used for, and directly traceable to, the purchase of tax-exempt bonds, or tax-exempt bonds are used as collateral for indebtedness, then no part of the interest paid or incurred on such indebtedness may be deducted. If borrowed funds are only partly or indirectly used to purchase or hold tax-exempt bonds, then the rule will disallow a deduction for that portion of the interest allocable to the tax-exempt bonds.

While the interest disallowance rule is broad in scope, it does not automatically deny an interest deduction whenever a taxpayer simultaneously maintains debt and earns tax-exempt income. For example, the rule generally will not apply if an individual, while holding tax-exempt bonds, takes out a mortgage to purchase a residence rather than selling the bonds to finance the purchase. In this circumstance, the personal purpose of the loan predominates, and the IRS considers it unreasonable to deny the mortgage interest deduction. Similarly, the interest disallowance rule will not apply with respect to bona fide business loans unless the indebtedness is determined to be in excess of reasonable business needs. For example, the interest disallowance rule generally will not apply if a taxpayer that owns tax-exempt bonds borrows funds to finance a major capital improvement. In addition, a taxpayer may invest the proceeds of bona fide business indebtedness directly in short-term tax-exempt bonds for a temporary period while the borrowed funds await their intended use.

The Internal Revenue Service has issued a Revenue Procedure (Rev. Proc. 72-18) that permits individual and corporate taxpayers to avoid the effect of this disallowance rule where the taxpayer's investment in tax-exempt bonds is insubstantial. In the case of an individual, investment in tax-exempt obligations is considered insubstantial if the average amount of tax-exempt obligations (valued at their adjusted basis) is less than or equal to 2 percent of the average adjusted basis of all portfolio investments of the taxpayer. In the case of a corporation (other than a dealer in tax-exempt obligations), investment in tax-exempt obligations is considered insubstantial if the average basis of such investments is less than or equal to 2 percent of the corporation's total assets.

The interest disallowance rule also prevents a bank or other financial institution from deducting that portion of its interest expense that is allocable to tax-exempt interest. The disallowed portion is determined by applying a ratio of (1) the taxpayer's average for the tax year of the adjusted bases of tax-exempt bonds acquired after August 7, 1986, to (2) the average for the tax year of the adjusted bases of all assets of the taxpayer. However, a financial institution may deduct 80 percent of its interest expense allocable to *qualified tax-exempt obligations*, which are a special type of tax-exempt obligation issued by qualified small issuers that reasonably anticipate issuing no more than $10,000,000 in tax-exempt obligations during the calendar year. Because of these special rules applying to banks and financial institutions, it is not clear whether the 2 percent rule discussed previously applies to banks or financial institutions.

Reporting of Tax-Exempt Interest

Notwithstanding the exemption from taxes for interest on municipal bonds, taxpayers are still required to report such interest on their federal income tax returns pursuant to section 6012(d) of the Code. The interest is reported for information purposes only and does not enter into the computation of any tax that is due, except as discussed with respect to the Alternative Minimum Tax and the Taxation of Social Security Benefits.

Alternative Minimum Tax

The tax-exempt status of municipal bonds does not extend in all instances to the *alternative minimum tax* (AMT). The AMT is a separate tax calculation that must be performed by both individual and corporate taxpayers, and the resulting tax is then compared to the regular tax. Whichever tax is higher is the one that must be paid. The AMT is calculated by starting with regular taxable income and then making certain adjustments to that income. The most common adjustments are the elimination of the personal exemption deduction, the elimination of a deduction for state and local taxes, and the inclusion in income of interest on private activity municipal bonds. In general, the bonds on which interest is taxable for AMT purposes are private activity bonds that were originally issued after August 7, 1986, except for (1) qualified 501(c)(3) bonds and (2) certain refunding bonds. *Private activity bonds* will typically include any municipal bond the proceeds of which are used to benefit or finance a facility for the use of a private business (see Chapter 9). Once AMT income is calculated, a taxpayer is permitted to reduce that income by a so-called *exemption amount* before calculating the tax due.

In general, investors in the 36 percent or 39.6 percent federal tax brackets will not encounter an AMT problem because their regular income tax will exceed their AMT. However, for investors in the 28 percent or 31 percent brackets, especially those with large capital gains that may result in the reduction or elimination of the exemption amount and those who live in states with high income taxes, the AMT may become a problem. An investor that is not otherwise subject to the AMT should take into account the effect of this provision in deciding whether, and to what extent, to purchase tax-exempt bonds that are subject to the AMT. Furthermore, an investor already subject to the AMT should take into account the additional AMT that would be owed as a result of the purchase of otherwise tax-exempt bonds.

Effect of Tax-Exempt Interest in Calculation of Social Security Benefits Subject to Taxation

Under some circumstances, a taxpayer who receives tax-exempt interest will have a greater portion of his or her social security benefits taxed than if he or she received no tax-exempt interest. Although this does not constitute a direct tax on the tax-exempt interest itself, it does increase the overall tax liability of the individual and should be taken into account in making the investment decision of whether or not to purchase the tax-exempt bond. The calculation of the amount of social security benefits subject to tax is governed by Section 86 of the Code and is fairly complex. Because of the complexity of such calculations, individuals subject to Section 86 may wish to consult their own tax advisors to perform these calculations.

State Tax Treatment of Tax-Exempt Bonds

This section is not intended as a comprehensive guide to the state tax treatment of tax-exempt bonds. However, in general, most states do not tax individuals on the interest income arising from tax-exempt bonds issued by that state, its agencies, or its political subdivisions. However, the reverse is true with respect to bonds issued by out-of-state agencies or political subdivisions—virtually all states tax the interest resulting from such bonds. The effect of such disparate treatment is to increase the effective yield on a tax-exempt bond issued in one's own state versus an out-of-state bond. For instance, if an investor pays state tax at an effective 5 percent rate (after taking into account the federal deduction allowed for such state taxes) and the state taxes out-of-state (but not in-state bonds), an in-state bond bearing a 6 percent interest rate is the equivalent of a 6.32 percent out-of-state bond.

The state tax exemption for interest on in-state bonds will not necessarily extend to capital gain resulting from the sale or disposition of such bonds (or ordinary income resulting from the application of the market discount rules). Thus, a holder who recognizes capital gain (or ordinary income resulting from market discount) may be required to pay state tax on such capital gain and should consult a tax advisor with respect to the state tax consequences of such a sale.

OTHER INVESTMENT FACTORS

Spread Relationships

Investors often invest in classes of securities whose yields are historically out of line with those of other securities in the market. Sometimes they do so in anticipation of a shift in these relationships caused by to changing market conditions. When interest rates are very high and investors are particularly concerned about a weakening in the economy, credit spreads (the gap between the yields of differently rated securities) often widen. Credit spreads generally narrow in a stronger economy, when many investors buy lower-rated bonds to increase the portfolio's yield. In addition, investors examine spreads between different sectors of the municipal market for increased yield opportunities.

Similarly, the spread between bonds with long maturities and short-term bonds also varies under different market conditions.

Investors are often concerned with the spread between tax-exempt and taxable securities. At times of very narrow spreads, different classes of investors will purchase municipal securities. Thus, experienced investors will look to the municipal market outperforming taxable markets during these periods of narrow spreads. Conversely, when the spread between tax-exempt and taxable instruments is relatively wide, investors may move out of tax-exempt securities. Yield relationships in comparison with taxable investments may also help determine the specific maturities that an investor will wish to purchase. The investor will monitor the option-adjusted spread, which is the average spread over the triple-A spot curve adjusted to reflect the put and call options that are embedded in the bond.

Measuring Performance

Investors evaluate the characteristics and performance of their portfolios with a wide range of financial and statistical measures that grade and rank the portfolio against itself and against other portfolios or indices.

In accordance with basic principles of investing—term to maturity, coupon rates, and redemption provisions—the investor looks for bonds that have the most favorable structure and features. The investor examines both the duration and convexity of the bond. *Duration* (or option-adjusted duration or effective duration) is the weighted maturity of a bond's cash flows, and it measures the price sensitivity of bond for a given change in interest rates. *Modified duration* is duration adjusted to price and yield levels to represent percentage change relationship of price and yield for noncallable bonds.

Convexity is the mathematical measure of the rate of change in the bond's duration as interest rates change. The more convex a bond is, the more its duration will change with interest rate shifts. *Negative convexity* happens when the bond price goes up less than the overall market, while in *positive convexity* the bond price goes up just as much as, or more than, the overall market. A bond that is noncallable may have greater value to an investor than one of the same maturity and coupon that contains a call option because the call features in municipal bonds may create negative convexity. In a low–interest rate environment, where price volatility is greater than in a higher–interest rate environment, the investor wants to avoid negative convexity because it will reduce the portfolio's total return.

The investor also works at managing the portfolio's duration because the greater the duration of a bond, the greater is its price volatility. A portfolio manager may employ hedging techniques or may purchase municipal futures to keep the portfolio's duration at a level where the total return is maximized.

There are many ways to compare the performance of institutional investors, particularly of mutual funds. Many publications compare the total return of a fund's portfolio on an annual, three-year, or longer basis. Investors and the fund's competitors can access websites and sort the performance of funds by sector, by state, by manager, or by other criteria. The fund's performance can also be compared to standard industry indices.

Evaluations for Individual Investors

Because municipal bonds are traded over the counter and because so many issues are traded infrequently, investors often request evaluations of their municipal holdings to determine the market value of their portfolios. Evaluations may also be necessary to satisfy legal or financial requirements for individuals and institutional investors as well as for bond funds.

The types of evaluations vary widely, but essentially they are designed to determine the price that would be received for each bond in a portfolio if the bond were sold that day. Evaluators generally value a portfolio by comparing each bond with the recent trade prices of matching or similar bonds. Beginning in November 1998, The Bond Market Association has posted on its website daily municipal price and yield reports on actively traded municipal issues. The basic data on the site list the issue and prices as reported the previous day by the MSRB. The MSRB daily report includes those bonds that trade four or more times on the prior trading day or approximately 1,000 issues out of 1.4 million outstanding municipal issues. The Bond Market Association and Standard & Poor's J.J. Kenny expanded the basic MSRB report to include such information as coupon, yield to maturity, yield to par call, credit ratings, and bond insurance, if any. Investors can sort the information by state, credit rating, high and low prices, maturities, yield, and other criteria.

INVESTOR CATEGORIES

Table 6.1 shows the holdings of municipal securities by major investor categories from 1955 to 1999. Over time, market share has shifted among investor groups. Household and household proxies represented 34.3 percent of all holdings in 1980, mostly as direct investments. By 1999, these combined categories had more than doubled their share of the holdings to 74.5 percent, with the growth coming out of direct investments by households and going to investments through various types of funds. Commercial banks were the single largest category of holders in 1980, at 37.3 percent. The 1986 Tax Reform Act made owning bonds by commercial banks less attractive, and by 1997, commercial banks accounted for only 7.2 percent of all holdings. Property and casualty companies' purchases of municipal bonds fluctuate with their earnings cycle and with tax rates. In 1980, these companies accounted for 20.2 percent of holdings; and by 1999, that share had declined to 13.7 percent.

Households

Households have been the largest single group of municipal investors since the 1980s. At the end of 1999, households directly held 35 percent of municipal securities (excluding mutual funds and other proxies). The activity of these investors in the market fluctuates, depending upon four major factors: the absolute level of interest rates, the relationship of municipal yields to those of taxable securities, competing returns in the equities markets, and income tax rates. Individuals generally purchase the greatest volume of municipal securities when municipal rates are near their highest levels; indeed, they are generally the last investor category in the business cycle to buy bonds.

TABLE 6.1 Trends in the Ownership of Municipal Securities, 1955–1999

Year	Households (%)	Open-Ended Funds (%)	Money Market Funds (%)	Closed-Ended Funds (%)	Bank Personal Trusts (%)	Commercial Banks (%)	Property and Casualty Insurance (%)	Other (%)	Total Outstanding ($ billions)
1955	42.0	—	—	—	—	28.2	9.2	20.6	45.7
1960	43.7	—	—	—	—	24.9	11.4	20.0	71.0
1965	36.4	—	—	—	—	38.6	11.3	13.7	100.4
1970	24.3	—	—	—	8.1	48.2	11.7	7.6	145.5
1975	22.4	—	—	—	7.5	46.1	14.9	9.0	223.0
1980	26.2	1.1	0.5	—	6.5	37.3	20.2	8.3	399.4
1985	40.3	4.1	4.2	0.1	5.6	27.0	10.3	8.5	859.5
1990	48.5	9.5	7.1	1.2	6.8	9.9	11.6	5.4	1,184.4
1995	35.4	16.3	9.9	4.6	8.4	7.2	12.4	5.8	1,293.5
1999	35.0	15.6	13.7	4.4	5.8	7.2	13.7	4.6	1,532.5

Note: Percentages may not add up to exactly 100.0 percent due to rounding. Dash = categories did not exist at that point in time.
Source: Federal Reserve System.

Some observers believe that, based merely on the progressive nature of tax rates, it would make sense for individuals to own more municipal bonds than they actually do. But many who are eligible because of high incomes have not accumulated the wealth to enable them to make substantial purchases, especially if they want to diversify their assets. The interest of individual investors in municipal securities is also affected by various tax law provisions, including the marginal tax rate of an individual under current tax provisions as discussed earlier in this chapter.

Mutual Funds

Unit Investment Trusts. The first municipal bond fund appeared in 1961 in the form of a unit investment trust. At that time, Congress did not yet allow managed mutual funds specializing in municipal bonds to pass tax-exempt interest income on to investors, though unit investment trusts could do so. A unit trust issues a set number of shares to investors and invests that finite sum in a portfolio of municipal bonds. The portfolio purchased by a unit trust is essentially unmanaged and usually held to maturity. The life of these trusts, then, is usually limited to the life of the bonds originally bought.

Investors can buy units in the funds. Although most investors intend to hold on to their investments until the bonds mature, the fund sponsors ordinarily maintain secondary markets for the units. Investors can also redeem the units through the fund trustees, although the price paid for the units will have declined if interest rates have risen. As the bonds in the unit trust mature or are called, the investors who have held their units are paid back the principal value. Some fund sponsors will reinvest interest income for investors in another fund set up for that purpose.

Managed Funds. In 1976, Congress allowed managed mutual funds to pass on tax-exempt income to investors, and thereafter, this category of funds grew rapidly. Managed funds include both closed- and open-end funds. Closed-end managed funds are similar to unit trusts in that a fixed number of shares is offered to investors and a finite sum is invested in a bond portfolio. Some closed-end funds are traded on an exchange market. Open-end bond funds may issue shares in relation to the demand for their product and the supply of appropriate investments. New investors may be accepted, and the portfolio may be expanded on an unlimited basis at the manager's discretion. Both types of managed funds investing in municipals can buy and sell bonds in the portfolio as often as they deem necessary. The objective is for active professional management to produce a higher return than would be available if bonds were simply bought and held. The prices of the bonds in the portfolio will determine the asset value of the funds, which will shift up and down with market conditions and with general changes in interest rates. Some funds carry sales charges, and others are *no-loads*.

The objectives and management styles of the managed funds vary widely. Some funds are devoted to short-term municipal bonds and provide investors with liquidity. Maximum liquidity in a tax-exempt instrument is available through the purchase of shares in a tax-exempt money market account. Other funds are dedicated to longer-term sectors of the market and have objectives that range from maximum total return funds (coupled with capital preservation) to high-yield funds, which invest in lower-quality or nonrated bonds and are designed for investors seeking maximum tax-exempt interest income with a higher element of risk.

The philosophies of individual fund managers often differ. Certain bond fund managers try to gauge swings in interest rates and to shift their portfolios among long-term and short-term maturities as well as cash. Other managers seek out undervalued securities as a method of increasing the return on their portfolios. Still others use financial products to increase the portfolio's yield. There is an enormous amount of competition among funds to generate the highest total return or income, and the fund's investors can compare the performance of funds in order to make an investment decision. Managed funds also include an index where the portfolios mirror that of accepted industry indices.

Both types of managed bond funds have steadily grown in popularity since their inception. In 1980, managed open-end funds owned 1.1 percent of all outstanding municipal bonds; at the end of 1999, this figure was 15.6 percent. Table 6.2 shows that municipal securities as a percentage of mutual funds reached a peak in 1990 and declined during the rest of the decade. During this time period there was a great increase in the denominator of all mutual funds, including equity fund.

Closed-end managed funds owned 0.1 percent of municipals in 1985 and accounted for 4.4 percent of municipal holdings in 1999. As shown in Table 6.3, municipal securities as a percentage of all closed end funds was in the low to mid-40 percent range during most of the 1990s.

Tax-exempt money market funds were offered beginning in 1979. Rule 2a-7 of the Investment Company Act of 1940 requires that the average overall maturities of securities held in a tax-exempt money market portfolio be 397 days or less. The average maturity in most money market funds is considerably less than that level. Such funds are created primarily to provide short-term liquidity along with the benefits of tax exemption to investors. The advent of tax-exempt money funds led to the growth and the creation of tax-exempt products such as variable-rate demand obligations and commercial paper. Table 6.4 shows that municipal securities as a percentage of all money market mutual funds peaked during the years surrounding the Tax

TABLE 6.2 Municipal Securities as a Percentage of Mutual Funds, 1976–1999

Year	Total Municipal Securities in Mutual Funds Outstanding ($ billions)	Total Mutual Funds Outstanding ($ billions)	Percent of Municipals in Mutual Funds Outstanding
1976	0.5	46.5	1.1
1977	2.2	45.5	4.8
1978	2.7	46.1	5.9
1979	4.0	51.8	7.7
1980	4.4	61.8	7.1
1981	5.1	59.8	8.5
1982	8.0	76.9	10.4
1983	13.4	112.1	12.0
1984	19.1	135.6	14.1
1985	34.9	245.9	14.2
1986	67.0	426.5	15.7
1987	74.8	480.2	15.6
1988	82.9	500.5	16.6
1989	98.6	589.6	16.7
1990	112.6	608.4	18.5
1991	139.7	769.5	18.2
1992	168.4	992.5	17.0
1993	211.3	1,375.4	15.4
1994	207.0	1,477.3	14.0
1995	210.2	1,852.8	11.3
1996	213.3	2,342.4	9.1
1997	219.8	2,989.4	7.4
1998	242.6	3,610.5	6.7
1999	239.7	4,552.4	5.3

Source: Federal Reserve System.

Reform Act of 1986. During the 1990s, they accounted for 15 to 20 percent of money market mutual fund assets, and in 1999 they accounted for 13.7 percent of municipal holdings. Tax-exempt money market funds as a percentage of all money market funds declined during the 1990s.

Bank Personal Trusts

Bank personal trust holdings of all municipal securities fluctuated in the 5–8 percent range from 1970 to 1999. Municipal holdings as a percentage of all bank personal trusts was at its highest during this time period in 1994 at 17 percent and at its lowest in 1999 at 8.1 percent. Table 6.5 shows the trend of

TABLE 6.3   Municipal Securities as a Percentage of Closed-Ended Funds, 1985–1999

Year	Total Municipal Securities in Closed-Ended Funds Outstanding ($ billions)	Total Closed-Ended Funds Outstanding ($ billions)	Percent of Municipals in Closed-Ended Funds Outstanding
1985	1.0	8.3	12.0
1986	2.0	14.5	13.8
1987	3.3	21.3	15.5
1988	7.5	43.2	17.4
1989	12.1	52.5	23.0
1990	14.1	52.9	26.7
1991	25.4	71.1	35.7
1992	39.7	93.5	42.5
1993	51.8	116.1	44.6
1994	53.4	117.8	45.3
1995	59.6	134.4	44.3
1996	61.7	144.7	42.6
1997	60.8	149.4	40.7
1998	61.7	143.0	43.1
1999	67.4	167.5	40.2

Source: Federal Reserve System.

municipal securities as a percentage of all bank personal trusts from 1975 to 1999.

Commercial Banks

Historically, the interest of banks in purchasing municipal bonds has been influenced by a combination of factors, including the level of loan demand, overall bank profitability, the attractiveness of municipal bonds versus alternative investments, and the level of interest expense deduction. Banks prefer short- and medium-term bonds because they are better matches for the maturities of the banks' liabilities.

Beginning in 1982, changes in federal tax legislation further reduced the banks' demand for municipal securities. Formerly, financial institutions were exempt from IRS rules that prohibited the deduction of interest paid on debt incurred to purchase or carry tax-exempt securities. In 1982, the law was changed to allow banks to deduct only 85 percent of such interest expense and was further tightened to 80 percent in 1984. Table 6.6 shows that in 1999 commercial banks accounted for only 7.2 percent of all municipal holdings, down from nearly half of all municipal holdings in the 1970s. At the close of

TABLE 6.4 Municipal Securities as a Percentage of Money Market Mutual Funds, 1975–1999

Year	Total Municipal Securities Held by Money Market Funds Outstanding ($ billions)	Total Money Market Mutual Funds Outstanding ($ billions)	Percent of Municipals Held by Money Market Mutual Funds Outstanding
1975	—	3.7	—
1976	—	3.7	—
1977	—	3.9	—
1978	—	10.8	—
1979	—	45.2	—
1980	2.2	76.4	2.9
1981	4.4	186.3	2.4
1982	13.3	219.9	6.0
1983	16.9	179.5	9.4
1984	24.0	232.2	10.3
1985	36.4	242.4	15.0
1986	64.1	290.6	22.1
1987	61.8	313.8	19.7
1988	66.1	335.0	19.7
1989	70.1	424.7	16.5
1990	84.0	493.3	17.0
1991	90.6	535.0	16.9
1992	96.0	539.5	17.8
1993	105.6	559.6	18.9
1994	113.4	602.9	18.8
1995	127.7	745.3	17.1
1996	144.5	891.1	16.2
1997	167.0	1,048.7	15.9
1998	193.0	1,334.2	14.5
1999	210.4	1,584.8	13.3

Source: Federal Reserve System, Flow of Funds Historical Data Chart L.121.

1985, municipals represented approximately 10 percent of total bank assets', and by the close of 1999, this figure had dropped below 2 percent. This decline in holdings from 1985 to the present was a direct result of the Tax Reform Act of 1986, which eliminated the interest expense deduction for all but the smallest local issues.

Property and Casualty Insurance Companies

Investment objectives and high tax rates have encouraged companies in the property and casualty insurance industry to invest in municipal bonds. Con-

TABLE 6.5 Municipal Securities as a Percentage of Bank Personal Trusts and Estates, 1975–1999

Year	Total Municipal Securities Held by Bank Personal Trusts and Estates ($ billions)	Bank Personal Trusts and Estates Outstanding Volume ($ billions)	Percent of Municipals Held by Bank Personal Trusts and Estates
1975	16.8	158.9	10.6
1976	20.4	184.8	11.0
1977	22.6	181.9	12.4
1978	24.3	192.8	12.6
1979	27.7	215.2	12.9
1980	26.0	244.8	10.6
1981	29.6	248.1	11.9
1982	31.2	264.2	11.8
1983	35.7	293.2	12.2
1984	39.9	306.1	13.0
1985	48.2	358.3	13.5
1986	56.9	404.4	14.1
1987	63.1	414.2	15.2
1988	65.9	443.7	14.9
1989	73.0	515.1	14.2
1990	80.8	522.1	15.5
1991	89.9	608.3	14.8
1992	96.0	629.6	15.2
1993	108.9	660.9	16.5
1994	114.2	670.0	17.0
1995	108.3	774.9	14.0
1996	104.0	841.6	12.4
1997	90.7	917.7	9.9
1998	89.5	976.3	9.2
1999	88.4	1092.3	8.1

Source: Federal Reserve System, Flow of Funds Historical Data Chart L.116.

siderable volatility in the investment activity of insurance companies is due to the cyclical nature of profits within the industry. The level of purchases depends mostly on their taxable profits. As profitability levels rise, insurers accelerate their purchases of tax-exempt securities.

The Tax Reform Act of 1986 altered the investment implications of tax-exempt bonds for property and casualty companies with the imposition of an alternative minimum income tax as well as changes in the calculation of loss reserves. However, changes in the way in which insurers' income is calculated

TABLE 6.6 Municipal Securities as a Percentage of Commercial Bank Assets Outstanding, 1975–1999

Year	Total Municipal Securities of Commercial Bank Assets Outstanding ($ billions)	Total Commercial Bank Assets Outstanding ($ billions)	Percent of Municipals of Commercial Bank Assets Outstanding
1975	102.9	885.1	11.6
1976	106.0	960.1	11.0
1977	115.2	1,066.9	10.8
1978	126.2	1,220.0	10.3
1979	135.6	1,355.2	10.0
1980	148.8	1,481.7	10.0
1981	154.0	1,618.6	9.5
1982	158.3	1,730.9	9.1
1983	162.1	1,887.2	8.6
1984	174.6	2,127.0	8.2
1985	231.7	2,376.3	9.8
1986	203.4	2,619.6	7.8
1987	174.3	2,774.5	6.3
1988	151.6	2,952.1	5.1
1989	133.8	3,231.4	4.1
1990	117.4	3,337.5	3.5
1991	103.2	3,442.2	3.0
1992	97.5	3,654.9	2.7
1993	99.2	3,891.8	2.5
1994	97.6	4,159.7	2.3
1995	93.4	4,493.8	2.1
1996	94.2	4,710.4	2.0
1997	96.7	5,174.6	1.9
1998	104.8	5,642.1	1.9
1999	110.7	5,994.1	1.8

Source: Federal Reserve System, Flow of Funds Historical Data Chart L.109.

may tend to increase their taxable income, thereby generating greater demand for municipal bonds in some cases.

Casualty insurers have typically favored long term maturities for their municipal bond portfolios. They have been interested principally in producing the highest yield possible, given adequate credit quality, and long-term municipal bonds produce the highest returns. Many casualty insurers prefer revenue bonds to GO securities to produce higher returns on their investments. However, portfolio managers are always looking for opportunities along the yield curve and among sectors to maximize their performance.

TABLE 6.7 Municipal Securities as a Percentage of Property and Casualty Company Assets, 1975–1999

Year	Total Municipal Securities in Property and Casualty Company Assets Outstanding ($ billions)	Total Property and Casualty Company Assets Outstanding ($ billions)	Percent of Municipals in Property and Casualty Company Assets
1975	33.3	80.3	41.5
1976	38.7	97.9	39.5
1977	49.4	118.3	41.8
1978	62.9	139.8	45.0
1979	72.8	161.7	45.0
1980	80.5	182.1	44.2
1981	83.9	194.4	43.2
1982	87.0	212.3	41.0
1983	86.7	235.2	36.9
1984	84.7	250.9	33.8
1985	88.2	298.6	29.5
1986	101.9	353.6	28.8
1987	124.8	405.0	30.8
1988	134.1	453.9	29.5
1989	134.8	503.0	26.8
1990	136.9	533.5	25.7
1991	126.8	575.8	22.0
1992	134.3	597.9	22.5
1993	146.1	642.5	22.7
1994	153.8	678.1	22.7
1995	161.0	740.3	21.7
1996	175.4	770.0	22.8
1997	191.6	840.6	22.8
1998	210.9	890.4	23.7
1999	209.4	883.6	23.7

Source: Federal Reserve System, Flow of Funds Historical Data Chart L.118.

Property and casualty companies held 20.2 percent of outstanding municipal securities in 1980, dropping to 13.7 percent in 1999. Table 6.7 shows that municipal assets as a percentage of overall insurance company assets were 45 percent in 1979 and declined to 23.7 percent of total assets in 1999.

CHAPTER 7

Credit Analysis

INTRODUCTION

Municipal credit analysis assesses both the ability and the willingness of an issuer to repay bonded debt as scheduled. The analyst uses quantitative tools and qualitative judgments to evaluate the creditworthiness of an issuer.

Municipal Credit Quality

Up to the mid-1970s, investors and dealers in municipal securities had been accustomed to comparatively secure payment of principal and interest. There had been few serious municipal credit problems since the Depression in the 1930s, when there were nearly 5,000 recorded defaults. One study found that between 1945 and 1965 only $10 million of principal and interest was permanently lost to municipal investors. Even the Depression defaults were almost entirely corrected by 1945, and most investors were paid what they were owed.

During the 1970s, however, the financial debt environment changed. Beginning with the note defaults by New York City, Cleveland, and the New York State Urban Development Corporation municipal credit analysis drew increased attention from investors and dealers. This attention was heightened in 1983 by the default of the Washington Public Power Supply System (WPPSS) on more than $2 billion of debt issued to finance the construction of nuclear power plants. The 1994 bankruptcy of affluent Orange County, California, made it clear that no jurisdiction was immune to financial uncertainty.

The Advisory Commission on Intergovernmental Relations (ACIR) analyzed the problem in its March 1985 report, *Bankruptcies, Defaults, and Other Local Government Financial Emergencies*. The commission found that the number of municipal bankruptcies grew to 21 between 1972 and 1984, compared with only 10 cases filed between 1960 and 1971. Changes in bankruptcy laws and the proliferation of special-district and industrial development bonds were partly responsible for this development. Under the revised Bankruptcy Code, which went into effect in 1979, municipalities gained the right to file for bankruptcy protection under Chapter 9. However, the municipality's state law must authorize a filing, and not every state authorizes Chapter 9 filings. There can be no involuntary bankruptcy filing as only the municipality can initiate the proceeding. The approval of creditors is no longer required for filing for bankruptcy, so that some entities—for example, the San Jose School District, California—were able to file for bankruptcy in order to avoid the burdens of a labor agreement. And in 1994, Orange County filed for protection under Chapter 9 as a result of substantial losses resulting from the county's investment activities.

The number of general purpose government filings has remained small, but defaults and bankruptcies can move independent of one another. For instance, the WPPSS defaulted on two projects without filing for bankruptcy, while the San Jose school district did file, although its debt payments remained intact. In fact, municipal bankruptcy filings are rare. Table 7.1 shows that there have been only 156 Chapter 9 filings from 1980 to March 2000.

TABLE 7.1   Chapter 9 Bankruptcy Filings (twelve months ended March 31)

Year	Number of Filings
2000	6
1999	4
1998	8
1997	7
1996	9
1995	13
1994	15
1993	10
1992	18
1991	21
1990	9
1989	6
1988	2
1987	12
1986	3
1985	3
1984	3
1983	4
1982	2
1981	1
Total	156

Source: Administrative Office of the U.S. Courts.

This compares to 38,109 business filings in just the 12 months ending March 31, 2000.

In 1999, Fitch analyzed municipal default risk and concluded that the default rate for municipal securities is very low. Fitch found that there were wide ranges in default risk depending on the type of bond with debt excluding industrial development bonds the lowest rate. Default rates also varied by the year that the bonds were issued.

Tax-supported bonds and revenue bonds are analyzed in different ways that give greater emphases to different factors. For tax-backed bonds, analysts concentrate on the financial health of the entire entity, noting the extent of its taxing power as well as the potential of its economic base. These are the major determinants of the entity's ability to raise the necessary taxes and fees to support debt service. The political environment, along with the debt; economic, financial, and management factors; and overall characteristics of the municipalities, are explored in detail by credit analysts. They seek more information about population, wealth, and local industry; they watch for trends in employment, per capita income, and the assessed valuation of property; they closely analyze the issuer's financial statements; and they seek fuller disclosure of data where necessary.

Revenue bond analysis is a broad field, with as many specializations as types of revenue bonds that are issued. Analysts tend to specialize in industries, such as utilities, housing, or health care, in order to stay on top of the trends that occur in each of the industries on a regional and national basis. A thorough economic analysis of the enterprise is necessary, as well as an assessment of the economic strength of the enterprise's service area. The legal provisions of the trust indenture protect bondholders from such risks as dilution of security through the issuance of additional bonds, and so the legal provisions and covenants are also carefully scrutinized.

Whether the analyst works on the sell side for a dealer or on the buy side for an investor, for a credit enhancer or for a rating agency, the analyst's job is to evaluate the issuer's creditworthiness. The next section describes the role of the ratings agencies in the municipal market.

THE RATING AGENCIES

Moody's Investors Service, Standard & Poor's Ratings Services, and Fitch are the three rating agencies that dominate the municipal market. At these three agencies, specialists in all facets of municipal credit evaluate new issues and perform surveillance on outstanding issues. Each agency publishes reports on new issues and on outstanding issues. They provide statistical information such as median debt ratios for states, utilities, health care institutions, and higher education institutions. They also follow on general trends, such as annual rating changes, and specific trends, such as policies on rating new credit structures. Rating criteria are also published. Many of these reports are available electronically and in traditional print form.

In addition to municipal debt, each agency rates many other kinds of debt, such as that of international, corporate, and asset-backed issuers. Each agency has it own rating definitions. Tables 7.2 through 7.4 are the rating definitions of Moody's, Standard & Poor's, and Fitch respectively.

TABLE 7.2   Moody's Rating Definitions

Debt Ratings - U.S. Tax-Exempt Municipals
There are nine basic rating categories for long-term obligations. They range from Aaa (highest quality) to C (lowest quality). Moody's applies numerical modifiers 1, 2, and 3 in each generic rating classification from Aa to Caa. The Modifier 1 indicates that the issue ranks in the higher end of its generic rating category; the modifier 2 indicates a mid-range ranking; and the modifier 3 indicates that the issue ranks in the lower end of its generic category. Advance refunded issues that are secured by escrowed funds held in cash, held in trust, reinvested in direct non-callable United States government obligations or non-callable obligations unconditionally guaranteed by the U.S. government are identified with a # (hatchmark) symbol, eg. # Aaa.

Aaa
Bonds that are rated Aaa are judged to be of the best quality. They carry the smallest degree of investment risk and are generally referred to as "gilt edge." Interest payments are protected by a large or by an exceptionally stable margin and principal is secure. While the various protective elements are likely to change, such changes as can be visualized are most unlikely to impair the fundamentally strong position of such issues.

Aa
Bonds that are rated Aa are judged to be of high quality by all standards. Together with the Aaa group they comprise what are generally known as high grade bonds. They are rated lower than the best bonds because margins of protection may not be as large as in Aaa securities or fluctuation of protective elements may be of greater amplitude or there may be other elements present that make the long-term risks appear somewhat larger than in Aaa securities.

A
Bonds that are rated A possess many favorable investment attributes and are to be considered as upper medium grade obligations. Factors giving security to principal and interest are considered adequate, but elements may be present that suggest a susceptibility to impairment some time in the future.

Baa
Bonds that are rated Baa are considered as medium grade obligations, i.e., they are neither highly protected nor poorly secured. Interest payments and principal security appear adequate for the present but certain protective elements may be lacking or may be characteristically unreliable over any great length of time. Such bonds lack outstanding investment characteristics and in fact have speculative characteristics as well.

TABLE 7.2 (Continued)

Ba

Bonds that are rated Ba are judged to have speculative elements; their future cannot be considered as well assured. Often the protection of interest and principal payments may be very moderate, and thereby not well safeguarded during both good and bad times over the future. Uncertainty of position characterizes bonds in this class.

B

Bonds that are rated B generally lack characteristics of the desirable investment. Assurance of interest and principal payments or maintenance of other terms of the contract over any long period of time may be small.

Caa

Bonds that are rated Caa are of poor standing. Such issues may be in default or there may be present elements of danger with respect to principal or interest.

Ca

Bonds that are rated Ca represent obligations that are speculative in a high degree. Such issues are often in default or have other marked shortcomings.

C

Bonds that are rated C are the lowest rated class of bonds, and issues so rated can be regarded as having extremely poor prospects of ever attaining any real investment standing.

Con. (...)

Bonds for which the security depends upon the completion of some act or the fulfillment of some condition are rated conditionally. These are bonds secured by: (a) earnings of projects under construction, (b) earnings of projects unseasoned in operating experience, (c) rentals that begin when facilities are completed, or (d) payments to which some other limiting condition attaches. Parenthetical rating denotes probable credit stature upon completion of construction or elimination of basis of condition.

Moody's Short-Term MIG/VMIG Ratings - US Tax-Exempt Municipals

There are four rating categories for short-term obligations that define an investment grade situation. These are designated Moody's Investment Grade as MIG 1 (best quality) through MIG 4 (adequate quality). Short-term obligations of speculative quality are designated SG.

In the case of variable rate demand obligations (VRDOs), a two-component rating is assigned. The first element represents an evaluation of the degree of risk associated with scheduled principal and interest payments, and the other represents an evaluation of the degree of risk associated with the demand feature. The short-term rating assigned to the demand feature of VRDOs is designated as VMIG. When either the long- or short-term aspect of a VRDO is not rated, that piece is designated NR, e.g., Aaa/NR or NR/VMIG 1.

(continued)

TABLE 7.2 (Continued)

Issues that are subject to a periodic reoffer and resale in the secondary market in a "dutch auction" are assigned a long-term rating based only on Moody's assessment of the ability and willingness of the issuer to make timely principal and interest payments. Moody's expresses no opinion as to the ability of the holder to sell the security in a secondary market "dutch auction." Such issues are identified by the insertion of the words "dutch auction" into the name of the issue.

Issues or the features associated with MIG or VMIG ratings are identified by date of issue, date of maturity or maturities or rating expiration date and description to distinguish each rating from other ratings. Each rating designation is unique with no implication as to any other similar issue of the same obligor. MIG ratings terminate at the retirement of the obligation while VMIG rating expiration will be a function of each issue's specific structural or credit features.

MIG 1/VMIG 1
This designation denotes best quality. There is present strong protection by established cash flows, superior liquidity support or demonstrated broad-based access to the market for refinancing.

MIG 2/VMIG 2
This designation denotes high quality. Margins of protection are ample although not so large as in the preceding group.

MIG 3/VMIG 3
This designation denotes favorable quality. All security elements are accounted for but there is lacking the undeniable strength of the preceding grades. Liquidity and cash flow protection may be narrow and market access for refinancing is likely to be less well established.

MIG 4/VMIG 4
This designation denotes adequate quality. Protection commonly regarded as required of an investment security is present and although not distinctly or predominantly speculative, there is specific risk.

SG
This designation denotes speculative quality. Debt instruments in this category lack margins of protection.

Prime Rating System
Moody's short-term issuer ratings are opinions of the ability of issuers to honor senior financial obligations and contracts. These obligations have an original maturity not exceeding one year, unless explicitly noted.

Moody's employs the following three designations, all judged to be investment grade, to indicate the relative repayment ability of rated issuers:

Issuers rated Prime-1 (or supporting institutions) have a superior ability for repayment of senior short-term debt obligations. Prime-1 repayment ability will often be evidenced by many of the following characteristics:

TABLE 7.2 (Continued)

Leading market positions in well-established industries.

High rates of return on funds employed.

Conservative capitalization structure with moderate reliance on debt and ample asset protection.

Broad margins in earnings coverage of fixed financial charges and high internal cash generation.

Well-established access to a range of financial markets and assured sources of alternate liquidity.

Issuers rated Prime-2 (or supporting institutions) have a strong ability for repayment of senior short-term debt obligations. This will normally be evidenced by many of the characteristics cited above but to a lesser degree. Earnings trends and coverage ratios, while sound, may be more subject to variation. Capitalization characteristics, while still appropriate, may be more affected by external conditions. Ample alternate liquidity is maintained.

Issuers rated Prime-3 (or supporting institutions) have an acceptable ability for repayment of senior short-term obligations. The effect of industry characteristics and market compositions may be more pronounced. Variability in earnings and profitability may result in changes in the level of debt protection measurements and may require relatively high financial leverage. Adequate alternate liquidity is maintained.

Issuers rated Not Prime do not fall within any of the Prime rating categories.

If an issuer represents to Moody's that its short-term debt obligations are supported by the credit of another entity or entities, then the name or names of such supporting entity or entities are listed within the parenthesis beneath the name of the issuer, or there is a footnote referring the reader to another page for the name or names of the supporting entity or entities. In assigning ratings to such issuers, Moody's evaluates the financial strength of the affiliated corporations, commercial banks, insurance companies, foreign governments or other entities, but only as one factor in the total rating assessment. Moody's makes no representation and gives no opinion on the legal validity or enforceability of any support arrangements.

Reprinted with permission from Moody's Investors Service
Source: Moody's Investor Service

TABLE 7.3 Standard and Poor's Ratings Definitions

A Standard & Poor's issue credit rating is a current opinion of the creditworthiness of an obligor with respect to a specific financial obligation, a specific class of financial obligations, or a specific financial program (including ratings on medium-term note programs and commercial paper programs.) It takes into consideration the creditworthiness of guarantors, insurers, or other forms of credit enhancement on the obligation and takes into account the currency in which the obligation is denominated. The issue credit rating is not a recommendation to purchase, sell, or hold a financial obligation, inasmuch as it does not comment as to market price or suitability for a particular investor.

(continued)

TABLE 7.3   (Continued)

Issue credit ratings are based on current information furnished by the obligors or obtained by Standard & Poor's from other sources it considers reliable. Standard & Poor's does not perform an audit in connection with any credit rating and may, on occasion, rely on unaudited financial information. Credit ratings may be changed, suspended, or withdrawn as a result of changes in, or unavailability of, such information, or based on other circumstances.

Issue credit ratings can be either long-term or short-term. Short-term ratings are generally assigned to those obligations considered short-term in the relevant market. In the U.S., for example, that means obligations with an original maturity of no more than 365 days - including commercial paper. Short-term ratings are also used to indicate the creditworthiness of an obligor with respect to put features on long-term obligations. The result is a dual rating, in which the short-term rating addresses the put feature, in addition to the usual long-term rating. Medium-term notes are assigned long-term ratings.

Long-Term Issue Credit Ratings
Issue credit ratings are based, in varying degrees, on the following considerations:

- Likelihood of payment-capacity and willingness of the obligor to meet its financial commitment on an obligation in accordance with the terms of the obligation;
- Nature of and provisions of the obligation;
- Protection afforded by, and relative position of, the obligation in the event of bankruptcy, reorganization, or other arrangement under the laws of bankruptcy and other laws affecting creditors' rights.

The issue rating definitions are expressed in terms of default risk. As such, they pertain to senior obligations of an entity. Junior obligations are typically rated lower than senior obligations, to reflect the lower priority in bankruptcy, as noted above. (Such differentiation applies when an entity has both senior and subordinated obligations, secured and unsecured obligations, or operating company and holding company obligations.) Accordingly, in the case of junior debt, the rating may not conform exactly with the category definition.

AAA
An obligation rated AAA has the highest rating assigned by Standard & Poor's. The obligor's capacity to meet its financial commitment on the obligation is extremely strong.

AA
An obligation rated AA differs from the highest-rated obligations only in small degree. The obligor's capacity to meet its financial commitment on the obligation is very strong.

A
An obligation rated A is somewhat more susceptible to the adverse effects of changes in circumstances and economic conditions than obligations in higher-rated categories. However, the obligor's capacity to meet its financial commitment on the obligation is still strong.

TABLE 7.3 (Continued)

BBB

An obligation rated BBB exhibits adequate protection parameters. However, adverse economic conditions or changing circumstances are more likely to lead to a weakened capacity of the obligor to meet its financial commitment on the obligation.

Obligations rated BB, B, CC, CC, and C are regarded as having significant speculative characteristics. BB indicates the least degree of speculation and C the highest. While such obligations will likely have some quality and protective characteristics, these may be outweighed by large uncertainties or major exposures to adverse conditions.

BB

An obligation rated BB is less vulnerable to nonpayment than other speculative issues. However, it faces major ongoing uncertainties or exposure to adverse business, financial, or economic conditions which could lead to the obligor's inadequate capacity to meet its financial commitment on the obligation.

B

An obligation rated B is more vulnerable to nonpayment than obligations rated BB, but the obligor currently has the capacity to meet its financial commitment on the obligation. Adverse business, financial, or economic conditions will likely impair the obligor's capacity or willingness to meet its financial commitment on the obligation.

CCC

An obligation rated CCC is currently vulnerable to nonpayment, and is dependent upon favorable business, financial, and economic conditions for the obligor to meet its financial commitment on the obligation. In the event of adverse business, financial, or economic conditions, the obligor is not likely to have the capacity to meet its financial commitment on the obligation.

CC

An obligation rated CC is currently highly vulnerable to nonpayment.

C

The C rating may be used to cover a situation where a bankruptcy petition has been filed or similar action has been taken, but payments on this obligation are being continued.

D

An obligation rated D is in payment default. The D rating category is used when payments on an obligation are not made on the date due even if the applicable grace period has not expired, unless Standard & Poor's believes that such payments will be made during such grace period. The 'D' rating also will be used upon the filing of a bankruptcy petition or the taking of a similar action if payments on an obligation are jeopardized.

Plus (+) or minus (-)

The ratings from AA to CCC may be modified by the addition of a plus or minus sign to show relative standing within the major rating categories.

(continued)

TABLE 7.3   (Continued)

p
The letter p indicates that the rating is provisional. A provisional rating assumes the successful completion of the project financed by the debt being rated and indicates that payment of debt service requirements is largely or entirely dependent upon the successful timely completion of the project.

L
The letter L indicates that the rating pertains to the principal amount of those bonds to the extent that the underlying deposit collateral is federally insured, and interest is adequately collateralized. In the case of certificates of deposit, the letter L indicates that the deposit, combined with other deposits being held in the same right and capacity, will be honored for prinicpal and pre-default interest up to federal insurance limits within 30 days after closing of the insured institution or, in the event that the deposit is assumed by a successor insured institution, upon maturity.

* Continuance of the ratings is contingent upon Standard & Poor's receipt of an executed copy of the escrow agreement or closing documentation confirming investments and cash flows.

r
The r is attached to highlight derivatives, hybrides and certain other obligations that Standard & Poor's believes may experience high volatitility or high variability i expected returns as a result of noncredit risks. Examples of such obligations are securities whose prinicpal or interest return is indexed to equities, commodities or other instruments. The absence of an 'r' symbol should not be taken as an indication that an obligation will exhibit no volatility or variability in total return.

NR
Not rated.

Short-Term Issue Credit Ratings

SP-1
Strong capacity to pay principal and interest. An issue determined to possess a very strong capacity to pay debt service is given a plus (+) designation.
SP-2
Satisfactory capacity to pay principal and interest, with some vulnerability to adverse financial and economic changes over the term of the notes.

SP-3
Speculative capacity to pay principal and interest.

Commercial Paper Ratings

A-1
This designation indicates that the degree of safety regarding timely payment is strong. Those issues determined to possess extremely strong safety characteristics are denoted with a plus sign (+) designation.

TABLE 7.3   (Continued)

A-2
Capacity for timely payment on issues with this designation is satisfactory. However, the relative degree of safety is not as high as for issues designated A-1.

A-3
Issues carrying this designation have an adequate capacity for timely payment. They are, however, more vulnerable to the adverse effects of changes in circumstances than obligations carrying the higher designations.

B
Issues rated B are regarded as having only speculative capacity for timely payment.

C
This rating is assigned to short-term debt obligations with a doubtful capacity for payment.

D
Debt rated D is in payment default. The D rating category is used when interest payments or principal payments are not made on the due date, even if the applicable grace period has not expired, unless Standard & Poor's believes such payments will be made during such grace period.

Reprinted with permission from Standard and Poor's
Source: Standard and Poor's

TABLE 7.4   Fitch Ratings Definitions

Fitch international credit ratings are applied to the spectrum of public finance, corporate and structured issues. The following ratings scale applies to foreign currency and local currency ratings.

Investment Grade

AAA
Highest credit quality. 'AAA' ratings denote the lowest expectation of credit risk. They are assigned only in case of exceptionally strong capacity for timely payment of financial commitments. This capacity is highly unlikely to be adversely affected by foreseeable events.

AA
Very high credit quality. 'AA' ratings denote a very low expectation of credit risk. They indicate very strong capacity for timely payment of financial commitments. This capacity is not significantly vulnerable to foreseeable events.

A
High credit quality. 'A' ratings denote a low expectation of credit risk. The capacity for timely payment of financial commitments is considered strong. This capacity may, nevertheless, be more vulnerable to changes in circumstances or in economic conditions than is the case for higher ratings.

(continued)

TABLE 7.4   (Continued)

BBB

Good credit quality. 'BBB' ratings indicate that there is currently a low expectation of credit risk. The capacity for timely payment of financial commitments is considered adequate, but adverse changes in circumstances and in economic conditions are more likely to impair this capacity. This is the lowest investment-grade category. Speculative Grade

BB

Speculative. 'BB' ratings indicate that there is a possibility of credit risk developing, particularly as the result of adverse economic change over time; however, business or financial alternatives may be available to allow financial commitments to be met. Securities rated in this category are not investment grade.

B

Highly speculative. 'B' ratings indicate that significant credit risk is present, but a limited margin of safety remains. Financial commitments are currently being met; however, capacity for continued payment is contingent upon a sustained, favourable business and economic environment.

CCC, CC, C

High default risk. Default is a real possibility. Capacity for meeting financial commitments is solely reliant upon sustained, favourable business or economic developments. A 'CC' rating indicates that default of some kind appears probable. 'C' ratings signal imminent default.

DDD, DD, D

Default. The ratings of obligations in this category are based on their prospects for achieving partial or full recovery in a reorganization or liquidation of the obligor. While expected recovery values are highly speculative and cannot be estimated with any precision, the following serve as general guidelines. 'DDD' obligations have the highest potential for recovery, around 90% - 100% of outstanding amounts and accrued interest. "DD' indicates potential recoveries in the range of 50% - 90% and 'D' the lowest recovery potential, i.e., below 50%.

Entities rated in this category have defaulted on some or all of their obligations. Entities rated 'DDD' have the highest prospect for resumption of performance or continued operation with or without a formal reorganization process. Entities rated 'DD' and 'D' are generally undergoing a formal reorganization or liquidation process; those rated 'DD' are likely to satisfy a higher portion of their outstanding obligations, while entities rated 'D' have a poor prospect of repaying all obligations.

International Short-Term Credit Ratings

The following ratings scale applies to foreign currency and local currency ratings. A Short-term rating has a time horizon of less than 12 months for most obligations, or up to three years for US public finance securities, and thus places greater emphasis on the liquidity necessary to meet financial commitments in a timely manner.

F1

Highest credit quality. Indicates the strongest capacity for timely payment of financial commitments; may have an added "+" to denote any exceptionally strong credit feature.

TABLE 7.4 (Continued)

F2

Good credit quality. A satisfactory capacity for timely payment of financial commitments, but the margin of safety is not as great as in the case of the higher ratings.

F3

Fair credit quality. The capacity for timely payment of financial commitments is adequate; however, near-term adverse changes could result in a reduction to non-investment grade.

B

Speculative. Minimal capacity for timely payment of financial commitments, plus vulnerability to near-term adverse changes in financial and economic conditions.

C

High default risk. Default is a real possibility. Capacity for meeting financial commitments is solely reliant upon a sustained, favourable business and economic environment.

D

Default. Denotes actual or imminent payment default.

"+" or "-" may be appended to a rating to denote relative status within major rating categories. Such suffixes are not added to the 'AAA' Long-term rating category, to categories below 'CCC', or to Short-term ratings other than 'F1'.

'NR' indicates that Fitch does not rate the issuer or issue in question.

'Withdrawn': A rating is withdrawn when Fitch deems the amount of information available to be inadequate for rating purposes, or when an obligation matures, is called, or refinanced.

Rating Watch: Ratings are placed on Rating Watch to notify investors that there is a reasonable probability of a rating change and the likely direction of such change. These are designated as "Positive", indicating a potential upgrade, "Negative", for a potential downgrade, or "Evolving", if ratings may be raised, lowered or maintained. Rating Watch is typically resolved over a relatively short period.

Reprinted with permission from Fitch.
Source: Fitch

THE RATING PROCESS

While each rating agency has its own style, the rating process is fairly similar among the three. For a new offerings, the issuer sends the rating agency all financing documents, financial projections, and audits and a preliminary official statement. Two or more analysts may be assigned to important issues, and one analyst usually assumes the role of lead analyst. The analysts review the documents and prepare questions for the issuer. These may be addressed in a formal meeting at the rating agency, on site with the issuer, or during a telephone call or teleconference. The issuer's experts, such as the financial advisor, the investment banker, and the feasibility consultant may be present at the meeting.

After all data have been gathered and all questions asked, the lead analyst presents the issue to a rating committee. The committee thoroughly reviews the issue and then assigns the rating. The news is given to the issuer before it is publicly disseminated to the market. Issuers who are dissatisfied with the result may offer new information or clarify existing points in their to attempt to raise the rating.

The rating agencies also perform surveillance on outstanding ratings. An issue may be upgraded or downgraded because of long-term trends such as improvement in the local economy or declining debt service coverage. Rating changes may also happen suddenly in the case of extraordinary events such as an unexpected bankruptcy filing. Each agency maintains its own public list of issues that are under review for possible upgrades or downgrades: Moody's Watchlist, Standard & Poor's CreditWatch, and Fitch Alert.

Representatives of issuers also visit the rating agencies on a regular basis to keep the analysts up to date on developments in their jurisdiction, even when there is no deal currently in the market. Such visits can be part of an issuer's long-term strategy for a rating upgrade. Issuers also meet with agencies to discuss new credit structures, to gauge how those structures would be rated, and to assess their impact on the rating of any existing credit.

Not all municipal issues are rated. Issuers and their financial advisors may decide that the issue is not of sufficient quality to receive an investment-grade rating or not large enough to warrant the expense of applying for a rating. They would prefer to market the issue as nonrated as opposed to non–investment grade. Investors then must be even more diligent in assessing the strengths and weaknesses of the credit. This may involve making a site visit to the facility and questioning the project's management. Table 7.5 shows the volume of long-term municipal issuance not rated by both Moody's and Standard & Poor's from 1989 to1999.

GENERAL OBLIGATION BONDS

Political Mood

One of the important lessons that the municipal market has learned is that changes in the political mood of taxpayers can prove as important for the value of the bonds as the issuer's financial ability to pay. Willingness to pay has always been an issue of municipal bond analysis, but the principle was brought home by several notable instances in the 1990s. The Orange County, California, bankruptcy is a good example. The county, which was wealthy by traditional economic measures, filed for bankruptcy in 1994. Many analysts

TABLE 7.5 Long-Term Municipal Issuance: Non-rated Issues by Moody's and Standard & Poor's, 1989–1999

Year	Nonrated Principal Amount ($ billions)	Nonrated Number of Issues	Percent Nonrated of Long-Term Municipal Debt	Long-Term Municipal Debt ($ billions)
1989	15.2	2,329	12.2	125.0
1990	16.5	2,397	12.9	128.0
1991	15.8	3,165	9.1	172.8
1992	16.3	3,151	6.9	234.7
1993	16.4	3,554	5.6	292.5
1994	17.4	3,274	10.5	165.1
1995	12.8	3,445	8.0	159.1
1996	13.4	3,368	7.2	185.0
1997	14.4	3,384	6.5	220.6
1998	19.9	4,011	7.0	286.2
1999	21.0	4,023	9.3	226.8

Source: Thomson Financial Securities Data, January 18, 2000.

did not question the county's ability to pay the debt but, rather, its willingness to do so. Another example was Brevard County, Florida, where a referendum was held to consider whether or not the county should decline to appropriate rentals on a new administrative center financed by certificates of participation. While that referendum was defeated, other COP issuers felt the repercussions over time. These episodes were preceded by events a decade earlier with the referenda in favor of property-tax cutbacks, most notably in California and Massachusetts. The limitation that these referenda placed on the tax-raising abilities of localities in these states did not affect their outstanding GO debt because any debt already approved was protected. However, lease-rental bonds, which are paid out of general tax revenues and are usually subject to appropriation, and tax-allocation bonds, which are backed by property tax revenues on increased property values, were affected.

In short, a community's actions can significantly alter the credit of municipal issues that are already outstanding. Although the contractual obligation of issuers to pay off GO debt has been strongly reinforced by the courts, such obligations cannot be met if the funds are not available.

Most revenue bonds are not affected by taxpayer limitations on property tax because these bonds are normally paid from other sources of income. But there is nothing to say that electric utility users, for example, will not stage their own revolt—as they did in the Pacific Northwest during the early 1980s. As a result, assessment of the prevailing political mood of states and localities can prove to be an important part of municipal bond analysis for revenue bonds as well as for GO bonds.

Analysts also rely on other information to assess a community's willingness to pay. The details of the state's constitution or of the statutes authorizing bonds and taxes provide an indication of how difficult it is for an issuer to raise more debt. Past action to meet budget deficits is another guide. Over the longer term, analysts prefer to see that the final maturity of bonds does not exceed the life of the project for which the proceeds are used. Future taxpayers may not be willing to pay for a public enterprise that is no longer in use or that is in need of substantial repair.

Debt Factors

Traditional GO bond analysis, where the bond is secured by the issuer's pledge of its full faith, credit, and taxing power, emphasized the debt burden of the community. The objective was, and still is, to determine whether the debt of the issuer is at a manageable level in proportion to property values, population, income, and similar data. Measures of debt burden have proved to be inadequate tools in themselves. However, coupled with other information, debt burden is still an important gauge of the ability of communities to pay their debts. Among the other measures most commonly used are a series of debt ratios that can be compared with benchmarks based on averages throughout the country. Trends in these ratios are watched closely for signals of improvement or deterioration. The analysis begins with the computation of the municipality's debt. A sample debt statement for the City of Austin, Texas, is shown in Table 7.6. This table is from the Comprehensive Annual Financial Report that can be viewed from the City's website.

The first step in the analysis is to compute the municipality's total bonded debt—that is, the total GO debt issued by the municipality, no matter what the purpose. Added to this is any unfunded debt, typically short-term notes. The sum of the two is usually called *total direct debt*. Austin had no outstanding short-term notes as of the date of this table. The next step is to deduct all debt that is not actually a potential burden on the municipality's tax resources. This deduction includes self-supporting enterprise debt, which is generally issued to support a project and is paid out of the revenues of the enterprise's operation. Austin has general obligation debt for several enterprise activities which are this type of deduction are not listed in Table 7.6. Analysts should also deduct any sinking funds or reserve funds established to pay off future debt. The buildup in such reserves reduces the burden to the issuer. *Tax anticipation notes* and *revenue anticipation notes* (TANs and RANs) are usually deducted. *Bond anticipation notes* (BANs), which are ultimately refinanced into long-term debt, are not deducted from total debt in the computation unless they have been issued for a self-supporting enterprise. Again, Austin did not have that type of debt.

TABLE 7.6 Computation of Direct and Overlapping Debt, City of Austin, Texas

Name of Governmental Unit	Total Debt Outstanding as of September 30, 1999 ($ thousands)	Percent Applicable to City of Austin[1]	Amount Applicable to City of Austin ($ thousands)
City of Austin	517,629	100.00	517,629
Greater than 10%			
Austin Community College	27,660	88.00	24,341
Austin Independent School District	535,569	90.00	482,012
Del Valle Independent School District	41,955	78.00	32,725
North Austin MUD #1	17,605	100.00	17,605
Northwest Austin MUD #1	8,000	100.00	8,000
Northwest Travis County RD #3	6,680	100.00	6,680
Travis County	351,189	75.00	263,392
Less than 10%			
Anderson Mill MUD #1	665	1.49	10
Eanes Independent School District	60,648	3.33	2,020
Leander Independent School District	171,267	0.67	1,147
Manor Independent School District	38,584	1.38	532
Pflugerville Independent School District	123,989	1.87	2,319
Round Rock Independent School District	284,831	4.79	13,643
Williamson County	44,005	2.62	1,153
Total direct and overlapping debt			1,373,208
Ratio of total direct and overlapping debt to assessed validation[2]		4.23	
Per capital overlapping debt[3]		$2,218.29	

[1]Source: Taxing jurisdictions.
[2]Based on assessed valuation of $32,458,349,755.
[3]Based on 1999 estimated population of 619,038.
Source: City of Austin, Texas. Comprehensive Annual Financial Report for year ended September 30, 1999.

When these items have been deducted from total direct debt, the figure remaining is called *net direct debt*. The debt of overlapping or underlying units of government is then added. Such units include but are not limited to school districts, park districts, and other entities that provide services in which the municipality shares, such as police or sanitation. Because the local population and economic wealth must also bear this debt, the pro rata or proportional part of the debt of these units is assigned to the governmental unit debt burden. The amount assigned is the proportion of the issuer's full market value to the full market valuation of the overlapping unit, including the issuer. Overlapping and underlying debt is totaled and added to the net direct debt to arrive at the final figure, which is called the *direct and overlapping net debt* or the *overall net debt*. The overall net debt for Austin was more than $1.37 billion as of September 30, 1999.

With overall net debt tallied, the analyst is ready to compute a variety of ratios. One popular measure is the ratio of overall debt to assessed valuation. (This ratio in Austin was 4.23 percent.) Analysts prefer to use full market value of property rather than assessed valuation. The latter is generally a percentage of the full value of the property as set by the municipality or state. Because these percentages vary widely, a comparison based on the assessed valuations of different municipalities is difficult to make. By using full valuation, the analyst does not have to worry about variations in state formulas. In Austin's case, assessed valuation and full valuation were the same. Many municipalities, however, have diversified their tax bases beyond the property tax (collecting sales and income taxes, for example), making debt to valuation a less important measure than it once was. Other debt ratios that incorporate fixed costs such as leases and pensions as a percentage of the operating funds can be more relevant than the ratio of overall debt to full valuation.

One commonly used ratio in credit analysis of local issuers is overall net debt to population, or debt per capita. Ratios can be calculated separately for cities, counties, and school districts according to the population of the governmental units. Ratios can also be calculated on such criteria as specific geographic area and sector. Comparison of per capita debt to per capita personal income is another useful measure in assessing the relative wealth levels of the issuer and its ability to repay the debt.

Debt per capita is also an important tool in analyzing the creditworthiness of the 50 states. Debt for this calculation generally includes all direct GO debt and nonvoted obligations such as appropriation-backed debt, lease-rentals, and COPs. Appropriation debt, which is subject to annual legislative action, is generally considered to be of lesser credit quality than direct GO debt.

Finally, comparing annual debt service to tax and other revenues provides another measure of an issuer's ability to pay. It is a common tool for analyzing the credit of states, where the property tax is not the major source of revenue. Further, this ratio has become a much more common tool in looking at those municipalities that have developed a broader mix of nonproperty tax revenues.

The moral obligation bonds issued by states present a special situation for analysts. While the full backing of the state is implied for these bonds, there is no legal obligation for the state to pay debt service. Thus, there is always some doubt as to how readily states will rescue troubled moral obligation issues. Analysts concentrate, therefore, on the degree to which these bonds are self-supporting.

It has become common for municipalities to issue limited-tax bonds. In these bonds, the tax that is pledged to the repayment of the bonds is limited with respect to either the rate or amount of the levy. It has also become more common for states and local governmental units to issue *appropriation* and *lease-rental* bonds and COPs. Generally, the debt analysis of these issues is the same as that for the full general obligation. The analyst looks at the mechanisms that are in place to assure that sufficient funds are budgeted and appropriated to pay debt service. The analyst also assesses how critical or essential the project is to the government in order to assess the likelihood of default. The legal documents involved in these financings are described in Chapter 3.

The best sources of financial information are the municipality's or unit's official statement and annual report. Much of this information is now available on the issuer's own websites or in NRMSIRS if the issuer has sold long-term debt after June 1995 (the effective date of secondary market disclosure amendments). Moody's, Standard & Poor's, and Fitch provide both print and electronic services that summarize much of the most important credit data for thousands of issues, some of which are available to the public on a nonsubscriber basis.

Economic Analysis

To many analysts, the current and prospective condition of the local economy is the single most important factor in determining a state or municipality's creditworthiness. Communities at different stages of growth may require more or less debt. A young, booming city often needs to issue more bonds than a mature or deteriorating city. However, an older community that has elected to keep up with capital improvements will probably need to embark on major borrowing to keep its economy healthy—or risk economic decline. A high per capita total debt or rising trends in total debt might be acceptable to investors in the first case and present a danger in the second.

Important indications of a community's economic strength include income levels, population trends and prospects, employment statistics, and industry or employer composition. Per capita income and its rate of growth are among the first measures analysts examine. Some analysts also look at income per household because per capita data can often be misleading. It may be distorted by large student or prison populations, for example.

Analysts caution against relying too heavily on unemployment numbers to measure the strength of employment. Patterns of unemployment can be disguised by a number of factors, including population shifts and changes in the composition of the labor force. Labor force growth is a more accurate measure.

A comparison of a state or local population's income levels and of its labor force growth with national averages can provide analysts with a measure of the community's economic standing. Moreover, comparing a state or municipality with its neighbors along similar lines can help identify problems that might otherwise go unnoticed.

Other readily available data that are good indicators of economic health include the valuation of property per capita, the age and condition of the local housing stock, and the community's rent levels. Population can also be a key indicator. A growing population is usually a sign of strength, although unusually rapid growth could lead to pressures to immediately provide infrastructure and service. A declining population is generally associated with deteriorating cities and regions. Occasionally, however, a city may lose population to its suburbs but retain its economic strength as a place of employment. This is especially relevant if the city has maintained its infrastructure in reasonably good shape.

Once the overall direction of the local economy has been established, scrutiny of the specific industries and companies that dominate the community's employment is important. The two principal questions are whether the main industries are healthy and growing and whether the region is economically diversified so that it does not depend too heavily on any one industry or on one sector, such as manufacturing. Expansion plans for major companies can be important, providing one way of assessing the likelihood of growth in employment. A mix of new, growing companies and mature, steady companies is usually most desirable.

Diversity not only protects a community from deterioration should a major employer leave town or suffer a business setback, it can also help to shield the municipality from a severe downturn during economic recessions. A good yardstick for a municipality's strength is how well it did during the last recession. Did employment recover in line with the rest of the economy? Did personal income hold up? Did the municipality run an operating deficit?

Financial Factors

Analysis of a locality's economic structure must be translated into how that structure affects its tax base. A strong economic structure will normally mean plenty of taxing potential, but there are several factors that should be analyzed further. Again, diversity is key. A single corporation may even be more dominant in terms of the proportion of taxes paid in the region than in the employment it provides.

Major sources of revenues besides the property tax are also welcome. How significant are revenues from sales taxes, income tax, fees, and concessions? Because most states do not levy property taxes, a careful analysis of their various sources of income is important. A well-structured tax system is one that encompasses a wide range of economic activity. For example, if a state's tax structure depends heavily on only one or two industries, budget constraints may occur when that industry enters a downturn.

Most analysts regard too much reliance on intergovernmental aid as a danger. For one thing, the flow of these funds is usually out of the control of the municipality (except in the case of school districts, where the state may supplement local property taxes). For another, the amount of aid can be changed not only by legislative actions but administrative decisions, all of which are subject to political vagaries.

Once the sources of revenue have been reviewed, analysts can determine what potential there is for raising or lowering tax rates. Generally, if taxes are already high, the potential for increases is less likely. The percentage of taxes collected in some state and local governments can run dangerously low, even when other factors look good. A poor collection rate, especially compared to rates in adjoining regions, could reflect either economic shifts or simply an inefficient government. A temporary drop in property taxes may sometimes occur as a result of property revaluation.

The emphasis on long-term factors in determining municipal financial health is an important credit consideration. The current financial status of the municipalities and their methods of reporting is also an area that is emphasized in credit analysis.

Deficits in any of the various funds municipalities use to account for their finances are red flags that require more investigation. The cause of any deficit, and whether the factors are temporary and easily remedied or chronic and longer term, must be understood. An occasional operating deficit is not necessarily a problem. A dip in the economy, a change in intergovernmental aid, or a local corporate bankruptcy could tilt a municipality's main operating fund into temporary deficit. A large or ongoing structural deficit, however, must be investigated further.

Analysts look carefully at the volume of short-term financing because it may indicate a weakening financial position. Many state and local governments have adopted active short-term financing programs to provide funds when the timing of revenues and expenditures does not match. Annual increases in the magnitude of such cash management financing may indicate that a government is finding it difficult to control expenditures against revenues. The volume of short-term notes or commercial paper can reach dangerously high levels, as in the case of New York City in the 1970s and of California in the early 1990s.

An operating deficit or surplus must be analyzed in light of a municipality's past operations. The surplus or deficit in the final balance is the sum of past surpluses and deficits. A surplus in that figure may more than compensate for an operating deficit in any given year. Balance sheets must also be examined. A healthy level of working capital and highly liquid current assets are beneficial. Reserves for items such as uncollected taxes and accounts payable should be adequate.

Close analysis of the budget is another valuable tool. How many years into the future is a budget prepared? Has the municipality stayed within its budget in the past? If not, what specific items account for the cost overruns or excesses? What measures can be used to balance the budget?

Management Factors

Analysts try to assess the general capability and responsibility of a state or local government's fiscal officers. Increasingly, analysts have come to examine how well a city or state is managed, how carefully programs are documented, and how diligently and imaginatively the future programs of the municipality are planned. Political structure can be particularly important. For example, a strong mayoral system or a council-manager form will often be able to control finances better than a weak mayor system. Analysts are placing increasing weight on such factors, however subjective they may be. In addition, better-managed governments are developing performance objectives that are both measurable and reported to their constituencies. It is beneficial to examine any such reports.

The state or municipality's investment and debt policies should be evaluated. Does the issuer have a written investment policy for its various (non-bond) funds, including the general fund and the pension funds? Does the issuer employ financial products, and if so, is this program managed prudently? Does the issuer have a debt policy that describes how much debt can be issued, and in what manner? All of these factors are used in assessing management strength.

There is also interest in the pension fund liabilities of municipalities. Analysts generally want to know how pension obligations will affect expenditures over both the short and the long term. Does the municipality have a defined benefit plan or a defined contribution plan? If there are heavy unfunded liabilities, will the state or local government be obliged to increase annual retirement expenses substantially? If pension liabilities are actuarially funded, are actuarial assumptions about inflation and investment returns on the funds realistic, or is funding set too high or too low? If the pension system is overfunded, who is entitled to the surplus?

The analyst examines the issuer's audit carefully. The Governmental Accounting Standards Board (GASB), the Government Finance Officers Association (GFOA), and rating agencies recommend that an independent audit of financial statements be undertaken annually. To the analyst, the independent audit helps ensure that the financial data being presented are accurate and consistent with prior financial statements. Because the audit is undertaken in accordance with the GASB's generally accepted accounting standards, the uniformity and consistency of accounting methods can be relied on. Municipal audits that are supervised by state officials (most states require some kind of audit) or are made to ensure compliance with a government program will not necessarily address the same areas as those covered in an audit conducted by an independent accountant using GASB principles.

Litigation that is material to the issuer's credit is examined to determine current and potential funding needs and expenditures. Some examples of material litigation include challenges to the basic systems of raising revenue, employment issues, and the general structure of the government. The analyst uses the issuer's official statement, annual financial statements, and the general news media to research the issuer's litigation. It is quite serious if material litigation is not disclosed to the market; government officials are subject to the SEC antifraud provisions.

REVENUE BONDS

Revenue bond analysis differs in many ways from the analysis of GO bonds. Although the analyst applies the basics—examining the debt, along with the economic, financial, and management/legal structure of the issuer—there are differing emphases in revenue bond analysis than are used for general obligation bonds. An economic analysis of the demand for services, the level of costs, operating efficiency, and actual and potential competition is imperative to revenue bond analysis. The economic health of the service area is an important and complicated factor.

The Bond Resolution or Indenture

Most revenue bonds are traditionally protected by a number of legal and financial agreements that can often be as important to bondholders as the project itself. The first step in any analysis is close examination of the provisions of the bond resolution. The provisions are summarized in the issuer's official statement, but attention is paid to the full text of all legal documents. It is important to keep in mind that final documents may differ in material respects from preliminary information in connection with the offering of new debt.

Revenue lien. From the beginning, however, the analyst determines what security there is for the bonds. Traditionally, revenue bonds are secured by a first lien on net revenues. This means that debt service is paid out of the *net revenues,* the funds that remain after the normal operating costs have been paid. A *gross lien bond,* on the other hand, is one where debt service is paid directly from the gross revenues before the payment of operating expenses. Most analysts do not give significantly higher ratings to gross lien bonds because it is healthier for the enterprise to operate effectively, to run a surplus, in order to survive in the long term. Some contract obligations have priority over even first-lien bonds; for example, a power supply contract for a public utility is usually treated as an operating expense and paid before debt service on the contracted bond. First-lien bonds are also called senior-lien bonds. Bonds that enjoy the same lien are said to be on *parity* with each other.

Subordinate-lien bonds, which are also called junior-lien bonds or second- or third-lien bonds, may be issued for any number of reasons. The senior-lien bonds may have been issued under a closed-end resolution (see following), meaning that any new bonds must have a subordinate position. Another reason to issue junior-lien bonds is that, over time, the credit quality of the senior-lien bonds may have risen. While bonds with second or third liens are generally rated significantly lower than those with first liens, the issuer may determine that the senior-lien credit is so strong that a well-structured junior-lien bond will be rated relatively close to senior bond.

Mortgage pledge. In addition to a claim on revenues, some bonds are also secured by a mortgage pledge on the facilities that are being financed. This means that in the event of default, the bond trustee can seize the property for the benefit of the bondholders. With bonds that have a mortgage pledge, usually there is also some kind of revenue pledge. In recent years, fewer bonds have contained mortgage pledges, primarily because municipal facilities have somewhat limited use outside of the purposes for which they were built.

General obligation. Revenue bonds can also be backed by a GO pledge of the issuer. This means that the issuer does not dedicate specific revenue to the repayment of the bonds but, rather, pledges its general credit, similar to the way a municipality pledges its general obligation. The essential difference is that the independent agencies that issue the revenue bonds do not have the ability to raise taxes that are unlimited as to rate or amount. It is common for colleges and universities to issue bonds backed by their general credit, especially if the university or college has a large endowment. It has also become increasingly common for highly rated health care issuers and strong state housing agencies to issue bonds with a GO pledge.

Flow of Funds

The flow of funds described in the bond resolution sets forth the order in which funds generated by the enterprise will be allocated to various purposes. In gen-

FIGURE 7.1 Typical Revenue Bond Flow of Funds

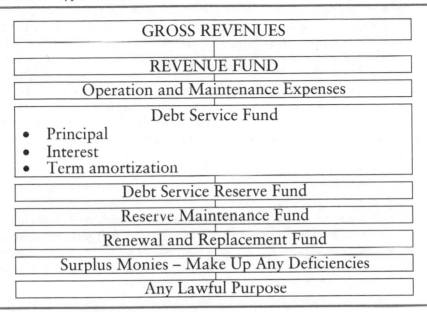

GROSS REVENUES

REVENUE FUND

Operation and Maintenance Expenses

Debt Service Fund
- Principal
- Interest
- Term amortization

Debt Service Reserve Fund

Reserve Maintenance Fund

Renewal and Replacement Fund

Surplus Monies – Make Up Any Deficiencies

Any Lawful Purpose

Source: The Bond Market Association.

eral, funds are used to pay for operations and debt service and to establish reserves. Different kinds of bonds require different flows of funds. But generally, all funds are first recorded in the revenue fund. The flow of funds described in Figure 7.1 is typical of many revenue bonds. When an issuer has several series of bonds, there may be separate debt service funds established for each series. This may happen even if all bond series are on parity with each other.

Operations and maintenance expenses. The money necessary to meet the ongoing budgeted expenses of the enterprise is placed in the enterprise's operations and maintenance fund. Normally, one-twelfth of an enterprise's annual budget is shifted from the revenue fund to the operations and maintenance fund each month. From there, expenditures are made to meet expenses. Occasionally, enough money is placed in the fund both to cover budgeted expenses and provide a reserve.

Debt-service fund. Money is set aside monthly that will equal, over the course of a year, the amount necessary to meet annual debt service. This fund frequently maintains separate accounts for principal and interest. In some resolutions, cash is transferred to the debt-service fund immediately before the semiannual coupon is to be paid. Sometimes, separate bond-redemption funds or accounts are set up. There may also be a note-repayment fund or account and a sinking fund account.

Debt-service reserve fund. This fund can be set up initially out of bond proceeds or be built up over time. If the latter, funds are apportioned to the debt-service reserve fund after annual debt-service payment is ensured. Reserve funds are tapped only if the debt-service fund itself is insufficient to meet annual payments. The reserve fund is usually set at an amount equal to six months or one year's debt service, with the smaller reserve fund used by stronger credits. Debt service can be defined as the maximum annual payment, the average annual payment, or some other negotiated amount. Many high-quality issuers are able to forego them, and other issuers may sometimes use a surety bond or other substitute for the reserve fund instead of employing bond proceeds.

Reserve maintenance fund. Allocations are made to this fund to meet unanticipated maintenance expenses, usually at the recommendation of the consultants in charge.

Renewal and replacement fund. The fund is established to replace equipment and make repairs over the life of an enterprise. A regular payment is made into this fund according to the enterprise's budget for such replacements. When more construction is planned, a separate construction fund is normally set up to pay for expansion or new projects.

Surplus monies. Most bond resolutions carefully itemize where the balance of revenues will be directed should they exceed what is required for all funds. The monies are sometimes used to redeem bonds or reduce tax payments. Many municipalities take surplus funds from revenue enterprises for use in their own general fund. The resolution also specifies what kinds of securities can be bought with the excess funds.

Covenants

A well-designed flow of funds and ample reserves are not the only assurances investors seek. In the case of user-charge bonds, it is important to have a rate covenant. By such a covenant, the issuer pledges that rates will be set high enough to meet operation and maintenance expenses, renewal and replacement expenses, and debt service. Another form of rate covenant requires that rates be set so as to provide a safety margin of revenues above debt service, after operation and maintenance expenses are met. Rate covenants vary greatly among different types of bonds. Bonds issued for stable and monopolistic enterprises, such as water systems, will have a lower rate covenant than bonds issued for less stable enterprises that face competition, such as health care institutions. There has been a general trend in most revenue bond sectors toward loosening, or lowering the margin, in the rate covenant.

Additional covenants might include a provision for insuring the project, requirements for a periodic review by a consulting engineer, or guarantees that no free services will be offered to municipalities or favored customers and that separate books will be kept to record the accounts of the project. Other covenants contain provisions for independent audits and prohibitions against the sale of the project or of its facilities before the bonds are paid off. In some cases, a covenant stipulates the retention of an outside expert for periodic reviews of the enterprise's operations or maintenance.

Additional bonds. Once the claim on revenues has been established, a very important covenant written into most revenue bond resolutions involves provisions for issuance of additional bonds. If the issuer retains the right to offer at a later time bonds that have an equal or prior claim on revenues, the bondholder may be placed in a riskier position. Most issuers will provide one of two types of protective bond clauses. The less common one stipulates that any additional bonds will be junior and subordinate to the current bonds except for bonds that may be necessary for the completion of the enterprise. This is called a closed-end provision; the drawback is that because the new bonds are subordinated they may be more difficult to market.

An open-end provision allows for bonds of equivalent lien on earnings to be issued, subject to certain requirements. Generally, the limitation is that the earnings coverage of debt service, including that for the new bonds, may not fall below a set minimum—for example, 125 percent. Earnings of the enterprise can be defined in several ways to meet this test. Some define the earnings as the most recent fiscal year's earnings or the average of earnings over the preceding 24 months. The latter is the most conservative of the methods commonly used. Another method is to base the test on future estimates of earnings, which usually requires reports by consultants with specific industry experience. Some methods permit adjustment of test period revenues to reflect planned rate increases or the anticipated expansion of the customer base.

Economic Analysis

Most revenue bonds are supported by enterprises that are subject to the same analysis as other business ventures. Of course, the factors affecting various kinds of revenue enterprises differ markedly from enterprise to enterprise. Two key factors are whether or not the enterprise enjoys a monopoly and how essential the service is that's provided. The issuer generally provides a great amount of data to investors through preliminary official statements, feasibility and other engineering studies, and annual reports.

Financial and legal considerations are often paramount in the analysis of this kind of debt. However, the effective demand for the service—which includes the ability of customers to pay for it—is a key consideration. Some of the most important factors affecting the credit of different kinds of revenue bonds are outlined below.

Utilities. *Electric utility bonds.* The strength of an area's economy and the cost of the service are key factors in determining that area's effective demand for electricity. With the recent deregulation of investor-owned electric utilities, and with particular reference to the U.S. Energy Policy Act of 1992, an even greater emphasis is placed on comparing the costs of the electric utility and its competitors. Analysts prefer to see that sources of power generation are diversified among different types of fuels. The power supply itself must be adequate to support the area's projected growth, and any future capital outlays should be considered. However, underutilization of generation facilities can become a burden.

Water and sewer system bonds. Water bonds usually relate to the supply of water for a community. This is an issue of importance both to established cities, where often the water supply system has to be either enlarged or renovated, and to new cities or communities, where water supply may have to be created. Sewer system bonds relate largely to the disposal of the wastewater. Sewer bonds often finance wastewater treatment plants that treat the sewage prior to its disposal into a river, lake, or ocean. Treatment plants have to meet federal environmental standards, and this may require special and expensive technologies. The economic base of the area being serviced and the potential for growth are factors important in determining demand for either water supply or wastewater disposal. Reduced direct federal financial support, especially in wastewater treatment, spurred the development of state revolving funds for wastewater treatment.

Solid waste bonds. Solid waste bonds finance the disposal of nonsewage waste generated by industrial, commercial, and residential usage. The economic analysis of solid waste bonds focuses on the likelihood that the service area will generate enough solid waste to make the project feasible. Price competitions among solid waste facilities in neighboring areas, flow control, and alternative methods of waste disposal, such as landfill, are examined. Pledged revenues may include tipping fees. If the facility is a waste-to-energy plant, where electric power is generated as a by-product of burning the trash, the market for that power is reviewed. Municipal guarantees, if any, are examined in light of the strength of the guarantee and the municipality's creditworthiness. Questions about the technology and the project operator, who is generally from the private sector, focus on experience and financial stability.

Health care, Higher Education, and Other Not-for-Profits. *Health care bonds.* Health care bonds are among the most complex of issues. The location, level, and quality of services offered are important. Competition among health care institutions has intensified tremendously over the past decade. How the institution has responded to a changed health care environment, where the low-cost provider has an important advantage under managed care, is a major part of the analysis. Most hospitals are affiliated with other hospitals, other health care institutions, or medical schools either through formal systems or through informal arrangements. Those affiliations may be within the same service area, in neighboring areas, or even in other states. Stand-alone facilities are less common.

In addition to traditional bonds issued for hospital construction, bonds are issued for facilities that provide a continuum of care for patients, including assisted living, continuing care, and nursing home facilities. Not-for-profit physician practices and health maintenance organizations have issued tax-exempt bonds for capital projects. For all health care bonds, the level of services, competition, and cost structure are the key economic factors. Both inpatient admissions and outpatient visits and procedures are measured.

College and university bonds. Private and public colleges have issued a significant amount of debt, either directly or through state-established finance authorities. The bonds are usually direct financial obligations of the institution itself and may be either a GO of the institution or a revenue bond for housing or a stadium. Because state-supported institutions receive a substantial part of their budget from appropriations and other state resources, the extent of state's commitment is a key analytical factor. Private institutions that successfully manage their endowments and their education programs are highly regarded in the bond market. Enrollment trends, diversity of curriculum, the demand for admission as evidenced by the institution's application pool, and the strength of an institution's asset base provide the major clues to its financial health and prospects. Private primary and secondary institutions are analyzed in a similar way.

Bonds for other not-for-profits. Not-for-profit issuers, including cultural institutions, research institutes, philanthropic foundations, membership groups, and service providers can also issue bonds. The economic analysis for these issuers focuses on market position and competition. Is there a positive trend in donations to the institution? Does a museum, say, rely solely on large exhibits to generate revenue, or is there a steady stream of revenues? What other organizations, both local and national, does the institution compete with for philanthropic or research dollars?

Student-loan bonds. Education loans are typically issued through a separately organized entity to meet students' needs for aid in covering tuition costs. Most of these student loan bonds are structured, in that they are based on assumptions regarding prepayments, delinquencies, investment income, insurance coverage, and guarantees.

Housing Bonds. There are essentially two types of housing revenue bonds: multifamily and single-family.

Multifamily housing revenue bonds. These bonds finance rental housing developments for low- and moderate-income families and the elderly. Multifamily bonds are usually secured by the principal and interest payments on a mortgage. These payments consist of the aggregate of monthly rental payments. Earlier multifamily issues were typically subsidized and/or insured under federal housing programs. As the federal government has reduced its involvement in housing programs, multifamily issues have come to use market-based rental units to subsidize a dedicated portion of units at below-market rents for defined beneficiaries. Credit enhancements such as bond insurance, surety bonds, collateralized mortgage pass-through certificates, and letters of credit are employed. Key analytical variables related to multifamily bonds include the occupancy rate and the ability of the occupants to pay. Proper construction of the housing as well as the quality of ongoing management are also important; maintenance of reserves, for example, should be adequate. Legal documents relating to redemption provisions and credit enhancement must be studied. Some highly rated state housing authorities have issued general obligation bonds meaning that all resources of the authority are pledged to the repayment of the bonds. These are not, however, general obligations of the state.

Single-family housing revenue bonds. These bonds provide mortgages at below-market rate to qualified individual borrowers financing one- to four-family owner-occupied dwellings. Security for these bond issues is derived from individual monthly mortgage payments generated by a portfolio of mortgages. Recent levels of delinquencies, foreclosures, and prepayments are key considerations in analyzing these bonds. The level of reserves, type of mortgage insurance coverage, and investment policies of an issuer help to define credit quality. The demand for mortgages in the area served is also an important point to be assessed, as a lack of demand can mean that a portion of the bond issue will have to be called, resulting in a lower coverage of program costs.

Transportation. *Toll-road bonds.* Once potential traffic for a highway is estimated, the major question for the success of this kind of enterprise concerns the elasticity of demand. In other words, if toll rates increase, would the amount of traffic decrease substantially? A mix of different types of users, especially if this includes heavy usage by commercial vehicles, helps ensure stable demand levels, but competition from other roadways, particularly those without tolls, needs to be assessed. Bond resolutions may contain provisions calling for limitations on the construction of potentially competitive projects by the same issuer. For new toll roads, the timely completion of the construction on budget is important to the issuer's ability to meet traffic and revenue projections. Economic trends in the area being serviced need to be analyzed, as do the price and availability of fuel. Bridge and tunnel authority bonds are often examined using these same criteria.

Transit revenue bonds. Both new and older public transportation systems have developed revenue bond programs to build, expand, or renovate their systems. As no public transit system in the United States is able to support itself entirely from fares, other financial resources have had to be provided. These additional funds include ongoing federal and state capital and operating subsidies and taxes such as a sales or gasoline tax. Debt financing may take the form of a gross revenue pledge from fares, as in the case of the special sales tax pledge. Key factors in such cases are the security offered, the need and demand for the service, the importance of the service to the local economy, the outlook for nonfare revenues, and management factors, particularly labor relations.

Airport bonds. Generally, a feasibility study is a must in analyzing the prospects for an airport. The potential traffic through the airport is the main consideration. Will the airport's traffic be generated primarily by residents of the metropolitan area around the airport, or will the airport be a hub, where passengers fly in to make connections with flights to other destinations? The economics of these two kinds of airports are significantly different. Another question is, are there competing airports in the same region? Some airport revenue bonds (special facilities bonds) are secured directly by leases with participating airlines and should be analyzed much like industrial revenue bonds. More often, revenues are derived from contracts with many airlines, based on usage, and from other airport services such as car rental and parking facilities. The economy of the service area and pricing policies of the airlines that fly to and from the airport are also factors.

Industrial Revenue and Pollution Control Bonds. These bonds are usually analyzed as unsecured corporate debt even though they may be backed by leases of highly rated corporations. Often, however, the bonds are guaranteed by a corporate subsidiary and not by the parent company. In the more secure issues, the investor has a first mortgage on the property involved.

Structured Bonds. Asset-backed municipal bonds are a relatively new development. They are secured by pools of municipal assets, which can be leases, tax receivables, or other receivables. The underlying strength of the pooled assets is looked at, as well as the legal and financial structure of the issue, including isolating the bonds from financial troubles of the governmental issuer.

Financial Factors

Financial ratio analysis is a useful way to assess the strength of a revenue project. The analyst is interested not only in a single year's results but also in the year-to-year trend of results. The analyst looks at the ratios in both income statement and balance sheet. The most frequently used measure of an enterprise's well-being is the *coverage ratio*—the ratio of revenues (less operation and maintenance expenses but before provision for depreciation) to debt service—which uses figures from the income statement projecting future debt service coverage is important. This coverage may be adequate when bonds are issued, but if additional bonds are planned or if revenues decline, the ratio could drop sharply. Analysis of the efficiency of current facilities and of the potential need for new facilities plays a role here.

In addition to coverage, the analyst looks at trends in operating ratios. For example, the trend of days in accounts receivable would show how efficient the issuer is in collecting money. Balance sheet ratios, such as days cash on hand, show how liquid the issuer is and how much financial cushion exists.

The rating agencies annually publish financial ratios for revenue bonds. These ratios are very helpful in comparing an issuer against its peer group or against a group that is rated higher or lower. Analysts can also create their own universe of ratios from issuers that they have examined and from other data sources to which they have access.

Electronic delivery of municipal credit information is based on documents (both official statements and continuing-disclosure documents) submitted by the issuer and on other available third-party information. Analysts use the data to evaluate the credit quality and to compare it to other credits in its sector, region or rating category or however the user sees fit. Some credit systems embed the issuer's financial statements and official statements directly into the software to maximize the amount of information available and to enhance the user's flexibility.

OTHER FACTORS AFFECTING CREDIT

In assessing how sound certain securities are, analysts must also take into account two final factors: the letters of credit backing an issue and any bond insurance policies, which perform much the same function. States also have enhancement programs for specific public purposes. These programs tend to be linked to the credit of the state.

Letters of Credit and Lines of Credit

Letters of credit (LOCs) are used to increase market access for an issuer that may have difficulty in selling its bonds due to a perceived weakness in its ability to meet its obligations. A letter of credit is generally issued by a commercial bank and represents a contract between the issuing bank and the bond trustee. Under the letter, the bank irrevocably agrees to pay to the trustee on demand monies in an amount necessary to cover all payments due on the bonds. As with all contracts, the specific terms are negotiated and can vary with each bond sale. Within the context of the municipal market, however, terms and conditions tend to be standardized, especially as far as the investor is concerned.

Letters of credit are used for two purposes: to enhance credit and to enhance liquidity. To enhance credit, the bank issuing the LOC irrevocably pledges to provide funds to meet debt service payments in the event that the bond issuer cannot do so. The terms of the LOC empower the bond trustee to draw on the letter of credit directly if the bond issuer fails to make deposits sufficient to provide for timely payment of interest or principal or both. Thus, the letter of credit is used to protect investors from a default.

The expanded use of tender or put option bonds spawned the second use of the LOC: to increase liquidity. Under the terms of this kind of contract, the bank issuing the LOC agrees to advance any funds necessary to purchase bonds tendered by investors. The bank, in effect, provides for extraordinary demands for cash if a substantial number of bonds are tendered.

An LOC is normally issued for up to 10 years, while the bonds may have a maturity of 20 to 30 years. It is necessary, therefore, that the letter be renewed periodically or a substitute obtained. The bond indenture typically provides that if the letter of credit is not renewed or if a suitable substitute cannot be found, the bonds must be redeemed before the expiration of the letter of credit.

Hence, the question of timely payment, while reduced, continues to exist. At the time of the bonds' issuance, a substitution of credit took place— the bank's for the issuer's. Attention must thus be paid to the creditworthiness of the bank itself, since a rating change for the bank's obligations will affect all financings supported by the bank. It is important, therefore, that the bank issuing the LOC has a sound financial history and a diverse loan portfolio and that it has adequate assets.

Lines of credit are used mainly to provide liquidity for commercial paper and other short-term programs. The critical difference between the letter of credit and the line of credit is that in a line there are conditions under which the provider would not have advance funds under a draw. These conditions can include default on other debt of the borrower, bankruptcy of the borrower, or a rating change, to name only a few. The analyst must look at each individual line of credit to assess the degree of credit enhancement it provides.

Bond Insurance Policies

A municipal bond insurance policy is a noncancellable guarantee designed to protect the bondholder from nonpayment on the part of the issuer. In the event that an issuer fails to meet a scheduled principal or interest payment, the insurer, acting as a third-party guarantor, will make service payment directly to the paying agent or trustee. The insurer has received an up-front premium for the guarantee, the amount of which is determined primarily by the perceived risk associated with the financing. Factors included here include the analyst's credit assessment, current market conditions, and other factors such as competition among the bond insurers for the business.

Analysts for bond insurers require much of the same information from issuers as do analysts for investors in order to approve an issuer's application for credit enhancement on a new issue. In addition to analyzing the credit, bond insurers may propose and negotiate specific covenants they may want added or changed in the indenture. The insurers want to strengthen the credit because they will be taking the on-credit risk for the lifetime of the bond. Not all insured issues have underlying ratings although many do.

In the event of a default, either technical or otherwise, the bond insurer generally works closely with the issuer to solve the problems that caused the default. Often, insurers will require that issuers bring in financial consultants and other experts to offer suggestions on how to improve operations.

The bond insurer's highest ratings are their most important asset to investors and issuers. Their credit quality is monitored by the rating agencies to detect declines, weaknesses, or improvements.

Still, it is important to remember that the issuer remains the first source of payment of principal and interest. Hence, the underlying credit characteristics of the issuer remain very important.

States also have enhancement programs for specific public purposes. These programs tend to be linked to the credit of the state. A state may withhold state aid payments for education, for example, to enhance the value of a school district's bonds. A state may also use its moral obligation to enhance its authorities' or localities' debt.

CHAPTER 8

Understanding Interest Rates

INTRODUCTION

To the professional municipal underwriter, trader, salesperson, or investor, fluctuations in the price of securities seem a constant, everyday affair. However, underlying the short-term shifts in securities prices and interest rates are less transitory factors that have a profound effect on long-term trends in interest rates. The basic factors that determine interest rates in general also determine the level of municipal rates; municipal bond yields tend to rise and fall in accordance with rates on other fixed-income securities, at least over time. A comparison of the 30-year Bond Buyer Revenue Bond Index with the rates on 30-year U.S. Treasury bonds clearly demonstrates the close relationship between markets for these securities (see Table 8.1).

Over shorter periods of time, however, municipal interest rates can move independent of general market rates. The supply of new issues and the cyclical buying habits of the principal investors particularly affect municipal rates. The tax exemption, as discussed in Chapter 6, limits the market to those who can best take advantage of it: households and household proxies, property and casualty insurance companies, and to a greater extent in the past, commercial banks.

Municipal rates are also usually lower than rates on other securities of equivalent maturity and risk because of the tax exemption. Municipal rates fluctuate more widely over time than taxable rates.

DETERMINANTS OF THE OVERALL LEVEL OF INTEREST RATES

The Business Cycle

One well-established observation of most economists is that as economic activity picks up, borrowing demand increases and interest rates rise. Financial institutions and capital markets compete with each other for a limited supply of funds. Consequently, banks raise both the rates they are willing to pay to lenders and the interest rates they demand from borrowers. To attract more capital to the money and bond markets, rates then have to rise further.

TABLE 8.1   Average Annual Yields, 1979–1999

Year	The Bond Buyer Revenue Bond Index (%)	U.S. Treasury Thirty-Year Bond (%)
1979	7.9	9.28
1980	9.44	11.27
1981	12.26	13.45
1982	12.48	12.76
1983	10.04	11.18
1984	10.52	12.41
1985	9.56	10.79
1986	7.76	7.78
1987	8.04	8.59
1988	8.03	8.96
1989	7.51	8.45
1990	7.53	8.61
1991	7.11	8.14
1992	6.59	7.67
1993	5.82	6.59
1994	6.45	7.37
1995	6.20	6.88
1996	6.01	6.71
1997	5.78	6.61
1998	5.32	5.58
1999	5.65	5.87

Sources: The Bond Buyer; Federal Reserve System.
Note: The Revenue Bond Index began on September 20, 1979; the thirty-year treasury series began in March 1977.

This process has been borne out in business cycle after business cycle. Interest rates peak at about the same time that the rate of real (inflation-adjusted) economic growth begins to decline. In inflationary periods, interest rates have generally peaked a little later in the cycle. Therefore, efforts to forecast the business cycle play an important part in interest rate forecasting.

The Federal Reserve

The nation's central bank is the *Federal Reserve*, or the *Fed*. It is one of the most powerful forces in the economy. It has considerable influence over key interest rates, both directly, in its ability to raise or lower the discount rate it charges to lend money to member banks, and indirectly, in its ability to add to or subtract from the nation's money supply. To many economists, the growth of the money supply and interest rates are the most important variables in determining the growth of aggregate spending. Others claim that fiscal policy—the primary tools being the tax policies of the federal government—is also influential.

The Federal Reserve has several methods by which it can influence interest rates and the money supply. It sets the discount rate, which is the rate at which banks that are members of the Federal Reserve System can borrow directly from the Fed. It also establishes reserve requirements for its members: banks must keep a set portion of every deposit or loan on hand as a reserve. The Fed's most flexible means of control, and the one it most frequently uses, works through the policy directions of its *Federal Open Market Committee (FOMC)*. The FOMC is a 12-member committee made up of the seven members of the Board of Governors, the president of the Federal Reserve Bank of New York, and on a rotating basis, the presidents of four other Federal Reserve Banks. It meets eight times per year to set guidelines regarding the Fed's purchase and sale of government securities in the open market as a means of influencing the volume of bank credit and money in the economy. It also establishes policy relating to the operations of the Federal Reserve System in foreign exchange markets.

Through guidelines established by this committee, the Fed buys, sells, and repos U.S. government securities in order either to add to or withdraw from reserves in the banking system. These actions directly affect the federal funds rate, which is the interest rate on overnight loans among banks and is the key for determining short-term rates. While the Fed also controls the discount rate, the federal funds rate is adjusted more frequently and is the Fed's main way to influence interest rates.

In the early 1980s the Fed focused on controlling the money supply. Since the mid-1980s, however, the Fed has been most focused on controlling the federal funds rate. The economists known as monetarists maintain that the Fed should, by and large, not attempt to control interest rates but, rather, concentrate on controlling the money supply. However, many other economists hold that the level of interest rates, which is partly determined by the federal funds rate, is more important than the money supply.

When the economy and/or inflation are growing too quickly, the Fed wants overall interest rates to move higher. It will attempt to accomplish this by raising the federal funds rate. When a decision to do so is made at a FOMC meeting, that decision has been announced immediately ever since the early 1990s.

From an operational perspective, following a decision to raise the federal funds rate, the Fed often will direct its open-market operation to sell government securities. This added supply of securities should drive prices down and yields up. At the same time, the Fed drains bank reserves from the system through the cash it receives in payment for the securities it is selling. This process can reduce the money supply. Conversely, if the Fed wants to drive down rates or to boost the money supply, it will usually buy government securities.

The Fed also implements its monetary policy in large part through open-market operations using repos. A *repo* is an agreement between a seller and a buyer, typically of U.S. government securities (it can also be for other securities). The seller sells the securities to the buyer, with a simultaneous agreement to repurchase the securities at an agreed on price at a future point in time. With a reverse repo, the buyer buys the securities from the seller and, at the same time, agrees to resell them at a future point in time. If the Fed wants to expand the money supply, it purchases securities in repo transactions from the non-bank dealers who deposit the proceeds into commercial banks, which increases reserves in the banking system. Conversely, if the Fed wishes to tighten the money supply, it will sell securities to non-bank dealers, who will draw on their reserves to purchase the securities.

An entire industry of Fed watchers has grown up over the past two decades. These economists try to anticipate the Fed's activities and explain the reasoning behind what the Fed does. In the late 1970s and early 1980s, the securities markets became very sensitive to Federal Reserve policy. Often, the market would rise or fall on the announcement of the weekly change in the money supply. If the money supply rose unexpectedly, interest rates rose in anticipation that the Fed would withdraw funds from the market and push rates up. An unanticipated drop in the money supply, however, sent rates lower in anticipation that the Fed would buy securities. By the mid-1980s through the present, almost the opposite is true; investors pay less attention to money growth, and the focus is on movements in the federal funds rate.

Inflation

Many economists believe that inflation expectations are built into interest rates. The basic theory is that there is a basic, real rate of interest that would prevail if prices were stable, and that nominal interest rates (the rates actually paid by borrowers and received by lenders) will be equal to the sum of this real rate and the expected rate of inflation.

For example, even if there were no inflation, lenders would demand compensation for giving up current purchasing power, while borrowers would be willing to pay for the credit in the expectation that they could use the money productively. History suggests that the real rate of interest for long-term corporate borrowing in the United States has averaged approximately 3 percent, with considerable variation around that average. For short-term securities, the real rate has been much lower.

When prices are rising, lenders demand a higher rate to compensate for their lost purchasing power. Borrowers are willing to pay higher rates because they will be paying back the loan in the future with money that has lost value. If investors expected inflation to stay at 4 percent for the life of a bond, for example, they would demand an additional 4 percent in interest on top of the real rate. According to this view, the 4 percent *inflation premium* plus the real rate of interest would approximate the long-term nominal interest rate under these conditions.

Because future inflation cannot be known with certainty, the degree to which inflation is built into nominal interest rates reflects investors' and borrowers' long-run expectations of inflation. Even short-term interest rates respond to these expectations. Most economists do agree that, for whatever reasons, as the inflation rate rises, so do interest rates. A clear indication of the direction of inflation is one of the most important factors in forecasting the level of interest rates.

The Nation's Flow of Funds

Interest rates are essentially the prices of different kinds of credit. These prices tend to equalize the supply and demand for credit throughout the economy. If there is a high demand for credit, interest rates will rise. This simultaneously makes it more expensive to borrow (thereby reducing credit demand) and attracts prospective lenders (increasing credit supply). If demand for credit falls, interest rates will fall. This makes it less expensive to borrow, so credit demand increases, and the supply of credit decreases because the lower rate is less attractive to prospective lenders.

Changes in the supply of credit will affect interest rates in the opposite way. If there are more funds available to buy fixed income securities, rates will be pushed down. If there are fewer funds available to buy these securities, rates will be pushed up. Many economists at brokerage firms and banks closely analyze the nation's capital flows to forecast interest rates. The object is to project the major demands for borrowing, on the one hand, and to project the major sources of the supply of lending, on the other. The projections, of course, are closely related to forecasts of the business cycle in general.

The Federal Reserve publishes an invaluable series of accounts to facilitate such an analysis. It is called the *Flow of Funds Accounts of the United States* and traces just how money flows through the entire economy. Economists use this tool to forecast the various components of the supply and demand for credit. Unusually heavy needs on the part of municipalities or the federal government, for example, can be assessed in this light. Heavy demand from these borrowers may be offset by diminished borrowing needs on the part of corporations. Regarding credit supply, economists can get a better notion of just how much strain will be placed on different kinds of financial institutions, as well as on the direct money and capital markets themselves. Any great increase in the demand for money by major institutions would lead to a tightening in the availability of credit and higher interest rates.

Flow of funds statistics are published quarterly in the Fed's Z.1 release. The data are also available electronically on the Fed's website.

TERM STRUCTURE OF INTEREST RATES

Why do fixed-income securities of about the same risk but with different maturities trade at different yields? The relationship between yield and maturity among bonds of different maturities is known as the *term structure of interest rates*. This relationship can be represented graphically by what is known as a *yield curve*.

The Treasury yield curves for May 17, 1999, is shown in Table 8.2. This curve is representative of a normal, positive upward-sloping yield curve. The vertical axis represents increasing yields, and the horizontal axis marks the years to maturity. The points that make up the curve are the actual yields for securities with the stated numbers of years left to maturity. Following the

TABLE 8.2 Active U.S. Treasury Yield Curves (May 17, 1999)

Maturity	May 17, 1999
3-month	4.64
6-month	4.77
1-year	4.85
2-year	5.27
5-year	5.50
10-year	5.64
30-year	5.89

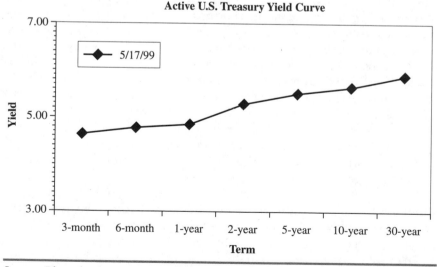

Active U.S. Treasury Yield Curve

Source: Bloomberg.

curve across to the vertical axis, one can see that on May 17, 1999, a security maturing in three months yielded 4.64 percent, one maturing in 10 years yielded 5.64 percent, and one maturing in 30 years yielded 5.89 percent. The difference in yield between the three-month maturity and the 30-year maturity was 125 basis points.

A very high positive upward-sloping yield curve occurred in December 1992 (See Table 8.3). Following the curve across to the vertical axis, a security maturing in three months yielded 3.29 percent, one maturing in one year yielded 3.71 percent, and one maturing in 30 years yielded 7.44 percent. There was a 415 basis point spread between the three-month and the 30-year

TABLE 8.3 Steep Upward-Sloping Yield
Curve (December 1992)

Maturity	December 1992
FF	2.92
3-month	3.29
1-year	3.71
5-year	6.08
10-year	6.77
30-year	7.44

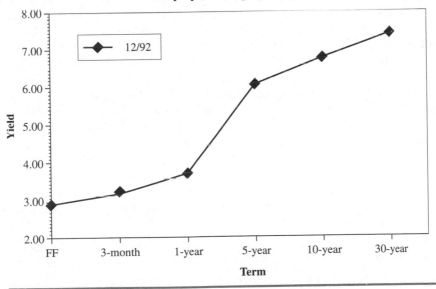

Source: Federal Reserve.

FIGURE 8.1   Active U.S. Treasury Inverted Yield Curve (17 May 2000)

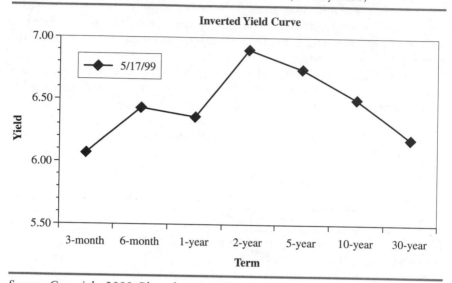

Source: Copyright 2000. Bloomberg L. P. Reprinted with permission.

maturities, a stark contrast to the flatter yield curves of 1999. The yield curve usually exhibits a more positive slope when the economy is near its cyclical low in a recession. The yield curve shown in Table 8.2 is flatter than this curve. That is, there is less slope or difference between yields in the earlier end of the curve and the later end of the curve. Conversely, a steeper yield curve such as the one in Table 8.3 has a greater difference between yields in the earlier end of the curve and the later end of the curve.

When the economy is at its peak growth rate and starting to put a strain its resources, the yield curve is usually inverted. The yield curve became inverted in 2000. Short-term rates became higher than long-term rates as money tightened at the height of economic growth . Short-term rates tend to fluctuate much more widely over an interest rate cycle than do long-term rates. Figure 8.1 shows an inverted yield curve from two years to 30 years. Following the curve across to the vertical axis, one can see that a security maturing in three months yielded 6.06 percent, one maturing in two years yielded 6.90 percent, and maturing in 30 years yielded 6.19 percent.

Several theories attempt to explain the shape of the yield curve. A summary of the most important ones follows.

Expectations

A theory to which most economists subscribe in one form or another is that investors' and borrowers' expectations of future changes in interest rates are the primary determinants of the term structure of rates. The theory in its pure form assumes that investors seek to maximize their returns, regardless of the maturity of the fixed-income securities they buy. Borrowers, too, are considered indifferent to the maturity of their debt. As a result, the long-term interest rate becomes the average of the current short-term rate and the expected level of future short-term rates. As expectations of short-term rate levels change, so do current levels of both short-term and long-term rates.

For example, when investors expect short-term rates to rise more than the general market does, some will buy short-term securities and sell longer-term securities, reasoning that they will earn a better return by rolling over their short-term investments than by keeping their funds in long-term securities. Their action forces current short-term yields to decline as they buy and long-term yields to rise as they sell. On the other side, using the same logic, borrowers seek out longer-term loans in anticipation that short-term rates will be higher in the future. These moves on the part of borrowers and investors have the effect of driving long-term rates up and forcing short-term rates down. The result is that the yield curve slopes upward more steeply, reflecting expectations that interest rates will indeed be higher in the future.

When investors and borrowers expect short-term rates to decline more than the general market declines, the opposite result occurs. Investors sell their short-term securities and buy longer-term securities because they want to lock in high rates. Over the long run, they believe the return will be greater. Borrowers defer their longer-term debt issues and instead borrow short term. Their combined actions cause short-term rates to rise and longer-term rates to fall, so that the yield curve flattens or turns downward.

Liquidity Preference

One major problem with the expectations theory, say many economists, is that longer-term securities fluctuate more in price than short-term securities when interest rates shift. If interest rates rise, the price of a long-term security falls much more than that of a short-term security. Thus, the long bond investor who wants to sell may have to take a significant loss.

Many of these economists subscribe to the liquidity preference theory, which suggests that, to make up for the risk of interest rate fluctuations, yields for longer-term securities must be higher than is implied by the expectations theory described above. The longer the maturity, the greater this premium. If investors and lenders all believe that future short-term rates will equal current short-term rates, the expectations theory predicts that the yield curve will be flat. Those who believe there must be a risk premium, however, argue that the curve will still be sloped upward.

Market Segmentation

At the other end of the theoretical spectrum are those economists who believe that interest rates are primarily a function of the supply and demand for bonds at different maturities. These economists argue that most investors and borrowers will not be willing to shift into different maturities simply because yields change. They will tend to buy and sell within a range of maturities for a variety of reasons, including legal constraints, regulatory constraints, habit, strategies that match the duration of an institution's assets with its liabilities, portfolio requirements, or market conditions. Banks, for example, tend to lend in the shorter-term ranges regardless of level of interest rates. The supply of, and demand for, funds at those maturities would then be the principal determinant of rates.

At one point, for example, there may be a very light investment demand for securities with maturities between 5 and 10 years. Or it may happen that very few borrowers come to market with issues that mature in more than 20 years. In each of these so-called segmented markets, according to proponents of this theory, rates will be set independent of what is going on in other maturities. The greater the supply of bonds compared to the demand in a maturity, the higher the rate will be, regardless of rates for other maturities. Conversely, the lower the supply, the lower the rate. In this view, then, the shape of the yield curve will depend mostly on the supply and demand for securities at different maturities.

MUNICIPAL BOND RATES

Economists generally take all the above factors into consideration when making forecasts of the overall level and term structure of interest rates. The municipal bond market, however, has several special features that must be emphasized. By far the most important of these is the unusual nature of the demand for municipal securities. The advantages of the tax exemption generally limit municipal bond purchases to higher-income households and their proxies, property and casualty insurance companies, and commercial banks.

Supply and Demand

Because of the specialized nature of the market for tax-exempt securities, highly cyclical demand factors are probably more important in determining municipal rates than in determining the rates of most other types of fixed-income securities. The particular characteristics of the major buyers of municipal bonds make for a cyclical pattern of demand.

Capital Gains Tax Effects

One other factor that has a different effect on municipal rates than on the rates of other securities is the treatment of capital gains. Although municipal bond interest payments are tax-exempt, capital gains earned on selling bonds are taxed. The buyers of discount municipal bonds, for example, will receive their interest payments tax free. But when the bonds are redeemed at maturity, the difference between the par value and the original purchase price of the bonds will be subject to federal income tax.

Volatility

In percentage terms, municipal rates are generally more volatile than other rates. A look back at Table 8.1 reveals how much wider the yield fluctuations are for the state and local securities than for U.S. government securities. The cyclical pattern of demand for municipal securities adds volatility to the market. Corporate and government bonds fluctuate less because the base of demand for taxable instruments is greater and because changes in tax rates have no effect on many of the large institutional buyers that dominate the taxable market.

Intermarket Yield Percentage

The difference in yield percentage between municipal securities and U.S. government securities is one of the most closely watched indicators in the municipal market. One can determine this difference, or spread, in yield between municipals and Treasuries and then calculate the ratio municipal yields to Treasury yields. The spread is expressed in basis points, with municipals nearly always lower than Treasuries, and the ratio of municipals to Treasuries is expressed as a percentage, nearly always less than 100 percent. The higher the percentage of municipal yields to Treasury yields, the greater is the relative value of municipals.

Table 8.5 shows two municipal intermarket yield curves. One is from May 17, 1999; the other is from May 17, 2000. There are many spread relationships that one can measure, including changes over time and differences on one day along the yield curve. On May 17, 1999, a 30-year, AAA general obligation municipal bond yielded 86.1 percent of a 30-year Treasury, with the Treasury security yields 81 basis points higher. On May 17, 2000, a 30-year AAA general obligation municipal bond yielded 95.8 percent of the 30-year Treasury, with the Treasury security yields 26 basis points higher. This means that during the course of 1999 and 2000, the municipal yields as a percentage of Treasuries rose, with the municipal investor getting a higher

TABLE 8.5 Active U.S. Treasury Yield Curve vs. AAA GO Municipal Bond Yield Curve, May 17, 1999 and May 17, 2000

Maturity	Active U.S. Treasuries		AAA GOs Municipals		Spread Munis to Treasuries	
	May 17, 1999	May 17, 2000	May 17, 1999	May 17, 2000	1999 (%)	2000 (%)
1-year	4.85	6.36	3.28	4.68	67.6	73.6
2-year	5.27	6.90	3.50	4.90	66.4	71.0
5-year	5.50	6.75	3.90	4.90	66.4	71.0
5-year	5.50	6.75	3.90	5.17	70.9	76.6
10-year	5.64	6.50	4.38	5.32	77.7	81.8
30-year	5.89	6.19	5.07	5.93	86.1	95.8

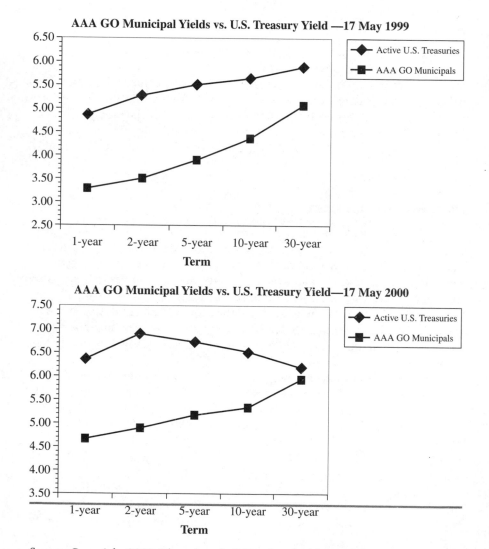

Source: Copyright 2000. Bloomberg L. P. Reprinted with permission.

relative yield in May 2000 than in May 1999. In May 2000, municipal bonds were considered cheap compared with Treasuries. A trader will look at these intermarket relationships throughout the day to spot buying or selling opportunities.

On any day, one can look all along the yield curve and see different relationships between securities. For example, on May 17, 2000, there was a 168 basis point spread between a one-year AAA GO bond and a one-year Treasury note; these municipals were 73.6 percent of Treasuries. Municipal professionals are acutely aware of these spread relationships. Going further out on the curve, we see the 10-year AAA GO bond at 81.8 percent of Treasuries. Again, traders and other municipal professionals are closely attuned to these differences between municipal and other markets to create trading and investment opportunities.

Upward-Sloping Yield Curves

The yield curve for municipal bonds is almost always upward sloping, as seen in Table 8.3 and steeper than the Treasury curve even when interest rates are near cyclical peaks. Short-term instruments trade very close to the after-tax return for corporations and individuals in the highest tax brackets, except during brief periods of abnormally heavy supply of short-term instruments or seasonal withdrawal of assets from money funds.

Long-term municipal securities will trade at somewhat higher relative rates. Even if the market expects rates in general to fall (when the corporate yield curve would be downward sloping), the municipal yield curve would generally slope upward. The primary reasons are: (1) the greater volatility of longer-term municipal bonds, (2) the heavy supply of intermediate- and long-term bonds as a percentage of the total market, and (3) the relatively limited demand for longer-term securities by corporate purchasers of tax-exempt bonds.

CHAPTER 9

Regulatory and Disclosure Requirements

INTRODUCTION

Until the late 1960s, the municipal securities market was relatively free from federal regulation. Despite the enactment in 1913 of the Sixteenth Amendment to the U.S. Constitution (which permitted the establishment of the modern federal income tax system), each version of the Internal Revenue Code enacted by Congress expressly exempted interest on municipal securities from federal income taxation. Similarly, when Congress enacted the Securities Act of 1933, the Securities Exchange Act of 1934, and related laws governing securities transactions, the lawmakers expressly exempted municipal securities and their issuers from the registration, reporting, and regulatory requirements imposed in connection with the issuance of securities by private corporations. However, issuers, underwriters, and other participants in a municipal securities transaction remain subject to the antifraud rules of the securities laws.

Federal involvement in the municipal securities markets began its significant increase with the enactment of legislation and with the promulgation of Treasury regulations in the late 1960s that imposed conditions for the interest on municipal securities to enjoy the federal tax exemption. The new federal tax restrictions were followed by the enactment in 1975 of federal securities laws that provided for the development of a comprehensive regulatory scheme under the jurisdiction of the MSRB to oversee the activities of brokers and dealers in municipal securities transactions.

More recently, the SEC adopted rule 15c2-12 in 1989 to impose express disclosure document review and distribution requirements on underwriters of municipal securities. The SEC amended the rule in 1994 to require an underwriter to determine, as a condition to underwriting certain municipal issues, that a commitment to provide continuing disclosure has been made by one or more persons obligated with respect to the payment of debt service on such issues. In the 1990s, reflective of the increased federal involvement in this area, the SEC established an Office of Municipal Securities and has increased greatly its enforcement activity with respect to antifraud compliance by municipal issuers.

THE BASIS OF FEDERAL TAX EXEMPTION

The tax-exempt status of municipal securities is closely intertwined with the development of the federal income tax system. The historical basis for the exemption initially rested upon an application of the constitutional doctrine of "intergovernmental tax immunity." The 1895 case that applied this doctrine to municipal securities, *Pollock v. Farmers' Loan and Trust Company,* also produced the need for the Sixteenth Amendment to the Constitution which authorized a modern income tax system.

At issue in *Pollock* was whether the Wilson-Gorman Tariff Act of 1894, which levied a federal tax on certain types of income, including interest on municipal securities, was constitutionally valid. Article I, Section 2 of the U.S. Constitution requires that direct taxes among the states be apportioned according to population; and Article I, Section 8 of the Constitution requires that indirect taxes, such as duties and imports, be uniform throughout the United States.

In *Pollock,* the Supreme Court decided that the 1894 Tariff Act was unconstitutional because taxes levied were not apportioned according to population. The Court also ruled that interest on municipal securities was not subject to federal income taxation because a tax on interest would impermissibly burden state government and interfere with its power to borrow money. Applying the doctrine of intergovernmental tax immunity, the Court reasoned that the states were immune from federal interference with their borrowing power. That doctrine, established in the landmark case of *McCulloch v. Maryland* (containing Justice Marshall's famous dictum, "The power to tax involves the power to destroy"), limits the ability of federal and state governments to levy taxes on each other that impermissibly intrude upon governmental sovereignty.

The *Pollock* decision produced the necessity for the Sixteenth Amendment to the U.S. Constitution in order to permit an effective federal income tax structure that would not be constrained by apportionment and population requirements. The amendment, which was enacted by Congress and submitted to the states for ratification in 1913, states that "The Congress shall have the power to lay and collect taxes on incomes, from whatever source derived, without apportionment among the several states, and without regard to any census or enumeration."

During the ratification process, an issue arose over the wording of the Sixteenth Amendment and its potential effect on the municipal securities tax exemption established by the *Pollock* decision. The concern was that the words authorizing a tax on incomes "from whatever source derived" expanded the areas of potential federal taxation to include the income on municipal securities. Several U.S. congressmen, including sponsors of the Sixteenth Amendment, disputed that interpretation and disavowed any congressional intent to achieve that result. Thus, for example, Senator William E. Borah of Idaho stated in the *Congressional Record* that

> *To construe the proposed amendment so as to enable us (the Congress) to tax the instrumentalities of the state would do violence to the rules laid down by the Supreme Court for a hundred years, wrench the whole Constitution from its harmonious proportions and destroy the object and purpose for which the whole instrument was framed.*

The Sixteenth Amendment, in the form proposed, was eventually ratified by the states. The question of whether the term "from whatever source derived" expanded the substantive areas of federal taxation was addressed by the Supreme Court in *Evans v. Gore,* decided in 1920, in which the Court concluded that

> *the genesis and words of the amendment unite in showing that it does not extend the taxing power to new or excepted subjects, but merely removes all occasion otherwise existing for an apportionment among the states of taxes laid on income, whether derived from one source or another. And we have so held in other cases.*

Although *Pollock* established the constitutional basis of tax exemption and later cases made clear that the Sixteenth Amendment did not expressly eliminate it, federal efforts to restrict or significantly limit the exemption have been made through the years, as discussed in the next section. Moreover, subsequent to *Pollock,* several Supreme Court decisions in other areas of federal-state relationships significantly limited the scope of the intergovernmental immunity doctrine, producing strong debate on the continuing vitality of *Pollock,* particularly as federal tax restrictions on municipal securities increased.

That debate eventually led to a challenge of federal restrictions and a re-examination of the *Pollock* holding in *South Carolina v. Baker,* decided by the Supreme Court in 1988. In that case, South Carolina contested the provisions of the Tax Equity and Fiscal Responsibility Act of 1982 that required most municipal securities to be issued in registered form and conditioned tax exemption on compliance with the registration requirement. The Supreme Court upheld the validity of the provisions and, in doing so, expressly overruled the *Pollock* holding that municipal bond interest is immune from a nondiscriminatory federal tax.

The *South Carolina v. Baker* decision removes the claim to historical constitutional protection for the municipal securities tax exemption and makes the continuation of that exemption and the nature of tax restrictions subject to the political dynamics of the federal legislative process. The Court's ruling in *South Carolina* produced discussion among some state and local governments about the need for a constitutional amendment expressly protecting the municipal securities tax exemption from federal intrusion.

HISTORY OF FEDERAL TAX LEGISLATION AFFECTING MUNICIPAL SECURITIES

Although the first Internal Revenue Code enacted after the adoption of the Sixteenth Amendment contained a specific stated exemption for interest on municipal securities, federal efforts to constrict or eliminate that exemption began soon after that enactment and have continued ever since. For example, the House of Representatives passed a proposed constitutional amendment in 1923 to authorize the taxation of income derived from future issues of municipal securities, but the proposal failed to pass the Senate. Other federal attempts to tax municipal bonds were made in the 1930s and 1940s without success. During consideration of the Revenue Revision of 1942, the Treasury Department strongly urged the imposition of a tax on the interest on all state and municipal bonds including both present and future issues. This proposal was rejected by the U.S. House of Representatives' Committee on Ways and Means but was accepted by the Senate Finance Committee with respect to future issues. After extensive debate on the floor of the Senate, the proposal was defeated and stricken from the bill. In 1969, the House passed a bill that included interest earned on all municipal securities within the Internal Revenue Code's minimum-tax provisions. The Senate did not accept the measure. Finally, in the late 1970s, a number of proposals were made in Congress to give municipal issuers the option of issuing taxable securities and receiving an interest subsidy from the federal government. Proposals of this nature (called the taxable bond option) were opposed by municipal issuers who feared that federal intervention would accompany the subsidies.

Since the taxable bond option proposals of the late 1970s, there have not been any general federal legislative attempts to eliminate completely or to provide a complete substitution for, the municipal securities tax exemption. Nevertheless, during that same period, the federal statutory authorization for such exemption has been the subject of significant restrictions. This process began in 1968, when Congress passed a law restricting the uses for which industrial development bonds could be issued and still retain the federal tax exemption. The list of eligible uses included in that law, as amended, included residential real property for family units; sports facilities; convention or trade show facilities; airports, docks, wharves, mass-commuting facilities, parking facilities, or storage or training facilities directly related to any of the foregoing; sewage and solid waste disposal facilities; facilities for the local furnishing of electric energy or gas; air and water pollution control facilities; facilities for the furnishing of water under certain conditions; development of industrial parks; and "small issue" industrial development bonds that are subject to dollar-amount limitations.

In 1969, Congress eliminated the statutory exemption for interest on *arbitrage bonds,* which are municipal securities the proceeds of which are used to acquire other securities with a yield higher than the yield on the municipal securities. Congress was concerned that some state and local governments were misusing the tax exemption for municipal securities by issuing arbitrage bonds solely for the purpose of investing their proceeds in higher-yielding federal or other obligations. The difference between the yields was pure profit to the municipalities. In addition, both the industrial development bond law and the arbitrage bond law have spawned extensive and intricate Treasury regulations governing the statutory concepts and their application to particular circumstances.

Further and increasingly extensive federal tax regulation of municipal securities occurred in 1980, with the enactment of the Mortgage Subsidy Bond Tax Act, which imposed substantial limits and requirements on tax-exempt residential mortgage bonds; in 1982, with the enactment of the Tax Equity and Fiscal Responsibility Act, which imposed additional restrictions on industrial development bonds and arbitrage bonds and required all municipal securities to be issued in registered form; and in 1984, with the enactment of the Deficit Reduction Act, which imposed volume limitations on *private activity bonds* (PABs), among other restrictions. Finally, as summarized in the next section, with the enactment of the Tax Reform Act of 1986, Congress further restructured and added additional restrictions to the provisions governing the issuance of tax-exempt municipal securities.

THE CURRENT STATUTORY EXEMPTION

The Tax Reform Act of 1986 continued the basic tax exemption for interest on municipal securities set forth in Section 103 of the Internal Revenue Code of 1954. However, the 1986 Tax Act significantly changed prior law by imposing new restrictions on all types of municipal securities, by further limiting the availability of tax-exempt bonds to finance private activities, by further restricting the aggregate volume of PABs, and by imposing additional arbitrage-related restrictions and procedures.

Although any discussion in full detail of the provisions of the 1986 Internal Revenue Code applicable to municipal securities is beyond the scope of this book, certain basic concepts are important and can be broadly, if somewhat imprecisely, summarized. In general, Section 103 of the 1986 Internal Revenue Code exempts interest on municipal obligations except for arbitrage bonds and certain PABs (see following).

Private Activity Bonds

Under the 1986 Code, PABs are defined as any municipal obligation, irrespective of the purpose for which it is issued or the source of payment, if (1) more than 10 percent of the proceeds of the issue will finance property that will be used by a nongovernmental person in a trade or business and (2) the payment of debt service on more than 10 percent of the proceeds of the issue will be (a) secured by property used in a private trade or business or payments in respect of such property or (b) derived from payments in respect of property used in a private trade or business. These two tests—the private business use test and the private payment or security test—must be examined in connection with the issuance of any municipal security. For example, care must be taken that municipal securities issued to finance a government office building do not violate the tests by virtue of underlying leases to, or operating arrangements with, nongovernmental persons. Interest on a municipal security that is a PAB will not be tax-exempt unless it is a *qualified bond* under the 1986 Code and meets certain other requirements.

Qualified bonds include those issued for exempt facilities such as governmentally owned airports, docks, wharves, and mass-commuting facilities; water-supply systems; sewage facilities; certain solid waste disposal facilities; qualified hazardous waste facilities; qualified residential rental projects; facilities for the local furnishing of electric energy or gas; and local district heating or cooling facilities. Qualified bonds also include municipal securities that meet specific requirements of the tax law and include securities issued to finance residential mortgages, qualified veterans' residential mortgages, qualified industrial development projects for manufacturing and certain farming purposes, qualified student loans, qualified redevelopment projects, and qualified expenditures of 501(c)(3) organizations such as hospitals and educational institutions.

Among the additional restrictions that apply to qualified PABs are specified state volume limitations imposed on an annual basis, a limitation on maximum bond maturity, public hearing and approval requirements, informational reporting requirements, and limits on the amount of proceeds that can be used for other than qualifying expenditures. In addition, certain restrictions applicable to all municipal securities, such as the arbitrage and rebate requirements discussed below, also apply to PABs.

Arbitrage Restrictions and Rebate

Another major area of restriction that is applicable to all municipal securities involves arbitrage and rebate. The arbitrage restrictions essentially preclude investment of the proceeds of municipal securities in higher-yielding securities. There are limited exceptions to this general rule for temporary periods, for reasonably required reserve funds not exceeding 10 percent of bond proceeds, and for a minor portion of the overall bond proceeds. In addition, under the 1986 Code, with limited exceptions, earnings on bond proceeds must be paid ("rebated") to the federal government at specified intervals to the extent that such earnings exceed the earnings that would have been derived if the proceeds had been invested at the bond yield. This rebate requirement includes an exemption for certain small-volume issuers and an exception for municipal securities issues where all the proceeds are expended for the applicable governmental purpose within specified periods after the date of issuance.

Other Restrictions

The 1986 Code also imposes restrictions on the advance refunding of municipal securities—that is, securities issued more than 90 days prior to the application of the proceeds of the securities to retire an outstanding issue of securities. Among other things, the 1986 Code prohibits the advance refunding of PABs (except for obligations issued for 501(c)(3) organizations) and restricts the number of times and conditions under which all other municipal securities can be advance refunded.

In addition to the restrictions summarized above on the types of municipal securities eligible for the federal tax exemption and the use of the proceeds of those securities, the 1986 Code also imposes a number of related restrictions affecting the municipal securities market. Thus, under the 1986 Code, interest on PABs (other than 501(c)(3) obligations) issued after August 7, 1986, is treated as a preference item for purposes of computing the corporate and individual alternative minimum tax. Similarly, interest on all municipal securities (whenever issued) is required to be entered into the minimum tax computation for corporations through the adjusted current earnings provisions of the 1986 Code. With limited exceptions, the 1986 Code also eliminated the prior law's provision that permitted financial institutions to deduct 80 percent of the amount of interest attributable to purchasing or carrying tax-exempt obligations. The effect of these and other provisions of the 1986 Code has been to alter significantly the type of investor participating in the municipal securities markets.

Recent Changes

The 1986 Code tax-exempt bond provisions have been revised by subsequent tax acts. The 1988 Act added limitations relating to pooled financing bonds, qualified 501(c)(3) bonds for residential housing and certain governmental housing bonds, and made technical corrections to the 1986 Act. The 1989 Act imposed (1) additional rules on so-called *hedge bonds* (bonds issued for the purpose of hedging against potential future increases in interest rates) and (2) additional Code provisions creating a new two-year spending exception to the rebate requirement for certain construction projects, which provisions were further amended by the 1990 Act. The 1993 Act permanently extended the "sunset" dates for qualified mortgage bonds, qualified veterans mortgage bonds, and qualified small-issue bonds used to finance manufacturing facilities. Final arbitrage and rebate regulations were issued in 1993 and have been amended several times since then to address issues such as hedging transactions and so-called "yield burning."

In 1996, regulations were published governing the circumstances under which modifications to the terms of debt instruments will cause such instruments to be treated as reissued for tax purposes.

In 1997, final regulations were published regarding application of the private business use and private payment or security tests described above. Also in 1997, legislation was enacted that partially repealed the $150 million limitation generally imposed by the 1986 act on bonds issued for the benefit of 501(c)(3) organizations (other than to finance hospital facilities). The $150 million limitation was repealed for 501(c)(3) bonds issued after August 5, 1997, if 95 percent or more of the proceeds of such bonds were used to finance capital expenditures incurred after that date. The $150 million limitation continues to apply, however, to (1) bonds issued to refund 501(c)(3) bonds subject to the $150 million limitation, (2) 501(c)(3) bonds issued to finance capital expenditures incurred on or before August 5, 1997, and (3) 501(c)(3) bonds issued after August 5, 1997, if less than 95 percent of the proceeds thereof are used to finance capital expenditures incurred after such date.

In 1998, temporary regulations were published regarding private business use of output facilities (i.e., electric and gas generation, transmission, distribution and related facilities and water collection, storage, and distribution facilities). In addition, in 1998, Congress enacted legislation to increase the dollar limitation (volume cap), beginning in 2003, on the amount of PABs that may be issued each year. The increase in the amount of available volume cap is phased in over the period from 2003 to 2007. Congress also enacted legislation in 1998 directing the IRS to permit tax-exempt bond issuers the right to an administrative appeal of an adverse determination by an IRS district office regarding the tax-exempt status of the issuer's bonds. At the end of 1998, the IRS published proposed procedures permitting issuers to appeal such adverse determinations made on or after July 22, 1998, to senior officers in the IRS Office of Appeals. Under proposed Revenue Procedure 98-58, the IRS is required to notify an issuer of municipal securities of a preliminary determination by the IRS that interest on such securities is taxable and to provide the issuer with the opportunity to appeal such a preliminary adverse determination.

In 1999, the IRS issued proposed regulations regarding the definition of "investment-type property" for purposes of the arbitrage and rebate rules and proposing a safe harbor for broker's fees in connection with *guaranteed investment contracts* (GICs) and bond defeasance escrows. In addition, the IRS began a major internal reorganization, doubled the number of agents responsible for audits of municipal securities, and announced its intention to increase the number of such audits.

APPLICATION OF FEDERAL SECURITIES LAWS TO MUNICIPAL SECURITIES

The Securities Act of 1933 established the SEC as the federal agency with regulatory authority over the issuance and trading of securities in the U.S. capital markets and imposed registration requirements governing the issuance of such securities. Congress, however, specifically exempted municipal securities from the registration and reporting requirements of the 1933 Act. Similarly, Congress exempted persons issuing municipal securities or engaging in municipal securities transactions from the reporting, registration, and related requirements of the Securities Exchange Act of 1934. The legislative history of the 1933 and 1934 Acts indicates that the municipal securities exemption stemmed not only from potential constitutional questions over the ability of Congress to regulate state and local governments in the issuance of securities but also from a sense that the municipal securities markets did not require the same type of regulation and oversight as the corporate capital markets.

In the early and middle 1970s, however, Congress refocused its attention on the municipal securities market as a result of the "boiler room" sales and questionable trading practices of a few municipal securities dealers. This renewed federal oversight resulted in the enactment of the Securities Acts Amendments of 1975. These amendments imposed the requirement that municipal securities dealers register with the SEC and provided for the establishment of the MSRB to regulate municipal securities transactions effected by brokers, dealers, and municipal securities dealers.

An important issue during congressional consideration of the Securities Acts Amendments was whether the legislation should permit regulation of issuers of municipal securities. This raised the possibility of the promulgation by the SEC of specific disclosure requirements for municipal bond issues and registration of offerings by municipal issuers. In response to those concerns, the proposed amendments were modified to prohibit the SEC and the MSRB from requiring an issuer, directly or indirectly, to make any filing with the SEC or MSRB before the sale of its securities in connection with their issuance, sale, or distribution. In addition, the Tower Amendment was added, prohibiting the MSRB from requiring an issuer of municipal securities, directly or indirectly, to furnish any information with respect to the issuer to the

MSRB or any purchaser or prospective purchaser of its securities. There was reserved to the MSRB, however, authority to require municipal securities brokers and dealers to furnish to the MSRB information with respect to the issuer generally available from a source other than the issuer.

Even though the imposition of federal disclosure requirements for issuers was thus restricted by the Securities Acts Amendments of 1975, those amendments confirmed the applicability to municipal market participants and transactions of the antifraud provisions of the federal securities laws. The most frequently referenced of the antifraud provisions, Rule 10b-5 promulgated pursuant to Section 10(b) of the 1934 Act, provides in part, that

it shall be unlawful for any person . . . (b) to make any untrue statement of a material fact or to omit to state a material fact necessary in order to make the statements made, in the light of the circumstances under which they were made, not misleading . . . in connection with the purchase or sale of any security.

The definition of a person under the 1934 Act was modified by the Amendments to include definitively municipal market participants for the purpose of §10(b) of the 1934 Act and of Rule 10b-5.

Specific disclosure practices in the municipal market were first addressed by SEC rule making in 1989 when the SEC, invoking its rule making authority under the antifraud provisions, adopted Rule 15c2-12 effective January 1, 1990. Rule 15c2-12 imposed, by rule for the first time, express disclosure document review and distribution responsibilities on municipal securities underwriters. In practical effect, the rule indirectly requires any issuer that wishes to sell securities covered by the rule through an underwritten primary offering to prepare and distribute an official statement for the offering. Rule 15c2-12 was amended in 1994, effective generally for primary offerings sold on or after July 3, 1995 and for issuer fiscal years ended on or after January 1, 1996, to require underwriters to obtain commitments from issuers (or other obligated persons) to provide continuing disclosure in connection with primary offerings.

Disclosure and the Antifraud Laws and Regulations of the Federal Securities Laws

Although the federal securities laws do not directly require municipal issuers to register or provide particular disclosure when offering municipal securities, several factors have caused municipal issuers and other municipal market participants to take greater care that their disclosure information is accurate and complete. First, the financial difficulties of some issuers in the 1970s stimulated investor requirements for greater disclosure in connection with the primary offering of municipal securities. Investor requirements, together with industry concerns about potential federal imposition of regulatory and disclosure requirements, prompted municipal market participants to develop recommended disclosure practices. The GFOA (then the Municipal Finance Officers Association or MFOA) led the development, in 1976, of "Disclosure Guidelines for State and Local Government Securities" (last revised in January 1991), which have become industry standards for municipal securities disclosure documents. Other industry initiatives, including improvements in government financial accounting and reporting under the auspices of the GASB, have also contributed to improved and more standardized disclosure practices. The National Federation of Municipal Analysts has an initiative underway at present to prepare its recommended best disclosure practices for various types of municipal securities.

A second major factor influencing the nature and extent of disclosure in connection with municipal securities are the antifraud provisions of both the Securities Act of 1933 and the Securities Exchange Act of 1934 and the increasing commitment of the SEC to enforce adherence to those provisions by municipal issuers and officials. The SEC Staff Report concerning the Washington Public Power Supply System (WPPSS), released in September 1988, refocused industry and federal agency efforts on improving disclosure practices for municipal securities and developing more effective means for assuring the availability, review, and distribution of disclosure information. Although enforcement actions against market participants were not recommended, the SEC Staff Report was critical of the disclosure practices for the WPPSS financings. The findings reflected in that report prompted the SEC to publish, and finally adopt, Rule 15c2-12 in 1989 (effective January 1, 1990), imposing specific disclosure document review and distribution requirements on municipal securities underwriters in connection with the primary offering of municipal securities.

In general, Rule 15c2-12 requires all underwriters participating in a primary offering of municipal securities with an aggregate principal amount of $1 million or more to obtain and review a nearly final official statement before bidding for, purchasing, offering for sale, or selling the securities. An offering of securities is exempt from the Rule if the securities are in minimum authorized denominations of $100,000 and the securities (1) have a maturity of nine months or less, (2) include variable rate tender features allowing a holder to tender the securities for purchase or redemption at a price not less than par at least as frequently as every nine months, or (3) are sold to 35 or fewer investors that the underwriter reasonably believes to be sophisticated and not to be purchasing for more than one account or with a view to distributing the securities. The Rule also requires each participating underwriter in negotiated offerings to deliver preliminary official statements to potential customers by the first business day following a customer request and to contract with an issuer for the receipt by the underwriter of final official statements in sufficient quantity and time to permit the underwriter to include a copy of that document with customer payment confirmations and to comply with MSRB Rules G-32 and G-36. A participating underwriter also has an obligation under Rule 15c2-12 to deliver a copy of the final official statement to each potential customer on request until the end of specified periods following the underwriting period.

The SEC release proposing original Rule 15c2-12 also set forth the staff's view of a municipal underwriter's responsibilities in connection with the delivery of primary offering documents to investors (Release No. 34-26100; S7-20-88; September 27, 1988). The staff modified its interpretation slightly in the release adopting Rule 15c2-12 (Release No. 34-26985; S7-20-88; June 28, 1989), but confirmed its view that by delivery of offering documents to an investor, an underwriter impliedly represents that "it has a reasonable basis for belief in the accuracy and completeness of the key representations contained in the documents." The releases discuss factors to be considered in determining whether the investigatory activities undertaken by an underwriter with respect to an offering would be sufficient to provide the requisite reasonable basis for belief in the accuracy and completeness of key representations. The interpretation acknowledges that an underwriter's investigation in a competitively sold offering is likely to be less extensive than for a negotiated offering because the underwriter is presumably involved in the preparation of the offering document for a negotiated offering.

The current requirement for continuing disclosure was added by amendments to Rule 15c2-12 effective generally for primary offerings sold on or after July 3, 1995, and for fiscal years that ended on or after January 1, 1996. With certain exceptions, the Rule now requires an underwriter to determine, as a condition to participating in the underwriting of a primary offering, that the issuer or obligated persons, that is, certain persons obligated with respect to payment of debt service, have agreed to provide, as long as the securities are outstanding, certain financial information and operating data annually and notice of the occurrence of specified events, if material, when and as they occur. Primary offerings exempt from the requirements of Rule 15c2-12 also are exempt from the continuing disclosure requirements.

The specific continuing disclosure requirements vary depending on the amount of nonexempt securities an issuer or obligated person has outstanding and the term to maturity of the securities being issued. If an obligated person with respect to an offering has outstanding more than $10,000,000 of nonexempt securities (including the proposed offering and any outstanding securities subject to the Rule or that would have been subject to the Rule if the Rule had been effective when they were issued), an underwriter must determine that the issuer or obligated person has agreed to provide to an appropriate state information depository (SID) and to each NRMSIR or the MSRB annual financial information and operating data of the type included in the final official statement for the primary offering, as well as audited financial statements (if and when available), for each obligated person. The commitment may set forth an objective standard for determining whether, for a particular fiscal year, continuing disclosure must be provided as to certain obligated persons. This approach would commonly be used in connection with pool financings in which the relative magnitude (and materiality) of a particular obligated person's payment obligations could vary over time.

The issuer or obligated person must also commit to provide notice of the occurrence of any one of the following 11 events, if material:

1. Principal and interest payment delinquencies
2. Nonpayment-related defaults
3. Unscheduled draws on debt service reserves reflecting financial difficulties
4. Unscheduled draws on credit enhancements reflecting financial difficulties
5. Substitution of credit or liquidity providers or their failure to perform
6. Adverse tax opinions or events affecting the tax-exempt status of the security
7. Modifications to rights of security holders
8. Bond calls
9. Defeasances
10. Release, substitution, or sale of property securing repayment of the securities
11. Rating changes

The continuing disclosure requirements are more limited if no obligated person has more than $10,000,000 of nonexempt securities outstanding (including the offered securities) or if the stated maturity of the issue is 18 months or less. Those obligated persons must commit to provide notice of the occurrence of any of the events described above, if material, and must also commit to provide either to a state information depository annually or to any person upon request, if the stated maturity of the issue is greater than 18 months, the financial information customarily prepared by the issuer and publicly available.

Municipal disclosure practices will continue to be the subject of industry and federal regulatory focus. The SEC has become much more aggressive in its enforcement activities in recent years, and those activities are likely to continue to cause issuers and underwriters to review disclosure practices. An area of increasing interest is the use of electronic means to disseminate disclosure information in connection with primary offerings and the implications of information available electronically, apart from disclosure documents, at the time of primary offerings and from time to time in the secondary market.

THE MUNICIPAL SECURITIES RULEMAKING BOARD

As noted above, the MSRB was created by Congress in 1975 as an independent, self-regulatory organization charged with primary rule-making authority for the municipal securities market. The MSRB's regulatory authority covers dealers, dealer banks, and brokers in municipal securities, but as discussed earlier, its jurisdiction does not extend to the issuers of municipal securities. All market participants subject to MSRB jurisdiction are required to register with the SEC. As a self-regulatory organization, the MSRB is financed solely by the municipal securities industry. Its operations are supported by fees and assessments paid by firms and dealer banks engaged in the municipal securities business. These payments include an initial fee paid by a firm or dealer bank before commencing municipal securities activities, an annual fee, and an assessment based on the volume of new-issue underwriting and trading in which a firm or dealer bank participates.

The Regulatory Structure

The MSRB was designated by Congress as the rule-making body for the municipal market with a view to the unique nature of the municipal market and its diverse participants—banks, securities firms engaged in a general securities business, and firms whose sole business is municipal securities. The MSRB has 15 members. Five members represent broker-dealers, another five represent dealer banks, and the remaining five, the *public representatives*, are independent and cannot be associated with or controlled by a municipal securities broker or dealer. One of the five public representatives must represent investors, and another must represent issuers of municipal securities.

The initial 15 Board members were appointed by the SEC in September 1975. Subsequently, new Board members have been nominated and elected by the MSRB under a procedure that allows for recommendations of individuals for nomination by the industry and by interested members of the public. While not involved directly in the election procedures, the SEC must, pursuant to statute, approve the selection of public MSRB members.

The Securities Acts Amendments of 1975 grant the MSRB general rule-making authority over municipal market participants and specify several areas of mandatory rule making in which the board is required, as a minimum, to propose and adopt rules. These enumerated areas include standards of operational capability and professional qualification, rules of fair practice, record keeping, the minimum scope and frequency of periodic compliance examinations, the form and content of quotations relating to municipal securities, sales of new-issue municipal securities to related portfolios during the underwriting period, the definition of "separately identifiable department or division" as it relates to banks for purposes of SEC registration and enforcement of MSRB rules, the internal operation and administration of the MSRB, and assessments.

The MSRB's rule making procedures involve several steps. Typically, the board drafts proposals for rule changes and then requests public comments for a period of 60 days. On adoption by the MSRB in final form, rule proposals are filed with the SEC and the federal bank regulatory agencies. Each proposed rule is published in the *Federal Register* and is subject to a public comment period of up to 35 days from the date of publication. The MSRB's rules are ordinarily subject to approval by the SEC before becoming effective. Exceptions are rules relating solely to the administration of the MSRB and to assessments that are effective on filing but that may be rescinded by the SEC within 60 days.

Even though the MSRB is charged with primary rule-making responsibility over municipal market professionals, the SEC retains ultimate regulatory authority and may add to or delete from the MSRB's rules if it finds such action necessary or appropriate.

In recognition of the existing regulatory structure for banks and securities firms, the MSRB does not have inspection or enforcement authority. Instead, the National Association of Securities Dealers, Inc., for its members, and the three federal bank regulatory agencies, as appropriate, are charged with the responsibility for inspection and enforcement of the board's rules, which have the force of federal law under the legislation.

The Rules

The MSRB wrote most of its rules in the first two years of its existence. Since then, the board has been concerned primarily with amendments to and interpretation of the existing rules. These rules are separated into three major categories, the first two of which are administrative and definitional. The third group, the general rules, are the substantive rules of the MSRB. The details of the most important of these rules have already been discussed. A brief summary of the major rules is given below, but the descriptions are at best simplifications, meant only as a guide. According to the MSRB's Rule G-29, each broker and dealer must keep a copy of the rules in each office in which municipal securities activities are conducted and make the rules available for examination by customers promptly on request.

The MSRB does not have authority to enforce its rules. There is overlapping authority for their enforcement with the SEC as to all brokers, dealers, and municipal securities dealers; with the National Association of Securities Dealers, Inc., for securities firms; and with various bank regulatory agencies for bank dealers.

Administrative Rules.   The administrative rules, A-1 through A-17, cover such areas as membership, powers, meetings of the board, and arbitration fees and deposits. The rules outline the rule-making procedures and set fees for registered dealers as well as rates for underwriters' assessments. Assessments are charged on the underwriting of primary offerings. In addition, transactions between dealers, and between dealers and customers, are also assessed at a fee.

Definitional Rules.   A short set of rules (D-1 through D-11) provides formal definitions of certain key but legally ambiguous terms. A bank dealer, a customer, and a discretionary account, for example, are carefully defined.

General Rules.   As of June 30, 2000, there were 39 general rules. Many of the key rules have been discussed in previous chapters of this volume. Rule G-1 defines exactly what operations qualify, under the rules, as independent dealer departments or divisions in banks. Professional qualifications, disciplinary actions, and fidelity bonding and other insurance coverage requirements are generally covered in Rules G-2 through G-7.

Rule G-3 is a far-reaching rule, classifying employees and establishing qualifying examinations. The Board has established four distinct classes of municipal securities employees—municipal securities representatives, municipal securities principals, municipal securities sales principals, and municipal securities financial and operations principals—and has developed a different qualifying exam for each class.

Most employees are classified as municipal securities representatives. They include anyone who (1) underwrites, trades, or sells municipal securities; (2) provides financial advisory or consultant services to issuers; (3) does research or offers investment advice; or (4) is involved in "any other activities which involve communication, directly or indirectly, with public investors in municipal securities" as it relates to activities described in (1) or (2). Clerical personnel are not, in general, included in this group. An important exemption from the qualifications test exists for anyone who has already passed the NASD examination for general securities representatives. New employees of securities firms may take the general securities exam in lieu of the municipal securities exam. In addition to taking the qualifying exam, all new municipal securities representatives must serve a minimum apprenticeship of 90 days before they can transact business with any member of the public. The passing score for the exam is set by the MSRB. An apprentice must pass the exam before the end of a 180-day time limit or cease to perform the functions of a municipal securities representative.

The three other classes of municipal securities employees are the municipal securities principals, the municipal securities sales principals, and the financial and operations principals. Rule G-27 requires the designation by each dealer of one or more persons as municipal securities principals, municipal securities sales principals, financial and operations principals, or general securities principals to be responsible for supervision of its municipal securities activities. The municipal securities principal is a person who has a supervisory role with respect to one or more areas of activity, and each firm must have at least one municipal securities principal; many firms have more. A municipal securities sales principal is a person whose supervisory activities are limited to supervising only sales to and purchases from customers of municipal securities. The financial and operations principal is the person designated to be in charge of preparing and filing financial reports with the SEC or any other regulatory agency for a securities firm. There are separate exams for municipal securities principals, municipal securities sales principals, and financial and operations principals. (Financial and operations principals who are qualified as such under the NASD examination are exempted from taking the exam.)

The principal record-keeping rule is G-8. Rule G-9 specifies how long records must be preserved, and Rule G-27 requires the adoption, maintenance, and enforcement of written supervisory procedures of the books and records required to be maintained and preserved by Rules G-8 and G-9 (including procedures for maintenance and supervision) by a designated principal.

Rule G-11 lists the MSRB's requirements for syndicate practices. The MSRB established uniform practices for clearing, processing, and settling transactions under Rule G-12. Rule G-15 lists requirements for written confirmations to customers.

Rule G-13 requires that all quotations by dealers must represent actual bids and offers—that is, the dealer must be prepared to make the trade at the yield or price quoted at the time the quotation is made. Dealers can, however, give mere indications of yields or prices when requested, as long as they make it clear that these indications are not actual quotations. Rule G-16 requires the examination of every municipal securities dealer for compliance with the rules by the assigned enforcement agency at least once every 24 months.

Most of the remaining rules—G-17 through G-39—are known as the fair-practice rules. In the words of the MSRB legislation, these are designed

> *to prevent fraudulent and manipulative acts and practices, to promote just and equitable principles of trade, to foster cooperation and coordination with persons engaged in regulating, clearing, settling, processing information with respect to, and facilitating transactions in municipal securities, to remove impediments to and perfect the mechanism of a free and open market in municipal securities, and, in general, to protect investors and the public interest.*

The first of these rules (G-17) simply states:

> *In the conduct of its municipal securities business, each broker, dealer, and municipal securities dealer shall deal fairly with all persons and shall not engage in any deceptive, dishonest, or unfair practice.*

An equally important rule is Rule G-19, on suitability, which requires that a dealer make suitable recommendations to customers. Some of the other fair-practice rules involve gifts, relationships between underwriters and issuers, dissemination of official statements or similar disclosure documents, advertising, the fairness of prices and commissions, quotations, and the improper use of assets.

Rule G-35 establishes arbitration procedures for dealers and customers who have disputes or claims involving municipal securities transactions. The MSRB has written an arbitration code that provides a procedure for the resolution of municipal securities disputes. The code covers the initiation of proceedings by a dealer or a customer, the conduct of hearings, and awards. A simplified procedure has been established for claims of $10,000 and less. Under Rule G-35, a customer or dealer may compel another dealer to arbitrate a dispute.

On May 31, 1990, the SEC approved Rule G-36, which requires underwriters to forward to the MSRB copies of official statements and advance refunding documents for bond issues subject to SEC Rule 15c2-12 and certain other issues if an official statement is prepared for the issue. This rule is intended to ensure that the MSRB has the necessary disclosure documentation for its Municipal Securities Information Library.

On April 7, 1994, the SEC approved Rule G-37, which prohibits a broker or dealer from engaging in municipal securities business with an issuer within two years after a political contribution has been made by the broker or dealer, any associated municipal finance professional, or a controlled political action committee for any particular officials of the issuer, under certain circumstances. This rule also requires the regular reporting of such contributions as well as any payments to political parties.

On January 17, 1996, the SEC approved Rule G-38, which requires the disclosure by a broker or dealer to an issuer of the retention by the broker or dealer of any person to obtain or retain municipal securities business through direct or indirect communication with that issuer. Any such retention must be evidenced by a written agreement, and reports of such arrangements are required to be made to the MSRB. Subsequent amendments to Rule G-38 require the reporting of political contributions by any such consultants retained by a broker or dealer.

On December 16, 1996, the SEC approved Rule G-39, which expressly regulates the telemarketing activities of brokers and dealers. The prohibitions do not apply generally to calls placed for the purpose of maintaining and servicing the accounts of existing customers. The placements of calls by brokers and dealers is also potentially subject to Rule G-17, which addresses fair dealing with investors as described previously.

Financial Products

INTRODUCTION

The use of financial products by municipal issuers and institutional investors has become an integral and recognized part of each one's financial management. Indeed, financial products have developed to meet the needs of both issuers and investors to manage their assets and liabilities more effectively. Products also exist to lower interest rate costs on the liability side of the balance sheet; others exist to maximize yield within tax law constraints on the asset side of the balance sheet. Financial products are chosen in light of each organization's own needs and the demands of the market. The following section is a basic discussion of financial products, with a focus from the issuer side.

A *derivative* is a financial product that gets or derives its value from an underlying security. In the tax-exempt market, there are primary and secondary derivative products. Primary tax-exempt derivative products are based on bonds issued by municipal issuers. Examples include inverse floater bonds, bonds with embedded swaps and caps, and bonds based on interest rate indices such as The Bond Market Association's swap index. Secondary tax-exempt derivative products are based on a custodial receipt, a trust certificate, or other security that is not directly issued by a state or local government. Examples include tender option bonds, trust certificates with interest rate swaps, and stripped interest rate bonds.

The following sections include a fundamental discussion of interest rate swaps, and of certain asset side based products.

INTEREST RATE SWAPS

The issuer uses interest rate swaps to manage the balance sheet and to lower overall interest costs. An *interest rate swap* is a contract between a party (in this case the issuer) and a counterparty. A counterparty can be any of a number of financial institutions including banks, insurance companies, and broker/dealers, who agree to swap interest payments for a set amount of time based on a *notional*, or hypothetical, amount of money. If the swap is entered

FIGURE 10.1   Fixed to Floating Rate Swap

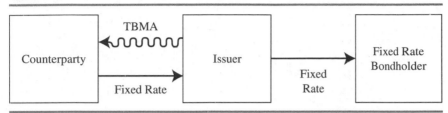

into at the time of a bond sale the notional amount can be a percentage or the full amount of the bond issue.

Municipal interest rate swaps can be categorized as fixed rate to floating rate, or floating rate to fixed rate. The issuer enters into a swap to convert existing fixed rate debt synthetically into floating rate debt, or vice versa. Issuers will do this to change the existing mix of fixed and floating rate debt without refunding the existing debt.

Assume that the issuer has fixed rate debt and wants to add some variable exposure because of a belief that floating debt rates will go lower. The issuer also does not want to formally refund a portion of the outstanding debt. A fixed to floating rate swap could be entered into with a counterparty, as shown in Figure 10.1. The counterparty can be a dealer, an insurance company, or other financial institution. The issuer pays the counterparty the current TBMA Municipal Swap Index (discussed in the nest sub-section). The counterparty pays the issuer an agreed-upon fixed rate. The issuer continues to pay the bondholders the normal interest rate associated with their bonds. Interest payments between the issuer and the counterparty are netted out, with only one payment made for the larger amount. The issuer now has some variable rate exposure, which should reduce the overall interest costs.

Now, assume that the issuer has more floating rate debt than it wants, and that it prefers to fix a portion of it synthetically. With an agreed-upon notional amount, the issuer would enter into a fixed rate swap. Figure 10.2 diagrams the flow of payments of a floating to fixed rate swap.

The issuer pays the counterparty a set fixed rate, based on the current market. The counterparty pays the issuer a floating rate, either TBMA or London Interbank Overnight Rate (LIBOR). Again, the payments are netted out.

Swaps become attractive when there is enough spread between different market rates to make the contract viable. For instance, assume that in the previous floating to fixed rate swap the issuer has two alternatives for creating fixed rate debt. The issuer can either sell twenty-year fixed rate debt at 5.25 percent, or can enter into a fixed rate swap for 4.70 percent plus expenses (assuming 30 basis points for expenses), for a total of 5.00 percent. Assume a TBMA floating index of 3.60 percent. The fixed swap rate is the present value

FIGURE 10.2 Floating to Fixed Rate Swap

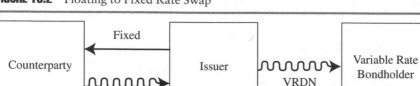

of TBMA index over the life of the swap, which may not necessarily be the same length as a twenty-year bond. The issuer picks up 25 basis points (5.25–5.00) by doing the swap and being in different markets.

The issuer and the counterparty must have the legal authority to enter into a swap. After that, there are inherent risks in any swap. These include, but are not limited to, the following:

- *Credit risk.* The issuer and the counterparty take a credit risk to each other over the life of the swap. Each must feel confident that the other will be able to perform under the contract. Both issuers and counterparties may set minimum credit levels for each other. Collateral is sometimes posted by one of the parties to mitigate the credit risk.
- *Basis risk.* The issuer and counterparty may enter into a swap under one set of yield curve conditions. If the yield curve changes dramatically, one may end up paying more in variable rate payment than in fixed payments.
- *Event risk.* The issuer and counterparty may encounter an unexpected event, such as a change in tax law, that would make the economics of the swap less attractive.
- *Modeling risk.* The counterparty has based the swap rates in part on its own proprietary modeling programs. A swap provider may be on the fixed rate receiving side of one swap and on the floating rate receiving side of another swap. The firm manages its swap book with certain assumptions about future rates and many other factors. If those assumptions prove to be incorrect, the swap provider may have entered into a swap rate that is too high or too low to be profitable.

Swap contracts will have termination events delineated and agreed to by both parties. Termination events will vary from issuer to issuer, and from counterparty to counterparty.

The Bond Market Association Municipal Swap Index

The Bond Market Association Municipal Swap Index, produced by Municipal Market Data, is a seven-day market index composed of tax-exempt

VRDOs, calculated weekly. The Index, which is also known in the market as TBMA, acts as a benchmark floating rate in a swap transaction.

In order for an issue to qualify for inclusion in the index it must

- be a weekly reset, effective on Wednesday (no lag resets considered).
- not be subject to alternative minimum tax.
- have an outstanding amount of $10 million or more.
- have the highest short-term rating (VMIG1 by Moody's or A-1+ by S&P).
- pay interest on a monthly basis, calculated on an actual/actual basis.

In addition, only one quote per obligor per remarketing agent will be included in the Index. Issues from all states are eligible for inclusion.

TBMA Index is calculated on a weekly basis, and released to subscribers on Thursday. The following are considered in TBMA Index calculation:

- The standard deviation of the rates is calculated. Any issue falling outside ±1.0 standard deviations is dropped.
- Each participating remarketing agent is limited to no more than 15 percent of the Index by an averaging method.

The actual number of issues that make up the Index will vary in time as issues are called, converted, mature, or are newly issued. In addition, if changes occur that violate the criteria or calculation methods, an issue will be dropped. Typically, TBMA Index has included 250 issues in any given week.

Table 10.1 shows the average TBMA Index for each year from 1989 to 1999. The lowest index in this time period was 1.64 percent on January 6, 1993, and the highest index was 7.90 on December 26, 1990.

INTEREST RATE CAPS, FLOORS, AND COLLARS

Issuers may use other derivative tools to manage interest rate risk preceding a bond offering or during a construction period. An *interest rate cap* is an agreement in which a party pays a premium up front or in installments to the counterparty. If the floating interest rate exceeds a stated fixed rate during the time of the cap agreement, the counterparty will pay the difference, based on the notional amount. The cap rate is also called the *strike rate*. An interest rate cap can protect the issuer against rising interest rates.

An *interest rate floor* is an agreement in which a party receives a premium up front or in installments from a counterparty. If the floating rate is lower than the stated fixed rate during the time of the floor agreement the party pays the difference based on the notional amount. The floor rate is also called the

TABLE 10.3 The Bond Market
Association Municipal Swap Index:
Average Annual Index, 1989–1999

Year	Average Index
1989	6.12
1990	5.91
1991	4.37
1992	2.81
1993	2.37
1994	2.84
1995	3.85
1996	3.43
1997	3.66
1998	3.43
1999	3.29

Source: The Bond Market Association,
Municipal Market Data.

strike rate. An interest rate floor lets a party receive up-front payments in exchange for the risk of making payments if interest rates fall.

An *interest rate collar* is an agreement that combines an interest rate cap and an interest rate floor. The party pays if the floating rate exceeds the cap rate and the counterparty pays if the floating rate drops below the floor rate.

Other swap-related products include a forward swap and swaptions. A *forward swap* is an agreement between the party and the counterparty to begin a swap at some future date. A *swaption* is an agreement that gives a party the option of requiring the counterparty to enter into a swap at some future date. Bonds can be issued as primary derivative products with these agreements embedded into their structures.

MANAGING THE ASSET SIDE

Bond documents often require that the issuer maintain specific funds such as debt service reserve and project funds. Arbitrage regulations and indenture requirements limit the amount of yield that the issuer can earn on these funds and the types of investments that are allowed. Following is a summary of some financial products into which the issuer can enter to maximize yield within the products' constraints. Again, new products are continuously being introduced.

- *Repurchase agreements.* A repurchase agreement, or *repo,* is the purchase of U.S. Treasury or agency securities, with an agreement by the seller of these securities to repurchase all or a portion of them back at the same price at some future date. The seller of the securities usually over-collateralizes them, allowing the purchaser to have additional security and to have some protection from price fluctuations. Repos are marked to market regularly and are held by a third party.

- *Reverse repurchase agreements.* In a reverse repurchase agreement, or *reverse repo,* a party purchases U.S. Treasuries or agencies, then immediately sells them to a dealer while simultaneously agreeing to repurchase them at a given price at a given future date. Similar custody and valuation arrangements for repos apply to reverse repos.
- *Investment agreements.* Investment agreements, offered by financial institutions, offer a guaranteed interest rate for the life of the agreement. Issuers will use these for construction funds, especially if there is a draw schedule for the funds.
- *Other products.* Other products include *treasury contracts* for debt service reserve funds, *rate lock agreements,* and *forward supply contracts* for escrows for refundings.

This is a brief summary of the products, which are continuously evolving to meet the needs of issuers and investors in their goals of stable and responsible financial management.

Municipal Securities Rulemaking Board Rule G-33

Calculations

Rule G-33. (a) *Accrued Interest.* Accrued interest shall be computed in accordance with the following formula:

$$\text{Interest} = \text{Rate} \times \text{Par Value of} \times \frac{\text{Number of Days}}{\text{Number of Days in year}}$$

For purposes of this formula, the "number of days" shall be deemed to be the number of days from the previous interest payment date (from the dated date, in the case of first coupons) up to, but not including, the settlement date. The "number of days" and the "number of days in year" shall be counted in accordance with the requirements of section (e) below.

(b) *Interest-Bearing Securities*

    (i) *Dollar Price.* For transactions in interest-bearing securities effected on the basis of yield the resulting dollar price shall be computed in accordance with the following provisions:

        (A) *Securities Paying Interest Solely at Redemption.* Except as otherwise provided in this section (b), the dollar price for a transaction in a security paying interest solely at redemption shall be computed in accordance with the following formula:

$$P = \left[\frac{\frac{RV}{100} + \frac{R}{M}}{1 + \left(\frac{E-A}{E} \cdot \frac{Y}{M} \right)} \right] - \left[\frac{A}{B} \cdot R \right]$$

For purposes of this formula the symbols shall be defined as follows:

"A" is the number of accrued days from the beginning of the interest payment period to the settlement date (computed in accordance with the provisions of section (e) below);

"B" is the number of days in the year (computed in accordance with the provisions of section (e) below);

"DIR" is the number of days from the issue date to the redemption date (computed in accordance with the provisions of section (e) below);

"P" is the dollar price of the security for each $100 par value (divided by 100);

"R" is the annual interest rate (expressed as a decimal);

"RV" is the redemption value of the security per $100 par value (divided by 100); and

"Y" is the yield price of the transaction (expressed as a decimal).

(B) Securities with Periodic Interest Payments. Except as otherwise provided in this section (b), the dollar price for a transaction in a security with periodic interest payments shall be computed as follows:

(1) for securities with six months or less to redemption, the following formula shall be used:

$$P = \left[\frac{\frac{RV}{100} + \frac{R}{M}}{1 + \left(\frac{E-A}{E} \cdot \frac{Y}{M} \right)} \right] - \left[\frac{A}{B} \cdot R \right]$$

For purposes of this formula the symbols shall be defined as follows:

"A" is the number of accrued days from the beginning of the interest payment period to the settlement date (computed in accordance with the provisions of section (e) below);

"B" is the number of days in the year (computed in accordance with the provisions of section (e) below);

"E" is the number of days in the interest payment period in which the settlement date falls (computed in accordance with the provisions of section (e) below);

"M" is the number of interest payment periods per year standard for the security involved in the transaction;

"P" is the dollar price of the security for each $100 par value (divided by 100);

"R" is the annual interest rate (expressed as a decimal);

"RV" is the redemption value of the security per $100 par value; and

"Y" is the yield price of the transaction (expressed as a decimal).

(2) for securities with more than six months to redemption, the following formula shall be used:

$$P = \left[\frac{RV}{\left(1 + \frac{Y}{2}\right)_{exp} N - 1 + \frac{E-A}{E}} \right] +$$

$$\left[\sum_{K-1}^{N} \frac{100 \cdot \frac{R}{2}}{\left(1 + \frac{Y}{2}\right)_{exp} N - 1 + \frac{E-A}{E}} \right] -$$

$$\left[100 \cdot \frac{A}{B} \cdot R \right]$$

For purposes of this formula the symbols shall be defined as follows:

"A" is the number of accrued days from beginning of the interest payment period to the settlement date (computed in accordance with the provisions of section (c) below);

"B" is the number of days in the year (computed in accordance with the provisions of section (e) below);

"E" is the number of days in the interest payment period in which the settlement date falls (computed in accordance with the provisions of section (e) below);

"N" is the number of interest payments (expressed as a whole number) occurring between the settlement date and the redemption date, including the payment on the redemption date;

"P" is the dollar price of the security for each $100 par value;

"R" is the annual interest rate (expressed as a decimal);

"RV" is the redemption value of the security per $100 par value; and

"Y" is the yield price of the transaction (expressed as a decimal).

For purposes of this formula the symbol "exp" shall signify that the preceding value shall be raised to the power indicated by the succeeding value; for purposes of this formula the symbol "K" shall signify successively each whole number from "1" to "N" inclusive; for purposes of this formula the symbol "sigma" shall signify that the succeeding term shall be computed for each value "K" and that the results of such computations shall be assumed.

(ii) *Yield.* Yields on interest-bearing securities shall be computed in accordance with the following provisions:

(A) *Securities Paying Interest Solely at Redemption.* The yield of a transaction in a security paying interest solely at redemption shall be computed in accordance with the following formula:

$$Y = \left[\frac{\left(RV + \left(\frac{DIR}{B} \cdot R \right) \right) - \left(P + \left(\frac{A}{B} \cdot R \right) \right)}{P + \left(\frac{A}{B} \cdot R \right)} \right] \cdot \left[\frac{B}{DIR - A} \right]$$

For purposes of this formula the symbols shall be defined as follows:

"A" is the number of accrued days from the beginning of the interest payment period to the settlement date (computed in accordance with the provisions of section (e) below);

"B" is the number of days in the year (computed in accordance with the provisions of section (e) below);

"DIR" is the number of days from the issue date to the redemption date (computed in accordance with the provisions of section (e) below);

"P" is the dollar price of the security for each $100 par value (divided by 100);

"R" is the annual interest rate (expressed as a decimal);

"RV" is the redemption value of the security per $100 par value (divided by 100); and

"Y" is the yield on the investment if the security is held to redemption (expressed as a decimal).

(B) *Securities with Periodic Interest Payments.* The yield of a transaction in a security with periodic interest payments shall be computed as follows:

(1) for securities with six months or less to redemption, the following formula shall be used:

$$Y = \left[\frac{\left(\frac{RV}{100} + \frac{R}{M} \right) - \left(P + \left(\frac{A}{E} \cdot \frac{R}{M} \right) \right)}{P + \left(\frac{A}{E} \cdot \frac{R}{M} \right)} \right] \cdot \left[\frac{M \cdot E}{E - A} \right]$$

For purposes of this formula the symbols shall be defined as follows:

"A" is the number of accrued days from the beginning of the interest payment period to the settlement date (computed in accordance with the provisions of section (e) below);

"E" is the number of days in the interest payment period in which the settlement date falls (computed in accordance with the provisions of section (e) below);

"M" is the number of interest payment periods per year standard for the security involved in the transaction;

"P" is the dollar price of the security for each $100 par value (divided by 100);

"R" is the annual interest rate (expressed as decimal);

"RV" is the redemption value of the security per $100 par value; and

"Y" is the yield on the investment if the security is held to redemption (expressed as a decimal).

(2) for securities with more than six months to redemption the formula set forth in item (2) of subparagraph (b)(i)(B) shall be used.

(c) *Discounted Securities*

(i) *Dollar Price.* For transactions in discounted securities, the dollar price shall be computed in accordance with the following provisions:

(A) The dollar price of a discounted security, other than a discounted security traded on a yield-equivalent basis, shall be computed in accordance with the following formula:

$$P = \left[RV \right] - \left[DR \cdot RV \cdot \frac{DSM}{V} \right]$$

For purposes of this formula the symbols shall be defined as follows:

"B" is the number of days in the year (computed in accordance with the provisions of section (e) below);

"DR" is the discount rate (expressed as a decimal);

"DSM" is the number of days from the settlement date of the transaction to the maturity date (computed in accordance with the provisions of section (e) below);

"P" is the dollar price of the security for each $100 par value; and "RV" is the redemption value of the security per $100 par value.

(B) The dollar price of a discounted security traded on a yield-equivalent basis shall be computed in accordance with the formula set forth in subparagraph (b)(i)(A).

(ii) *Return on Investment.* The return on investment for a discounted security shall be computed in accordance with the following provisions:

(A) The return on investment for a discounted security, other than a discounted security traded on a yield-equivalent basis, shall be computed in accordance with the following formula:

$$IR = \left[\frac{RV - P}{P}\right] \cdot \left[\frac{B}{DSM}\right]$$

For purposes of this formula the symbols shall be defined as follows:

"B" is the number of days in the year (computed in accordance with the provisions of section (e) below);

"DSM" is the number of days from the settlement date of the transaction to the maturity date (computed in accordance with the provisions of section (e) below);

"IR" is the annual return on investment if the security is held to maturity (expressed as a decimal);

"P" is the dollar price of the security for each $100 par value; and

"RV" is the redemption value of the security per $100 par value.

(B) The yield of a discounted security traded on a yield-equivalent basis shall be computed in accordance with the formula set forth in subparagraph (b)(ii)(A).

(d) *Standards of Accuracy; Truncation*

(i) *Intermediate Values.* All values used in computations of accrued interest, yield, and dollar price shall be computed to not less than ten decimal places.

(ii) *Results of Computations.* Results of computations shall be presented in accordance with the following:

(A) Accrued interest shall be truncated to three decimal places, and rounded to two decimal places immediately prior to presentation of total accrued interest amount on the confirmation;

(B) Dollar prices shall be truncated to three decimal places immediately prior to presentation of dollar price on the confirmation and computation of extended principal; and

(C) Yields shall be truncated to four decimal places, and rounded to three decimal places,*provided, however* ,that for purposes of confirmation display as required under rule G-15(a) yields accurate to the nearest .05 percentage points shall be deemed satisfactory.

Numbers shall be rounded, where required, in the following manner: if the last digit after truncation is five or above, the preceding digit shall be increased to the next highest number, and the last digit shall be discarded.

(e) *Day Counting.*

(i) *Day Count Basis.* Computations under the requirements of this rule shall be made on the basis of a thirty-day month and a three-hundred-sixty-day year, or, in the case of computations on securities paying interest solely at redemption, on the day count basis selected by the issuer of the securities.

(ii) *Day Count Formula.* For purposes of this rule, computations of day counts on the basis of a thirty-day month and a three-hundred-sixty-day year shall be made in accordance with the following formula.

$$\text{Number of Days} = (Y2 - Y1)\ 360 + (M2 - M1)\ 30 + (D2 - D1)$$

For purposes of this formula the symbols shall be defined as follows:

"M1" is the month of the date on which the computation period begins;

"D1" is the day of the date on which the computation period begins;

"Y1" is the year of the date on which the computation period begins;

"M2" is the month of the date on which the computation period ends;

"D2" is the day of the date on which the computation period ends; and

"Y2" is the year of the date on which the computation period ends.

For purposes of this formula, if the symbol "D2" has a value of "31," and the symbol "D1" has a value of "30" or "31," the value of the symbol "D2" shall be changed to "30." If the symbol "D1" has a value of "31," the value of the symbol "D1" shall be changed to "30." For purposes of this rule time periods shall be computed to include the day specified in the rule for the beginning of the period but not to include the day specified for the end of the period.

Table of contents | *Home Page* | *Interpretive Letter* | *Interpretive Notices* | *Next Rule*

Page from Basis Book

YEARS and MONTHS   6% ↓

Yield	8-3	8-6	8-9	9-0	9-3	9-6	9-9	10-0
4.00	113.93	114.29	114.64	114.99	115.33	115.68	116.01	116.35
4.20	112.43	112.76	113.06	113.37	113.67	113.98	114.27	114.58
4.40	110.96	111.24	111.51	111.79	112.04	112.31	112.57	112.83
4.60	109.51	109.76	109.98	110.22	110.44	110.68	110.89	111.12
4.80	108.09	108.30	108.48	108.69	108.87	109.07	109.25	109.44
5.00	106.68	106.86	107.01	107.18	107.32	107.49	107.63	107.79
5.20	105.30	105.44	105.56	105.69	105.81	105.94	106.05	106.18
5.40	103.94	104.05	104.13	104.23	104.31	104.41	104.49	104.59
5.60	102.60	102.68	102.73	102.80	102.85	102.97	102.96	103.03
5.80	101.29	101.33	101.35	101.39	101.41	101.45	101.46	101.55
6.00	99.99	100.00	99.99	100.00	99.99	100.00	99.99	100.00
6.10	99.35	99.34	99.32	99.32	99.29	99.29	99.26	99.26
6.20	98.71	98.69	98.65	98.64	98.60	98.58	98.54	98.53
6.30	98.08	98.05	97.99	97.96	97.91	97.88	97.83	97.80
6.40	97.45	97.41	97.34	97.30	97.23	97.19	97.12	97.08
6.50	96.83	96.77	96.69	96.63	96.55	96.50	96.42	96.37
6.60	96.22	96.14	96.05	95.98	95.88	95.81	95.72	95.66
6.70	95.61	95.52	95.41	95.33	95.22	95.14	95.03	94.96
6.80	95.00	94.90	94.78	94.68	94.56	94.47	94.35	94.26
6.90	94.40	94.28	94.15	94.04	93.91	93.80	93.68	93.58
7.00	93.80	93.67	93.53	93.41	93.26	93.15	93.01	92.89
7.10	93.21	93.07	92.91	92.78	92.62	92.49	92.34	92.22
7.20	92.62	92.47	92.30	92.15	91.98	91.84	91.68	91.55
7.30	92.03	91.87	91.69	91.53	91.35	91.20	91.03	90.89
7.40	91.46	91.28	91.09	90.92	90.73	90.57	90.38	90.23
7.50	90.88	90.70	90.49	90.31	90.11	89.94	89.74	89.58
7.60	90.31	90.11	89.89	89.71	89.49	89.31	89.11	88.93
7.70	89.75	89.54	89.31	89.11	88.88	88.69	88.48	88.29
7.80	89.18	88.97	88.72	88.51	88.28	88.08	87.85	87.66
7.90	88.63	88.40	88.14	87.92	87.68	87.47	87.23	87.03
8.00	88.07	87.83	87.57	87.34	87.09	86.87	86.62	86.41
8.10	87.53	87.28	87.00	86.76	86.50	86.27	86.01	85.79
8.20	86.98	86.72	86.44	86.19	85.91	85.67	85.41	85.18
8.30	86.44	86.17	85.88	85.62	85.33	85.09	84.81	84.58
8.40	85.90	85.63	85.32	85.05	84.76	84.52	84.22	83.98
8.50	85.37	85.08	84.77	84.49	84.19	83.93	83.64	83.38
8.60	84.84	84.55	84.22	83.94	83.63	83.35	83.05	82.79
8.70	84.32	84.01	83.68	83.39	83.07	82.78	82.48	82.21
8.80	83.80	83.48	83.14	82.84	82.51	82.22	81.91	81.63
8.90	83.29	82.96	82.61	82.30	81.96	81.66	81.34	81.06
9.00	82.77	82.44	82.08	81.76	81.41	81.11	80.78	80.49
9.10	82.27	81.92	81.55	81.23	80.87	80.56	80.22	79.92
9.20	81.76	81.41	81.03	80.70	80.34	80.02	79.67	79.37
9.30	81.26	80.90	80.52	80.17	79.80	79.48	79.12	78.81
9.40	80.76	80.40	80.00	79.65	79.27	78.94	78.58	78.26
9.50	80.27	79.90	79.50	79.14	78.75	78.41	78.05	77.72
9.60	79.78	79.40	78.99	78.63	78.23	77.89	77.51	77.18
9.70	79.30	78.91	78.49	78.12	77.72	77.37	76.99	76.65
9.80	78.82	78.42	77.99	77.62	77.21	76.85	76.46	76.12
9.90	78.34	77.93	77.50	77.12	76.70	76.34	75.94	75.60
10.00	77.86	77.45	77.01	76.62	76.20	75.83	75.43	75.08
10.20	76.93	76.50	76.05	75.64	75.21	74.83	74.41	74.05
10.40	76.00	75.56	75.10	74.68	74.24	73.84	73.42	73.04
10.60	75.09	74.64	74.16	73.73	73.28	72.87	72.44	72.05
10.80	74.20	73.73	73.24	72.80	72.33	71.92	71.47	71.08
11.00	73.31	72.84	72.34	71.88	71.41	70.98	70.53	70.12
11.20	72.45	71.96	71.44	70.98	70.49	70.06	69.60	69.19
11.40	71.59	71.09	70.57	70.10	59.60	69.15	68.68	68.26
11.60	70.75	70.24	69.70	69.22	68.71	68.26	67.79	67.36
11.80	69.91	69.40	68.85	68.36	67.85	67.39	66.90	66.47
12.00	69.10	68.57	68.01	67.52	66.99	66.53	66.03	65.59

Source: Reproduced from Publication No. 83, Expanded Bond Value Tables. Copyright 1970. Page 446, Financial Publishing Company, Boston, Massachusetts.

Accrued interest. (1) The dollar amount of interest accrued on an issue, based on the stated interest rate on that issue, from its date to the date of delivery to the original purchaser. This is usually paid by the original purchaser to the issuer as part of the purchase price of the issue. (2) Interest deemed to be earned on a security but not yet paid to the investor calculated from settlement date to payment date.

Ad valorem tax. [Latin: to the value added] A tax based on the value (or assessed value) of real property.

Account. Also known as a syndicate.

Advance refunding. A financing structure under which new bonds are issued to repay an outstanding bond issue before its first call date. Generally, the proceeds of the new issue are invested in government securities, which are placed in escrow. The interest and principal repayments on these securities are then used to repay the old issue, usually on the first call date.

Agency transaction. A sale and purchase of bonds when the dealer places bonds with the buyer on a commission basis rather than selling bonds that the dealer owns.

Agreement among underwriters (AAU). Legal document used principally in negotiated sales by underwriters acting as a group, not individually. The document consists of the instructions, terms and acceptances, and standard terms and conditions.

Allotment. Distribution of bonds to syndicate members by the book-running manager.

All or none (AON). Where the offerer of a block of bonds will only sell all of the available bonds and not just a portion of them.

Alternative minimum tax (AMT). An alternative way of calculating tax under the Internal Revenue Code. Interest on private activity bonds (other than 501(c)(3) obligations) issued after August 7, 1986, is used for such a calculation.

Arbitrage. Arbitrage in the municipal market is the difference between the interest paid on tax-exempt bonds and the interest earned on normally higher-yielding taxable securities. Federal tax law restricts the yield that can be earned on the investment in taxable bonds.

Arbitrage certificate. Transcript certificate evidencing compliance with the limitations on arbitrage imposed by the Internal Revenue Code and the applicable regulations.

Ascending or positive yield curve.   The interest rate structure that exists when long-term interest rates exceed short-term interest rates.

Ask price.   Price being sought for the security by the seller. Also called the offer.

Assessed valuation.   The value of property against which an ad valorem tax is levied, usually a percentage of true or market value.

Auction rate bonds.   Floating-rate tax-exempt bonds where the rate is periodically reset by a dutch auction.

Authority.   A separate state or local governmental issuer expressly created to issue bonds or run an enterprise or do both. Certain authorities issue bonds on their own behalf, such as a transportation or power authority. Authorities that issue bonds on the behalf of qualified nongovernmental issuers included health facilities and industrial development authorities.

Authorizing resolution.   Issuer document that states the legal basis for debt issuance and states the general terms of the financing.

Basis point.   One one-hundredth of one percent (.01 percent). Yield differences among fixed income securities are stated in basis points.

Bearer security.   A security that has no identification as to owner, that is, the bonds are not registered. It is presumed to be owned by the bearer or the person who holds it. Bearer securities are freely and easily negotiable, as ownership can be quickly transferred from seller to buyer. Tax-exempt municipal bonds are no longer being issued in bearer form.

Bid.   Price at which a buyer is willing to purchase a security.

Bid list.   Schedule of bonds distributed by holder or broker to dealer in order to get a bid or current price on the bonds.

Blue sky memorandum.   A memorandum for use by the account specifying the way a specific issue will be treated under state securities laws, frequently of all 50 states, Puerto Rico, the District of Columbia, and territories. This memorandum is prepared first in preliminary form, which may note that certain steps need to be taken in various jurisdictions in order to qualify the issue for sale within these jurisdictions. The memorandum is then issued in supplemental form, which generally reports that the required actions in the various jurisdictions have been taken.

Bond.   (1) The written evidence of debt, bearing a stated rate or stated rates of interest or stating a formula for determining that rate and maturing on a date certain, on which date and on presentation a fixed sum of money plus interest is payable to the holder or owner. A municipal bond issue is usually comprised of many bonds that mature over a period of years; (2) For purposes of computations tied in to per bond, a $1,000 increment of an issue (no matter what the actual denominations are); (3) Bonds are long-term securities debt with a maturity of greater than 13 months.

Bond anticipation note (BAN). A note issued in anticipation of later issuance of bonds, usually payable from the proceeds of the sale of the bonds or of renewal notes. BANs can also be general obligations of the issuer.

Bond bank. Agencies created by a few states to buy entire issues of bonds of municipalities. The purchases are financed by the issuance of bonds by the bond bank. The purpose is to provide better market access for small, lesser-known issuers.

The Bond Buyer. The daily newspaper of the municipal bond market. The Bond Buyer publishes news stories, new issuer calendars, results of bond sales, notices of redemptions, and other items of interest to the market. *The Bond Buyer* also publishes weekly indices of bond yields that are widely followed by the market.

Bond counsel. A lawyer or law firm that delivers a legal opinion to the bondholders that deals with the issuer's authorization to issue bonds and the tax-exempt nature of the bond. Bond counsel is retained by the issuer.

Bond funds. Registered investment companies whose assets are invested in portfolios of bonds.

Bond insurance. Legal commitment by insurance company to make scheduled payment of interest and principal of a bond issue in the event that the issuer is unable to make those payments on time. The cost of insurance is usually paid by the issuer in case of a new issue of bonds, and the insurance is not purchased unless the cost is offset by the lower interest rate that can be incurred by the use of the insurance. Insurance can also be obtained for outstanding bonds in the secondary market.

Bond purchase agreement (BPA). The contract between the issuer and the underwriter setting forth the terms of the sale, including the price of the bonds, the interest rate or rates which the bonds are to bear, and the conditions to closing. It is also called the purchase contract.

Bond resolution. Issuer legal document that details the mechanics of the bond issue, security features, covenants, events of default, and other key features of the issue's legal structure. Indentures and trust agreements are functionally similar types of documents, and the use of each depends on the individual issue and issuer.

Bond year. An element in calculating average life of an issue and in calculating net interest cost and net interest rate on an issue. A bond year is the number of 12-month intervals between the date of the bond and its maturity date, measured in $1,000 increments. For example, the number of bond years allocable to a $5,000 bond dated April 1, 2000, and maturing June 1, 2001, is 5.830 (1.166 [14 months divided by 12 months] × 5 [number of $1,000 increments in $5,000 bond]). Usual computations include bond years per maturity or per an interest rate and total bond years for the issue.

Book-entry. A method of registering and transferring ownership of securities electronically that eliminates the need for physical certificates.

Broker. A firm or person who acts as an intermediary by buying and selling securities to dealers on an agency basis rather than for its own account.

Bullet. A security with a fixed maturity and no call feature.

Call. Actions taken to pay the principal amount prior to the stated maturity date in accordance with the provisions for call stated in the proceedings and the securities. Another term for call provisions is *redemption provisions.*

Callable. Subject to payment of the principal amount (and accrued interest) prior to the stated maturity date, with or without payment of a call premium. Bonds can be callable under a number of different circumstances, including at the option of the issuer, or on a mandatory or extraordinary basis.

Call premium. A dollar amount, usually stated as a percentage of the principal amount called, paid as a penalty or a premium for the exercise of a call provision.

Call protection. Bonds that are not callable for a certain number of years before their call date.

Carry. The cost of borrowing funds to finance an underwriting or trading position. A positive carry happens when the rate on the securities being financed is greater than the rate on the funds borrowed. A negative carry is when the rate on the funds borrowed is greater than the rate on the securities that are being financed.

Certificates of participation (COP). COPs are a structure where investors buy certificates that entitle them to receive a participation, or share, in the lease payments from a particular project. The lease payments are passed through the lessor to the certificate holders with the tax advantages intact. The lessor typically assigns the lease and lease payments to a trustee, which then distributes the lease payments to the certificate holders.

Closing date. The date for delivery of securities and payment of funds for a new issuance of bonds.

Commission. The fee paid to a dealer when the dealer acts as agent in a transaction, as opposed to when the dealer acts as a principal in a transaction (see *net price*).

Competitive underwriting or sale. A sale of municipal securities by an issuer in which underwriters or syndicates of underwriters submit sealed bids (or oral auction bids) to purchase the securities. The securities are won and purchased by the underwriter or syndicate of underwriters who submit the best bid according to guidelines in the notice of sale. This is contrasted with a negotiated underwriting.

Concession. Fractional discount from the public offering of new securities at which the underwriter sells the bonds to dealers not in the syndicate.

Confirmation. (1) A written document confirming an oral transaction in municipal securities that provides pertinent information to the buyer and seller concerning the securities and the terms of the transaction. (2) a document that states in writing the terms and execution of a verbal arrangement to buy or sell a security.

Continuing disclosure. Under amendments to Rule 15c2-12, the obligation from the issuer to the underwriter issuer's part to provide annual updating of financial information and operating data of the type included in the official statement for the primary bond offering. The issuer must also provide notice of material events.

Counterparty. One of two entities in a traditional interest rate swap. In the municipal market a counterparty and a party can be a state or local government a broker dealer or a corporation.

Covenant. The issuer's pledge, in the financing documents, to do or to avoid doing certain practices and actions.

Convexity. A measure of the change in a security's duration with respect to changes in interest rates. The more convex a security is, the more its duration will change with interest rate changes.

Coupon. The detachable part of a bond that denotes both the amount of interest due and on what date and where the payment is to be made. Coupon is also used to refer to the interest rate on the bond. Coupons are generally payable semiannually.

Credit enhancement. The use of the credit of a stronger entity to strengthen the credit of a lower-rated entity in bond or note financing. This term is used in the context of bond insurance, bank facilities, and government programs.

Cover bid. The second highest bidder in a competitive sale.

Current yield. The ratio of interest to the actual market price of the bond, stated as a percentage. For example, a bond with a current market price of $1,000 that pays $60 per year in interest would have a current yield of 6 percent.

CUSIP. The Committee on Uniform Security Identification Procedures, which was established under the auspices of the American Bankers Association to develop a uniform method of identifying municipal, U.S. government, and corporate securities. CUSIP numbers are unique nine-digit numbers assigned to each security.

Dated date (or issue date). The date of a bond issue from which the bondholder is entitled to receive interest, even though the bonds may actually be sold or delivered at some other date.

Dealer. A securities firm or bank that engages in the underwriting, trading, and sales of municipal (or other) securities.

Debt limit. Statutory or constitutional limit on the principal amount of debt that an issuer may incur (or that it may have outstanding at any one time).

Debt service.   Required principal and interest on a bond.

Debt service requirements.   Amounts required to pay debt service, often expressed in the context of a time frame (such as annual debt service requirements).

Debt service reserve fund.   The fund into which are paid monies that are required by the trust agreement or indenture as a reserve against a temporary interruption in the receipt of the revenues or other amounts that are pledged for the payment of the bonds. A common deposit requirement for a debt service reserve fund is six months' or years' debt service on the bonds. The debt service reserve fund may be initially funded out of bond proceeds, over a period of time from revenues, or by a combination of the above.

Debt service coverage.   The ratio of net revenues to the debt service requirements.

Deep discount.   A discount greater than traditional market discounts.

Default.   Failure to pay principal or interest when due. Defaults can also occur for failure to meet nonpayment obligations, such as reporting requirements, or when a material problem occurs for the issuer, such as a bankruptcy.

Defeasance.   Termination of the rights and interests of the trustee and bondholders under a trust agreement or indenture on final payment or provision for payment of all debt service and premiums and other costs, as specifically provided for in the trust instrument.

Denomination.   The face amount or par value of a bond or note that the issuer promises to pay on the maturity date. Most municipal bonds are issued in a minimum denomination of $5,000.

Derivative.   A derivative is a financial product that derives its value from an underlying security. In the tax-exempt market, there are primary and secondary derivative products.

Discount.   (1) Amount (stated in dollars or a percentage) by which the selling or purchase price of a security is less than its face amount. (2) Amount by which the amount bid for an issue is less than the aggregate principal amount of that issue.

Discount bond.   A bond sold at less than par.

Discount rate.   The rate the Federal Reserve charges on loans to member banks.

Divided account.   Account structure that is divided as to liability and not as to sales. Also called *Western account.*

Dollar bond.   A bond that is quoted and traded in dollar prices rather than in terms of yield.

Double-barreled bond.   A bond is said to be double-barreled when it is secured by the pledge of two or more sources of payment. In some states a bond secured in the first instance by a user charge, for example, water or sewer, may be additionally secured by ad valorem taxes.

Double exemption. Securities that are exempt from state as well as federal income taxes are said to have double exemption. In states where this exemption occurs, the exemption is usually only for bonds issued by the state or its local governments. Debt of Puerto Rico and U.S. territories is also double tax exempt.

Duration. The weighted average maturity of a fixed-income investment's cash flows, used in the estimation of the price sensitivity of fixed-income securities for a given small change in interest rates.

Exempt facilities bond. Refers to those types of privately owned or privately used facilities that are authorized to be issued on a tax-exempt basis under the Internal Revenue Code.

Extraordinary redemption. This is different from optional redemption or mandatory redemption in that it occurs under an unusual circumstance such as destruction of the facility financed.

Face amount. The par value (i.e., principal or maturity value) of a security appearing on the face of the instrument.

Federal funds rate. The interest rate charged by banks on overnight loans of their excess reserve funds to other banks.

Financial advisor. A consultant to an issuer of municipal securities who provides the issuer with advice with respect to the structure, timing, terms, or other similar matters concerning a new issue of securities.

Financial and operations principal. A municipal securities employee who is required to meet qualifications standards established by the MSRB. The individual is the person designated to be in charge of the preparation and filing of financial reports to the SEC and other regulatory bodies.

Firm. Free option to buy securities for a stated time at a stated price.

Flow of funds. Refers to the structure that is established in the bond resolution or the trust documents that sets forth the order in which funds generated by the enterprise will be allocated to various purposes.

Forward cap. An agreement to enter into a cap at some date in the future.

Forward floor. An agreement to enter into a floor at some date in the future.

Forward swap. An agreement to enter a swap at some date in the future.

Fully registered. A security that is registered as to principal and interest, payment of which is made only to or on the order of the registered owner.

Futures contract. In the municipal market, an agreement to purchase or sell the municipal bond index (*The Bond Buyer* 40-Bond Index) for delivery in the future.

General obligation bond (GO). A municipal bond secured by the pledge of the issuer's full faith, credit, and taxing power.

Good faith requirement. Security deposit on new securities, ranging from 1 percent to 5 percent of the par amount, provided to the issuer at the time of a competitive bid by each underwriting syndicate. Also called good faith deposit. A surety bond can be used as a good faith deposit.

High-yield bonds. Bonds where the rating is below investment grade.

Indenture. Issuer legal document that details the mechanics of the bond issuer, security features, covenants, events of default and other key features of the issue's legal structure. Bond resolutions and trust agreements are functionally similarly types of documents, and the use of each depends on the individual issue and issuer.

Indexed rate bonds. Tax-exempt bonds where the rate is periodically reset on a formula
that incorporates an index, such as the Bond Market Association Swap Index.

Initial delivery. The delivery of a new issue by the issuer to the original purchaser on payment of the purchase price. Also called *original delivery.*

Initial offering price. The price (based on yield to maturity) stated as a percentage of par at which the account determines to market the issue during a set period of time, called the initial offering period. Members of the account may not offer any part of the issue at any other price during that period.

Interest. Compensation paid or to be paid for the use of money, generally expressed as an annual percentage rate. (See also *coupon.*)

Interest rate cap. An agreement where a party pays a premium up front or in installments to the counterparty. If the floating interest rate exceeds a stated fixed rate during the time of the cap agreement, the counterparty will pay the difference, based on the notional amount. The cap rate is also called the *strike rate.* An interest rate cap can protect the purchaser against rising interest rates.

Interest rate collar. An agreement that combines an interest rate cap and an interest rate floor. One party pays if the floating rate exceeds the cap rate, and the counterparty pays if the floating rate drops below the floor rate.

Interest rate floor. An agreement where a party receives a premium up front or in installments from a counterparty. If the floating rate is lower than the stated fixed rate during the time of the floor agreement the party pays the difference based on the notional amount. The floor rate is also called the *strike rate.* An interest rate floor lets a party receive up-front payments in exchange for the risk of making payments if interest rates fall.

Interest rate swap. A contract where two parties agree to make payments to each other. One party pays a fixed rate. The counterparty makes floating rate payments, generally based on an index such as the Bond Market Association Swap Index. The payments are based on the notional amount of the swap and are generally netted against each other, with the party owing the greater amount paying the other on a periodic basis.

Inverse floater bonds. A primary derivative tax-exempt bond. The interest payable is based on a formula that has a ceiling rate less a specified floating rate index or bond.

Inverted or negative yield curve. The interest rate structure that exists when short-term interest rates exceed long-term interest rates. (See also *ascending or positive yield curve.*)

Investment grade. Bonds considered suitable for preservation of invested capital; ordinarily, those rated Baa3 or better by Moody's Investors Service, BBB– or better by Standard & Poor's Corporation, or BBB– by Fitch.

Issuer. A state, political subdivision, agency or authority that borrows through the sale of bonds or notes. The public entity is the issuer even in those cases where the actual source of the money to pay debt service is to be an entity other than the issuer.

Joint managers. Underwriting accounts are headed by a manager. When an account is made up of several underwriting firms that normally function as separate accounts, the larger account is often managed by several underwriters, usually one from each of the several groups, and these managers are referred to as joint managers.

Legal opinion. An opinion concerning the validity of a securities issue with respect to statutory authority, constitutionality, procedural conformity, and usually the exemption of interest from federal income taxes. The legal opinion is usually rendered by a law firm recognized as specializing in public borrowings, often referred to as *bond counsel.* Other legal opinions in an issue may include tax opinions, defeasance opinions, underwriters' counsel opinion, and so forth.

Letter of credit (LOC). A commitment, usually issued by a bank, used to guarantee the payment of principal and interest on debt issues. The LOC is drawn if the issuer is unable to make the principal and/or interest payments on a timely basis.

Level debt service. A debt service schedule where total annual principal plus interest is approximately the same throughout the life of the bond. This entails a maturity schedule with increasing principal amounts each year.

Level principal. A debt service schedule where total annual principal plus interest declines throughout the life of the bond. This entails a maturity schedule with the same amount of principal maturing each year, with a resulting smaller interest component each year. This is also called declining debt service.

Limited tax bond. A bond secured by a pledge of a tax or category of taxes limited as to rate or amount.

Line of credit. A commitment by a bank to provide funds to a borrower if certain conditions have been met or if certain conditions do not exist.

Long. Securities that are owned by a dealer or investor.

Manager (or senior manager). The underwriter that serves as the lead underwriter for an account. The manager generally negotiates the interest rate and purchase price in a negotiated transaction or serves as the generator of the consensus for the interest rate and purchase price to be bid in a competitive bidding situation. The manager signs the contracts on behalf of the account and generally receives either a fee or slightly a larger spread for its services in this capacity. (See also *joint managers.*)

Mandatory sinking fund redemption.   A requirement to redeem a fixed portion of term bonds, which may make up the entire issue, in accordance with a fixed schedule. Although the principal amount of the bonds to be redeemed is fixed, the specific bonds that will be called to satisfy the requirement as to amount are selected by the trustee by lot.

Marketability.   A measure of the ease with which a security can be sold in the primary and secondary market without an undue price concession.

Material events.   In the municipal market, with regards to Rule 15c2-12, one of 11 specified events that must be disclosed to investors if they occur.

Maturity date.   The date when the principal amount of a security becomes due and payable.

Maturity schedule.   The listing, by dates and amounts, of principal maturities of an issue.

Modified duration.   Duration adjusted to price and yield levels to represent percentage change relationship of price and yield.

Monetary default.   Failure to pay principal or interest when due.

Moral obligation bond.   A municipal bond that, in addition to its primary source of security, possesses a structure whereby a state pledges to make up shortfalls in a debt service reserve fund, subject to legislative appropriation. There is no legal obligation for the state to make such a payment, but market participants recognize that failure to honor the moral pledge would have negative consequences for the state's own creditworthiness.

Mortgage revenue bond.   A security issued by a state, certain agencies or authorities, or a local government to make or purchase loans (including mortgages or other owner financing) with respect to single-family or multifamily residences.

Municipal bond.   A bond issued by a state or local governmental unit.

Municipal over bond (MOB).   Spread measures the relative difference between the municipal bond index future price and the U.S. Treasury bond futures price.

Municipal securities principal.   A municipal securities employee under MSRB rules who has supervisory responsibility for the municipal securities operations of the firm.

Municipal securities representatives.   The broadest class of municipal securities professionals who are required to pass a qualification examination under the rules of the MSRB. This group includes individuals who underwrite, trade, or sell municipal securities, do research or offer investment advice, provide financial advisory services, or communicate with investors in municipal securities.

Municipal Securities Rulemaking Board (MSRB). An independent, self-regulatory organization established by the Securities Acts Amendments of 1975, that is charged with primary rule making authority over dealers, dealer banks, and brokers in municipal securities. Its 15 members are divided into three categories—securities firms representatives, bank dealer representatives, and public members, each category having equal representation on the board.

Mutual fund. Mutual funds invest pooled cash of many investors to meet the fund's stated investment objective.

Negative convexity. A characteristic callable or prepayable securities that causes investors to have their principal returned sooner than expected in a declining interest rate environment or later than expected in a rising interest rate environment. In the former scenario, investors may have to reinvest their funds at lower rates (*call risk*); in the latter, they may miss an opportunity to earn higher rates (*extension risk*).

Negotiated underwriting. In a negotiated underwriting the sale of bonds is by negotiation and agreement with an underwriter or underwriting syndicate selected by the issuer before the moment of sale. This is in contrast to a competitive or an advertised sale.

Net direct debt. Total direct debt of a municipality less all self-supporting debt, any sinking funds, and short-term debt such as tax anticipation notes and revenue anticipation notes.

Net interest cost. An old method of calculating bids for new issues of municipal securities. The total dollar amount of interest over the life of the bonds is adjusted by the amount of premium or discount bid and then reduced to an average annual rate. The other method is known as the true interest cost. (See also *true interest cost.*)

Net order. Bond sold to investors at the price or yield shown in the reoffering scale. This is the price with no concessions.

Net price. Price paid to a dealer for bonds when the dealer acts as principal in a transaction, i.e., the dealer sells bonds that he owns, as opposed to an agency transaction. (See also *agency transaction.*)

Noncallable bond. A bond that cannot be called for redemption at the option of the issuer before its specified maturity date or in extraordinary circumstances.

Non–investment grade bond. Bonds not considered suitable for preservation of invested capital; ordinarily, those rated Ba1 or below by Moody's Investors Service or BB+ or below by Standard & Poor's Corporation or BB+ or below by Fitch. Bonds that are non–investment grade are also called high-yield bonds.

Notes. Promises to pay specified amounts of money, secured usually by specific sources of future revenues, such as taxes, federal and state aid payments, and bond proceeds (often mature within 13 months).

Notice of sale. An official document disseminated by an issuer of municipal securities that gives pertinent information regarding an upcoming bond issue and invites bids from prospective underwriters.

Notional amount. A stated principal amount in an interest rate swap on which the swap is based.

NASD (National Association of Securities Dealers). Largest securities industry self-regulatory organization in the United States.

NRMSIRS: Nationally Recognized Municipal Securities Information Repositories. An information vendor, meeting certain SEC conditions, that disseminates final official statements and secondary market disclosure information.

Odd lot. Block of bonds of $250,000 or, sometimes, $100,000.

Offer. The price at which a seller will sell a security (see also *ask price*).

Offering price. The price at which members of an underwriting syndicate for a new issue will offer securities to investors.

Official statement (OS). The offering document for municipal securities that is prepared by or for the issuer. The OS discloses security features and economic, financial, and legal information about the issue. The final OS contains the pricing information on the issue that is not contained in the preliminary official statement.

Option adjusted duration (effective duration). A measure of the bond's movement for a shift in the yield curve. For noncallable bonds, modified duration and effective duration are the same.

Option adjusted spread. The average spread over the AAA spot curve based on potential paths that can be realized in the future for interest rates. The potential paths of the cash flows are adjusted to reflect the options (puts/calls) embedded in the bond.

Optional redemption. A right to retire an issue or a portion thereof before the stated maturity thereof during a specified period of years. The right can be exercised at the option of the issuer or, in pass-through issues, of the primary obligor. Optional redemption usually requires the payment of a premium for its exercise, with the amount of the premium decreasing the nearer the option exercise date is to the final maturity date of the issue.

Order period. Specific length of time when orders for new issues are placed by investors.

Original delivery. See *initial delivery*.

Original issue discount bond (OID). A bond initially issued at a dollar price less than par that qualifies for special treatment under federal tax law. Under federal tax law for tax-exempt bonds, the difference between the issue price and par value is treated as tax-exempt interest rather than capital gain.

Over-the-counter market (OTC). A securities market where transactions are executed through dealers, not through a centralized exchange.

Overlapping debt. On a municipal issuer's financial statement, overlapping debt is the debt of other issuers that is payable in whole or in part by taxpayers of the subject issuer.

Parity debt. Securities issued or to be issued with equal and ratable claim on the same underlying security and source of payment for debt service.

Par. Price equal to the face amount of a security; 100 percent.

Par amount. The principal amount of a bond or note due at maturity.

Participation. Principal amount of bonds to be underwritten by each syndicate member.

Party. One of two entities in a traditional interest rate swap. In the municipal market a counterparty and a party can be a state or local government, a broker dealer, or a corporation.

Paying agent. Place where principal and interest are payable. Usually a designated bank or the office of the treasurer of the issuer.

Performance. An investment's return (usually total return) compared to a benchmark that is comparable to the risk level or investment objectives of the investment.

Point. Shorthand reference to 1 percent. In the context of a bond, a point means $10 as a bond with this reference means $1,000 (no matter what the actual denominations of the bonds of the issue). An issue or a security that is discounted two points is quoted at 98 percent of its par value.

Primary tax-exempt derivative products. These are based on bonds issued by state and local governments. Examples include inverse floater bonds, bonds with embedded swaps and caps, and bonds based on interest rate indices such as the Bond Market Association's Swap Index. Secondary tax-exempt derivative products are based on a custodial receipt, a trust certificate, or another security that is not directly issued by a state or local government. Examples include tender option bonds, trust certificates with interest rate swaps, and stripped interest rate bonds.

Private activity bonds. Under the 1986 Code, PABs are defined as any municipal obligation, irrespective of the purpose for which it is issued or the source of payment, if (1) more than 10 percent of the proceeds of the issue will finance property that will be used by a nongovernmental person in a trade or business, and (2) the payment of debt service on more than 10 percent of the proceeds of the issue will be (A) secured by property used in a private trade or business or payments in respect of such property, or (B) derived from payments in respect of property used in a private trade or business. These two tests—the "private business use test" and the "private payment or security test"—must be examined in connection with the issuance of any municipal security.

Private placement. The negotiated offering of new securities directly to investors without a public underwriting.

Preliminary official statement (POS). The offering document for municipal securities, in preliminary form, which does not contain pricing information. It is also called a POS, or a red herring.

Premium. The amount by which the price of a security exceeds its principal amount.

Premium bond. Bonds priced greater than par.

Prepayment provision. Provision specifying that, and at what time and on what terms, repayment of the principal amount may be made by the issuer before the stated maturity. Includes call, but prepayment usually connotes less formal procedures than a call.

Price. The dollar amount to be paid for a security, stated as a percentage of its face value or par.

Primary market (new-issue market). Market for new issues of municipal bonds and notes.

Principal. The face amount of a bond, exclusive of accrued interest and payable at maturity.

Principal transaction. A sale and purchase of bonds when the dealer commits their own capital in effecting the transaction.

Put bond. A bond that gives the holder the right to require the issuer or the issuer's agent to purchase the bonds at a price, usually at par, at some date or dates before the final stated maturity.

Put option. A put option allows the holder of a bond to put, or present, the bond to the issuer (or trustee) and demand payment at a stated time before the final stated maturity of the bond.

Rate covenant. A covenant in the financing proceedings requiring the charging of rates or fees for the use of specified facilities or operations at least sufficient to achieve a stated coverage level.

Ratings. Alpha and/or numeric symbols used to give indications of relative credit quality. In the municipal market these designations are published by the investors' rating services. Internal ratings are also used by other market participants to indicate relative credit quality.

Red herring. A preliminary official statement.

Redemption provisions. Another term for call provisions.

Refunding. Sale of a new issue, the proceeds of which are to be used, immediately or in the future, to retire an outstanding issue by, essentially, replacing the outstanding issue with the new issue. Refundings are done to save interest cost, extend the maturity of the debt, or relax existing restrictive covenants.

Registered bond. A bond whose owner is registered with the issuer or its agent. Transfer of ownership can only be accomplished when the securities are properly endorsed by the registered owner.

Remarketing. A formal re-underwriting of a bond for which the form or structure is being changed. Most commonly used in connection with changing variable rate to fixed rate financings. Typically remarketings are done because the construction phase is over, rates are at a level the issuer feels comfortable with for the long term, or because of indenture requirements (probably relating to arbitrage).

Remarketing agent. A dealer responsible for the pricing of variable rate demand bonds. The remarketing agent periodically sets and resets the interest rate of a variable rate demand note. If bonds are tendered, the remarketing agent will use his/her best efforts to sell tendered bonds to another purchaser.

Request for proposals. Widely referred to as an "RFP." A series of questions sent by a potential issuer to evaluate the qualification of potential underwriters of their negotiated issues. Written and sometimes oral (the "orals") responses to questions may include a marketing plan for the bonds, the plan of finance, and estimated costs. Also referred to as *Request for Qualifications* or *RFQ*s.

Revenue anticipation note (RAN). RANs are issued in anticipation of other sources of future revenue other than taxes. This may include intergovernmental aid.

Revenue bond. A bond on which the debt service is payable solely from the revenue generated from the operation of the project being financed or a category of facilities or from other nontax sources.

Risk. A measure of the degree of uncertainty and of financial loss of an investment or decision. There are many different risks including:
- Credit risk. The risk that the obligor on the bonds will be unable to make debt service payments because of a weakening of their credit.
- Event risk. The risk that an issuer's ability to make debt service payments will change because of unanticipated changes, such as a corporate restructuring, a regulatory change, or an accident, in their environment.
- Interest rate risk. Potential price fluctuations in a bond caused by changes in the general level of interest rates.
- Underwriting risk. The risk of pricing and underwriting securities and then ultimately being able to sell them to the investor.

Round lot. Block of bonds $100,000 or higher or 250,000 or higher depending on the market.

Scale. Listing by maturity of the price or yields at which a new issue will be offered.
- Consensus scale. In a negotiated issue, the very early price indications.
- Preliminary scale. Initial prices and yields, before a bid is submitted.
- Final scale. Scale that is submitted to the issuer at the time of the sale.

■ Reoffering scale. Scale offered to the investor by the underwriter who has purchased bonds. Also called the winning scale.

Secondary market.   Ongoing market for bonds previously offered or sold in the primary market.

Section 501(c) (3).   The section of the Internal Revenue Code under which not-for-profit organizations receive their tax-exempt status.

Security.   Specific revenue sources or assets pledged by an issuer to the bondholder to secure repayment of the bond.

Selling group.   A selling group includes dealers or brokers who have been asked to join in the offering of a new issue of securities, but who are neither liable for any unsold syndicate balance nor share in the profits of the overall syndicate. They obtain securities for sale less the take-down.

Senior manager.   The underwriter who coordinates the sale of a bond or note issue and manages a syndicate or selling group. The senior manager will run the books. If other securities firms share in the management responsibilities, they may be called co–senior managers, or to a lesser extent, co-managers.

Serial bonds.   All or a portion of an issue with stated maturities in consecutive years. (As opposed to mandatory sinking fund redemption amounts.)

Settlement date.   The date for the delivery of securities and payment of funds.

Short.   Borrowing and then selling securities that one does not own in anticipation of a price decline. When prices fall, the short is covered by buying the securities back and returning them to the lender.

Short-term debt.   Generally, debt that matures in one year or less. However, certain securities that mature in up to three years may be considered short-term debt.

Sinking fund.   Separate accumulation of cash or investments (including earnings on investments) in a fund in accordance with the terms of a trust agreement or indenture, funded by periodic deposits by the issuer (or other entity responsible for debt service), for the purpose of assuring timely availability of moneys for payment of debt service. Usually used in connection with term bonds.

Special tax bond.   A bond secured by a special tax, such as a gasoline tax or a sales tax.

Spread.   (1) The difference between the price at which an issue is purchased from an issuer and that at which it is reoffered by the underwriters to the first holders. (2) The difference in price or yield between two securities. The securities can be in different markets or within the same securities market between different credits, sectors, or other relevant factors.

Swap.   (1) A transaction in which an investor sells one security and simultaneously buys another with the proceeds, usually for about the same price and frequently for tax purposes. (2) An interest rate swap.

Syndicate.   A group of underwriters formed for the purpose of participating jointly in the initial public offering of a new issue of municipal securities. The terms under which a syndicate is formed and operates are typically set forth in an agreement among underwriters. One or more underwriters will act as manager of the syndicate and one of the managers will act as lead manager and run the books. A syndicate is also often referred to as an account or underwriting account.

Take-down.   The discount from the list price allowed to a member of an underwriting account on any bonds purchased from the account.

Tax anticipation note (TAN).   TANs are issued by states or local governmental units to finance current operations in anticipation of future tax receipts.

Tax-backed bond.   A broad category of bonds that are secured by taxes levied by the obligor. The taxes are not necessarily unlimited as to rate or amount, so while all GO bonds are tax backed, not all tax-backed bonds are GOs. Examples of tax-backed bonds include moral obligations and appropriation-backed bonds. This category is also known as *tax supported*.

Tax base.   The total property and resources subject to taxation. (See also *assessed valuation*.)

Tax-exempt bond.   A common term for municipal bonds. The interest on the bond is excluded from the gross income of its owners for federal income tax purposes under Section 103 of the Internal Revenue Code of 1986, as amended. Municipal bonds that are also exempt from state and local as well as federal income taxes are said to have double or triple tax exemption.

Tax-exempt commercial paper (TECP or TXCP).   A short-term promissory note issued for periods up to 270 days is often used in lieu of fixed-rate BANs, TANs, and RANs because of the greater flexibility offered in setting both maturities and determining rates. The purpose for issuing TECP or TXCP can be the same as BANs, TANs, and RANs.

Tax-exempt/taxable-yield equivalent formula.   A formula that converts the lower yield of a tax-exempt security into the higher yield of a taxable security. The tax-exempt yield is divided by 100 percent, less the investors marginal tax rate, and the resulting quotient is expressed as a percentage. This allows investors to compare equivalent yields on the two securities.

Taxable municipal bond.   A municipal bond where the interest on the bond is not excluded from the gross income of its owners for federal income tax purposes. Certain municipal bonds are taxable because they are issued for purposes that the federal government deems not to provide a significant benefit to the public at large.

Technical default.   A default under the bond indenture terms, other than nonpayment of interest or principal. Examples of technical default are failure to maintain required reserves or failure to maintain adequate fees and charges for service.

Term bonds.   Bonds of an issue that have a single stated maturity date. Mandatory redemption provisions require the issuer to call or purchase a certain amount of the term bonds using money set aside in a sinking fund at regular intervals before the stated maturity date.

Total bonded debt.   Total GO bond debt outstanding of a municipality, regardless of the purpose.

Total direct debt.   The sum of the total bond debt and any unfunded debt (typically short-term notes) of a municipality.

Total return.   Investment performance measure over a stated time period that includes coupon interest, interest on interest, and any realized or unrealized gains or losses.

Trade date.   The date that a trade, or sale and purchase, is consummated with settlement to be made later. (See also *settlement date.*)

Transcript of proceedings.   Final documents relating to a municipal bond issue.

Transparency.   The concept of disseminating price, volume, and other information to the public about transactions in the financial markets for securities.

True interest cost.   A method of calculating bids for new issues of municipal securities that takes into consideration the time value of money (see also *net interest cost*).

True yield.   The rate of return to the investor taking into account the payment of capital gains at maturity on a bond bought at a discount.

Trust agreement.   Agreement between the issuer and the trustee (1) authorizing and securing the bonds; (2) containing the issuer's covenants and obligations with respect to the project and payment of debt service; (3) specifying the events of default; and (4) outlining the trustee's fiduciary responsibilities and bondholders' rights.

Trustee.   A bank designated by the issuer as the custodian of funds and official representative of bondholders. Trustees are appointed to insure compliance with the bond documents and to represent bondholders in enforcing their contract with the issuer.

Underwrite.   The purchase of a bond or note issue from an issuer to resell it to investors.

Underwriter.   The securities dealer who purchases a bond or note issue from an issuer and resells it to investors. If a syndicate or selling group is formed, the underwriter who coordinates the financing and runs the group is called the senior or lead manager.

Underwriting spread.   The difference between the offering price to the public by the underwriter and the purchase price the underwriter pays to the issuer. The underwriter's expenses and selling costs are usually paid from this amount.

Undivided account. Syndicate account structure that is undivided as to sales and liability. Also called an *Eastern account.*

Unit investment trust (municipal). A fixed portfolio of tax-exempt bonds sold in fractional, undivided interests (usually $1,000).

Unlimited tax bond. A bond secured by the pledge of taxes that are not limited as to rate or amount.

Variable-rate demand obligation (VRDO). A bond that bears interest at a variable or floating rate established at specified intervals (e.g., flexible, daily, weekly, monthly, or annually). It contains a put option permitting the bondholder to tender the bond for purchase when a new interest rate is established. VRDOs are also referred to as VRDNs (Notes), VRDBs (Bonds), or low floaters.

Volatility. A statistical measure of the variance of price or yield over time. Volatility is low if the price does not change very much over a short period of time and high if there is a greater change.

Volume cap. Dollar limitation of private activity bonds allowed to be issued, by a state, each year. Legislation enacted by Congress sets the volume cap.

Yield. The annual percentage rate of return earned on a security. Yield is a function of a security's purchase price and coupon interest rate.

Yield curve. The graphic relationship between yield and maturity among bonds of different maturities and the same credit quality. This line shows the term structure of interest rates.

Yield to call. A yield on a security calculated by assuming that interest payments will be paid until the call date, when the security will be redeemed at the call price.

Yield to maturity. A yield on a security calculated by assuming that interest payments will be made until the final maturity date, at which point the principal will be repaid by the issuer. Yield to maturity is essentially the discount rate at which the present value of future payments (investment income and return of principal) equals the price of the security.

Yield to worst. This is the lowest yield generated given the potential stated calls before maturity.

Zero-coupon bond. A bond where no periodic interest payments are made. The investor receives one payment at maturity equal to the principal invested plus interest earned compounded semiannually at the original interest rate to maturity.

bibliography

Websites

American Bankers Association
www.aba.com

American Capital Access
www.aca-insurance.com

Advisory Commission on Intergovernmental Relations Research Collections
www.library.unt/edu/gpo/acir

Association for Investment Management and Research
www.aimr.org

Ambac Financial Group
www.ambac.com

Bloomberg Online
www.bloomberg.com

The Blue List of Current Municipal and Corporate Offerings
www.bluelist.com

The Bond Buyer Online—The Daily Authority on Public Finance
www.bondbuyer.com

The Bond Market Association
www.bondmarkets.com

Board of Governors of the Federal Reserve System
www.bog.frb.fed.us

The Chicago Board of Trade
www.cbot.com

Commodity Futures Trading Commission
www.cftc.gov

CNNfn, The Financial Network
www.cnnfn.com

CUSIP
www.cusip.com

DPC Data
www.dpcdata.com

EDGAR Online: The Source for Today's SEC Filings
www.edgar-online.com

The Federal Judiciary Homepage: Publications and Directories
www.uscourts.gov/publications

Government Accounting Standards Board
www.gasb.org

Financial Security Assurance
www.fsa.com

Financial Guaranty Insurance Company
www.fgic.com

FitchIBCA
www.fitchibca.com

Forbes Mutual Fund Tool
www.forbes.com

Government Finance Officers Association
www.gfoa.org

Investment Company Institute
www.ici.org

Library of Congress
lcweb.loc.gov

Lipper, Inc.
www.lipperweb.com

Moody's Investors Service
www.moodys.com

MoodysResearch.com
www.moodysresearch.com

Morningstar
www.morningstar.com

MBIA
www.mbia.com

Municipal Reinvestment Home
www.thedesks.com

The Municipal Securities Rulemaking Board
www.msrb.org

National Association of Securities Dealers Regulation
www.nasdr.com

Standard and Poor's
www.standardandpoors.com

U.S. Bureau of the Census
www.census.gov

U.S. Securities and Exchange Commission
www.sec.gov

Books

Auletta, Kenneth. 1979. *The Streets Were Paved with Gold*. New York: Random House.

The Bond Buyer. Various years. New York: The Bond Market Association.

The Bond Buyer's Municipal Marketplace. Various volumes. Skokie, Ill.: Thomson Financial.

The Bond Market Association. *Investor's Guides*. New York. Author.

Conlon, Steven D., and Vincent M. Aguilino. 1995. *Tax Exempt Derivatives*. Chicago: American Bar Association.

Fabozzi, Frank J. 1993. *Bond Markets, Analysis and Strategies* (2nd ed.). Englewood Cliffs, N.J.: Prentice-Hall.

Fabozzi, Frank J. 1993. *Fixed Income Mathematics* (rev. ed.). Chicago, Ill.: Probus.

Fabozzi, Frank J., Sylvan G. Felstein, Irving M. Pollack, and Frank G. Zarb. (eds.) 1983. *The Municipal Bond Handbook* (vol. 1 and 2) Homewood, Ill.: Down Jones–Irwin.

Federal Reserve Board. *Flow of Funds*. Washington, D.C.

Feldstein, Sylvan G., Frank J. Fabozzi, and Irving M. Pollack. (eds.) 1983. *The Municipal Bond Handbook* (vol. 2). Homewood, Ill.: Down Jones–Irwin.

Financial Publishing Company. 1970. *Expanded Bond Values* Tables. Boston, Mass.

FitchIBCA. *Fitch Ratings Book U.S. Public Finance*. New York.

FitchIBCA. *Public Finance Guidelines*. New York.

Gehrig, William L. (ed.) 1997. *Fundamentals of Municipal Bond Law*. Wheaton, Ill.: National Association of Bond Lawyers.

Gurwitz, Aaron. 1992–1998. *Municipal Market Research*. New York: Goldman, Sachs & Co.

Government Finance Officers Association. 1988. *Disclosure Guidelines for State and Local Governments*. Chicago, Ill.: Author.

Governmental Accounting Standards Board of the Financial Accounting Foundation. *Governmental Accounting Standards* series. Norwalk, Conn.

Homer, Sidney, and Martin L. Liebowitz. 1972. *Inside the Yield Book: New Tools for Bond Market Strategy*. Englewood Cliffs, N.J.: Prentice-Hall and New York Institute of Finance.

Investment Company Institute. *Fact Books*. Published annually. Washington, D.C.

Kurish, J. B., and Patricia Tigue. 1993. *An Elected Official's Guide to Debt Issuance*. Chicago: Government Finance Officers Association.

Lamb, Robert, and Stephen P. Rappaport. 1987. *Municipal Bonds*. (2d ed.) New York: McGraw-Hill.

Leonard, Paul A. 1996. An empirical analysis of competitive bid and negotiated offerings of municipal bonds. *Municipal Finance Journal* (17).

Miller, Girard. 1982. *A PublicInvestor's Guide to Money Market Instruments*. Chicago: Government Finance Officers Association.

Moody's Investors Services. 1997. *Guide to Moody's Ratings, Rating Process and Rating Practices*. New York: Author.

Moody's Investors Services. *Moody's Bond Record: Corporates, Convertibles, Governments, Municipals and Commercial Paper Ratings, Preferred Stock Ratings*. Published monthly. New York: Author.

Moody's Investors Services. *Moody's Ratings Reports*. Published daily.

Municipal Securities Rulemaking Board. 1985. *Glossary of Municipal Securities terms*. Washington, D.C.: Author

Municipal Securities Rulemaking Board. *MSRB Rule Book*. Reprinted semiannually.

National Association of Bond Lawyers. 1995. *The Function and Professional Responsibilities of Bond Counsel* (2d ed). Wheaton, Ill.: Author.

National Federation of Municipal Analysts. 1992. *Disclosure Handbook for Municipal Securities*.

Orrick Herrington and Sutcliffe. 1994. *An Issuer's Guide to Water and Wastewater Finance*. San Francisco.

Panel Publishers. *Municipal Finance Journal*. Published quarterly New York.

Public Securities Association. 1991. *A Guide to Certificates of Participation*. New York.

Standard & Poor's. *Credit Week*. New York.

Standard & Poor's. 1986. *Credit Week, Municipal Credit Week*. New York: Author.

Standard & Poor's. *Municipal Rating Handbook*. Published monthly. New York.

Stigum, Marcia. 1983. *The Money Market* (rev. ed). Homewood, Ill.: Dow Jones–Irwin.

index

about the writer

Judy Wesalo Temel has spent her career in the municipal bond business, on both the broker/dealer and issuer sides. She worked seventeen years at Goldman, Sachs & Co. after stints at Lehman Brothers and the Office of the Comptroller of the City of New York. She brings her extensive industry experience and insight to this book.

Wesalo Temel's perspectives on credit quality has influenced decisions on underwriting and trading, both on the dealer side and on the asset management side, and has advised issuers on many aspects of their transactions, including the rating agency process. She has worked with many different types of issuers, ranging from the largest states, cities, and their authorities to the most prestigious institutions of higher education and health care. She also understands the needs of the issuer, having served on the boards of several large nonprofit agencies.

A graduate of Cornell University, Wesalo Temel holds an MPA from New York University and has spoken and written widely about many aspects of the business.

WILEY FINANCE